THE
PRINCIPLES
OF
FINANCIAL
INTERMEDIATION

Alex N. McLeod

**UNIVERSITY
PRESS OF
AMERICA**

LANHAM • NEW YORK • LONDON

4720 Boston Way
Lanham, MD 20706

3 Henrietta Street
London WC2E 8LU England

Library of Congress Cataloging in Publication Data

McLeod, Alex N., 1911-
The principles of financial intermediation.

Bibliography: p.
Includes index.
1. Finance. 2. Credit. 3. Money. I. Title.
II. Title: Financial intermediation.
HG173.M397   1984   332   83-27418
ISBN 0-8191-3831-2 (alk. paper)
ISBN 0-8191-3832-0 (pbk. : alk. paper)

All University Press of America books are produced on acid-free
paper which exceeds the minimum standards set by the National
Historical Publications and Records Commission.

In acknowledging my debts to others with respect to this book, where should I begin? And where should I stop? Surely I must recognize my debts to my parents, for starting me on my way, and to other familiy members—especially my wife Rosalind—for aid and encouragement. Colleagues, friends, . . . the list is endless.

My teachers at various levels deserve special acknowledgement, severally and collectively. In the 1920's the Canadian Prairies still retained the optimism of an expanding frontier, and most teachers in the primary and secondary schools I attended in Regina were young, enthusiastic, able, and dedicated. At the university level my recognition of debts to individuals is sharper: at Queen's University, particularly Dean Matheson and others in the Mathematics Department and Professors F.A. Knox and W.A. Mackintosh in the Economics Department; at Harvard, Professors A.H. Hansen, J.A. Schumpeter, and John Williams.

The International Monetary Fund gave me invaluable experiences of the financial institutions and problems of individual countries as well as international financial affairs. I particularly appreciated the example of E.M. Bernstein, Director of the Research Department in the early years, as a conscientious and able international civil servant. Also, working with the late George A. Blowers in Libya and Saudi Arabia was especially valuable. In later years I benefitted from the friendship of Frank A. Southard Jr.

The Toronto-Dominion Bank merits special acknowledgement in two distinct ways. First, The Bank provided me with direct experience in the world of Canada's chartered banks and other financial intermediaries as a result of hiring me as their first Chief Economist in 1955. Second, and more specifically, The Bank contributed materially to the work that went into this book. At an early stage in working up the material The Bank provided financial and secretarial assistance; now they have again provided financial assistance in preparing the manuscript for publication. It is a pleasure to acknowledge this debt, and to extend best wishes to my former colleagues and their successors.

TABLE OF CONTENTS

v

CHAPTER 11. Selected Policy Inferences

This book is an attempt to provide a general theory of financial intermediation, in which the roles of various types of intermediary are seen as parts of an integrated whole.

The *practice* of banking and other forms of financial intermediation can be traced back through many ancient civilizations—Roman, Greek, Babylonian, Chinese, Indian, and other. Institutions that may reasonably be considered the forerunners of today's corporate presences in these fields had appeared in Europe by the early years of the 15th century, but a large and prestigious organization is not necessary to successful intermediation. The essential feature is that a trustworthy operator must offer his own financial obligations to the public at large, or to some segment of the public, in exchange for the standard money of the community, and must make loans to third parties out of the proceeds. (Alternatively, he may use the proceeds for his own purposes—in which case he may be thought of as lending money from himself in one capacity to himself in another.) These functions have often been performed as small-scale local operations—perhaps as a sideline to money-changing, goldsmithing, or some mercantile activity. Small private banking operations have persisted until quite recent times even in countries with sophisticated financial structures, and some commercial enterprises still carry on a quasi-banking operation.

A satisfactory *theory* of financial intermediation, or even of the mechanical aspects of banking, is a recent development. It is a commonplace that the theory of money was virtually a separate and independent compartment within general economic theory until the "classical dichotomy" was discredited by the events of the 1930's and the new theories those events gave rise to. Some thirty years ago Schumpeter observed that the literature on banking and finance had been almost equally a compartment within the literature on money and credit (*History of Economic Analysis*, page 1110f). A compartment within a compartment! A long if intermittent debate over the ability of the banks to create money and credit was not conclusively ended until the 1920's, as noted in the opening pages of this book. The next advance was the recognition, which became widespread in the 1950's, that credit creation was possible through other intermediaries as well as banks.

This volume has had a long gestation period. As a graduate student at Harvard just after World War II I became convinced that the traditional distinction between banks and other financial intermediaries on the basis of their ability or inability to create credit was invalid. In a memorandum in October 1949 I proposed writing a paper for a forthcoming international seminar, demonstrating that a multiple credit expansion could occur in a country in which the only money was a full-bodied gold coin (as in the model introduced in Chapter 1 below), but I did not have an opportunity to pursue it then. In May 1958 I presented a paper entitled "Credit Creation" to the International Monetary Fund staff seminar, and met Richard Thorn, who was developing similar ideas. "The Mysteries of Credit Creation" appeared in *The Canadian Banker* in the 1949 Winter issue, fulfulling the suggestion made ten years earlier. "Credit Expansion in an Open Economy" in the September 1962 issue of the *Economic Journal* carried the analysis further. Then, soon after I joined the faculty of Atkinson College of York University, I began to incorporate these ideas into a draft general textbook on money and banking. *The Principles of Financial Intermediation* is the theoretical core of that draft, with a limited amount of elaboration and comment.

Toronto   Alex N. McLeod
October 1983

INTRODUCTION

1. The Argument

The argument in this book assumes some familiarity with the theory of money and financial institutions, at least at the level presented in typical introductory courses in economics, and preferably at the level of an undergraduate course in money and banking. A major purpose is to develop the pure theory of financial intermediation in a way that is as free as possible from the carryover of past prejudices, yet retains as much as possible of past insights. Unfortunately the distinction between prejudice and insight is every bit as subjective as that other source of endless contention, the distinction between superstition and religious truth.[1] Nevertheless we will make a gallant attempt at the well-nigh-impossible.

The problem centres around the differences between banks and other financial intermediaries. Until about the end of World War II it was pretty generally accepted that banks were unique in that they could "create" credit by simultaneously "creating" money, whereas other intermediaries could only relend money that had been placed with them. It is a matter of some irony that the ability of banks themselves to create credit (and money) had only become generally accepted fairly recently, largely thanks to Phillips in the U.S.A. and Crick in Britain,[2] over the objections of practical bankers who stoutly maintained that they could only relend money deposited with them; the now-familiar deposit-loan-redeposit sequence showed that in a sense both sides were right. Interestingly enough, essentially the same point was argued to essentially the same conclusion in Britain a century earlier, primarily in terms of note-issuing rather than deposit-taking banks (though some participants did extend the analysis to deposits)[3], but apparently that debate had been largely forgotten in the meantime. During the 1950's the uniqueness of banks was newly challenged, notably but not exclusively by Gurley and Shaw,[4] and the current literature

---

[1] One version has it that religious truth is what *we* believe, superstition is what *they* believe.

[2] C.A. Phillips, *Bank Credit,* New York, The Macmillan Company, 1921, and W.F. Crick, "The Genesis of Bank Deposits", *Economica,* no. 20, June 1927, pp. 191–202.

[3] See J. Viner, *Studies in the Theory of International Trade,* New York and London, Harper & Bros., 1937, pp. 234–243, and E. Wood, *English Theories of Central Banking Control 1819–1858,* Cambridge Mass., Harvard University Press, 1939, pp. 35f, 42f, and 46f.

[4] See for example J.G. Gurley and E.S. Shaw, "Financial Aspects of Economic

1

began to emphasize the similarities between banks and other financial intermediaries rather than their differences. We will argue that in this case, too, both sides are substantially right.

Another major purpose is to elaborate on some of the macroeconomics of credit expansion first pioneered by Rutledge Vining in 1940.[5] This approach offers a number of useful insights, including considerable help in reconciling the "creation" of credit with its ultimately having to be saved out of income. It also helps to illuminate the very real differences between money and near-money, or between banks and near-banks, which remain undeniable even though economists' understanding of them has now changed radically.

The book is addressed to the purely theoretical aspects of financial intermediation, as the title indicates. However, every effort will be made to keep real-world applications in mind. Theory and practice must work together. Good theory requires continual practical testing, just as good practice requires continual reference to sound principles.

2. Techniques

2.1. Long-Run-Equilibrium Analysis

The bulk of the analysis is in terms of long-run general-equilibrium models. Such models are not fashionable nowadays, for very practical reasons,

---

Development", *American Economic Review*, Vol. XLV, no. 4, September 1955, pp. 515–538; "Financial Intermediaries and the Savings-Investment Process", *The Journal of Finance*, Vol. XI, no. 2, May 1956, pp. 257–276; "The Growth of Debt and Money in the United States, 1800–1950", *The Review of Economics and Statistics,* Vol. 39, no. 3, August 1957, pp 250–262; and *Money in a Theory of Finance*, The Brookings Institution, Washington, 1960. See also "Are Our Monetary Controls Outmoded?", an address by S. Clark Beise, President, Bank of America, before the Economic Club of New York on 19th November 1956; Richard S. Thorn, "Non-Bank Financial Intermediaries, Credit Expansion, and Monetary Policy," *I.M.F. Staff Papers,* Vol VI, no. 3, November 1958, pp. 369–383; E.A. Birnbaum, "The Growth of Financial Intermediaries as a Factor in the Effectiveness of Monetary Policies", *ibid.*, pp. 384–426; A.N. McLeod, "The Mysteries of Credit Creation", *The Canadian Banker*, Vol. 66, no. 3, Winter 1959, pp. 20–28; and A. Lamfalussy, "Radcliffe under Scrutiny: Money Substitutes and Monetary Policy", *The Banker* [London], Vol. CXI, January 1961, pp. 44–50.

This list is not exhaustive. The ideas involved had become widely recognized by the early 1950's (personal workingpapers go back to 1949), though until 1955 they do not seem to have been committed to writing in any systematic way. Thus Gurley and Shaw, who seem to have been the first to put them on paper, did so as an incidental aspect of their treatment of more general subjects and not as an exercise in credit theory as such.

[5] "A Process Analysis of Bank Credit Expansion", *The Quarterly Journal of Economics*, Vol. LIV, no. 4, August 1940, pp. 599–623.

epitomized by Keynes's quip that "in the long run we are all dead," yet they have their uses in identifying some of the forces that are at work in a disequilibrium situation. Their main limitation in policy applications is that the real world never allows these forces to operate undisturbed for long enough to bring the economy to anything even approaching an equilibrium position: new "disturbances" are always occurring before the old ones have worked themselves out. Instead of identifying it with death, therefore, we might say that long-run equilibrium is like tomorrow, which never - comes; we must always wrestle with today's new problems before we have fully solved those of yesterday.

As best, therefore, long-run-equilibrium analysis suffers from serious limitations. The dynamics of economic adjustment processes are essential to a great deal of economic analysis if it is to have any useful application to day-to-day policy decisionmaking. Unfortunately "dynamic analysis" is one of those things that are more easily said than done. Yet some attempt at it must be made, and even the limited techniques we will be able to employ do offer substantial help in understanding the operation of the financial system. In particular, they enable us to focus clearly on the differences between the roles of banks and the roles of other financial intermediaries in the process of credit expansion, as in section 2 of Chapter 5 and section 2 of Chapter 6 below, whereas long-run considerations tend to emphasize the similarities.

Nevertheless the limitations of long-run analysis must not be exaggerated. It is clear that full long-run general equilibrium may be taken to imply the passage of unlimited time during which all contracts are repeatedly renegotiated at successively closer approximations to the final equilibrium, but it is equally clear that some variables may quite rapidly approach their hypothetical equilibrium values. The very fact that a given disturbance is not allowed to work itself out in isolation contributes to this conclusion: a random distribution of positive and negative disturbances, miscalculations, and misadventures should produce a series of partly-offsetting leads and lags in response. Some possibilities are noted on pages 32 and 118f below in respect of the equilibrium position in credit expansions through financial intermediaries, and somewhat similar considerations apply to income-expansion sequences. It therefore appears that a reasonable approximation to the theoretical long-run-equilibrium position may be attained fairly promptly in these cases.

2.2. Closed-Economy and Open-Economy Models

Closed-economy models will be used extensively in elaborating the credit-expanding and the income-expanding potential of financial intermediation, but open-economy models will be used whenever they can contribute materially to the analysis. In those applications in which we are primarily concerned with the balance sheets of domestic financial intermediaries and the implications for credit expansion, as in Part One, most closed-economy models may be reinterpreted as representing the equilibrium position in an open economy after the various external drains have had their full effect: the relative magnitudes of the domestic assets and liabilities will be unaffected by the drains. In those applications in which we are concerned with the links between the credit and the income expansions, as in Part Two, this simple reinterpretation will not apply to the income components. However, the most significant effect of open-economy conditions is to very materially reduce the potential expansions of both credit and income that will occur as a result of a given disturbance or departure from equilibrium; since we will generally be more interested in basic principles than in quantitative conclusions, closed-economy models can materially simplify the analysis without serious distortion even in these applications.

Quite aside from their practical convenience, however, closed-economy models have more relevance in the real world than may appear at first sight. Their key feature is that there is no loss of external reserves to nor gain of reserves from other economies, and this condition or something very like it may arise in a variety of ways. In the first place the lags mentioned on pages 32 and 118f below may produce something very like closed-economy conditions in the very short run. In the second place the external repercussions may reverse an external drain in the moderately long run and raise the credit multiplier to something very close to its simple closed-economy value.[6] In the third place, and much more immediately relevant to our models, modern money-management techniques have virtually eliminated any reliable link between increments of domestic financial claims and increments of external reserves. This is particularly true for a country that is following a so-called "clean float" policy with respect to the external value of its currency, but it is also substantially true even for a country that is attempting to maintain a fixed exchange-rate relative to some other currency or currencies. Since credit-based standard monies are now the rule rather than the exception, it would appear that many national financial structures may for considerable periods of time resemble our closed-economy model with an acceptance ratio (explained on page 14 below) of unity and a reserve ratio of zero—with of course the very important difference that these financial systems are discretionary not automatic, i.e. they are consciously managed in pursuit of recognized economic goals.

2.3. Nominal Values and Real Values
The discussions will be mostly in terms of the acquisition and holding of financial assets, and of the associated changes in money-income. Except where clearly indicated to the contrary, the analysis will involve only

---

[6] See Chapter 8, below.

nominal monetary values for income, savings, wealth, and various financial assets. Cumulative totals will be simply the sum of the values in previous periods without consideration of or adjustment for any price changes that may have occurred. Whether real values change, and if so whether the change is proportionate or more or less than proportionate, will depend on factors not discussed here—price changes, the upward and downward flexibility of prices, elasticities of demand and supply, the existence or otherwise of the money illusion, and so on. The discussion of The Revaluation Effect in section 2.4 of Chapter 3 below is the only important exception.

2.4. A Neutral Presentation

The presentation is addressed to general principles, and is specifically designed to avoid identification with the currency or the institutions of any particular country. To emphasize this neutrality in Parts One and Two, which are primarily addressed to domestic financial systems, a different currency is used in each chapter for the illustrations: dinars in Chapter 1, francs in Chapter 2, marks in Chapter 3, crowns in Chapter 4, riyals in Chapter 5, and dollars in Chapter 6. All are purely hypothetical currencies, despite the fact that there actually are currencies bearing these names—in most cases, several distinct and unrelated currencies. Part Three is addressed to international financial arrangements, however, and there is little risk of confusion with particular domestic financial institutions. Three real-world currencies are used in the illustrations in these chapters, though all the numerical examples are purely hypothetical.

3. Definitions

Let us adopt D.H. Robertson's definition of *money*: "... anything which is widely accepted in payment for goods, or in discharging other kinds of obligations."[7] The justification for this choice will appear in section 2.3 of Chapter 6 on pages 145ff below. We will sometimes expand the term to "money proper", to emphasize the distinction between it and certain close substitutes.

The *standard money* of a given country is the basic monetary unit in which debts are recorded and payments made within the domestic economy. If there is a central bank or other monetary authority then the standard money may be taken to be the monetary obligations of that institution. If the standard money is a commodity money (e.g. gold, in gold-standard days), or is effectively convertible into a commodity-money or into a foreign currency at a fixed or an approximately-fixed exchange-rate, then

---

[7] *Money* (Cambridge Economic Handbooks), 4th ed., London, Nisbet, 1948, p. 2.

that commodity money or that foreign currency is the *ultimate standard money* of the country.

Near-money is anything (usually a financial claim, but conceivably a commodity or a physical object) which is easily convertible into money-proper with little risk of capital loss, and therefore a close substitute for money-proper for some purposes.

A *financial intermediary* is an institution that borrows[8] from one set of people and lends to another, thus mediating between primary lenders and ultimate borrows.

A *bank* is a financial intermediary whose public obligations are transferable and are in fact accepted as money; an issuer of money-proper (banknotes, currency notes, chequeable deposits). A *bank of issue* is a bank whose public obligations are banknotes or currency notes that pass as hand-to-hand money. A *bank of deposit* is a bank whose public obligations are freely transferable among its creditors, usually by cheque or the equivalent, and are commonly accepted as money. A *central bank* is a bank whose purpose is to regulate domestic money-and-credit conditions and which is endowed with adequate powers to do so. Typically, it is a bank of issue and deposit; it has either a monopoly or a dominant share of the domestic note issue; and it accepts deposits only or primarily from the national government and its agencies, from domestic commercial banks, and from foreign central and commercial banks. A *commercial bank* is a financial intermediary whose public obligations include both money and near-money; a combination bank and near-bank. Typically, it offers a wide variety of deposit, lending, and other services not only to commercial enterprises but also to non-commercial enterprises, individuals, and other financial intermediaries.[9]

A *near-bank*[10] is a financial intermediary whose obligations are classed as near-money.

Credit. There is some confusion in the use of this term in relation to financial intermediation. Some writers identify "credit" and "debt" as the

---

[8] "Borrowing" should be construed in terms of the economic effect rather than of how the creditor views the transaction. It may not be the purpose of a depositor or a banknoteholder to make a loan to a bank, but that is the economic effect.

[9] The term "commercial" is derived from their historical origins, not their current practices. Before the evolution of a recognized lender of last resort and active markets for liquid securities, the survival rate was much higher for banks that emphasized *commercial* loans for the marketing of staple goods—hence the early interest of bankers in "self-liquidating paper" and "real bills".

[10] This usage has led a central banker with a sense of humour to suggest that financial intermediaries whose obligations are not close substitutes for money (such as insurance companies, pension funds, mutual funds, etc.) should be classed as "far banks."

obverse terms to describe the two aspects of a lending-and-borrowing contract, but this is objectionable because of the obvious confusion with "credit" and "debit" in bookkeeping operations; it seems preferable to follow ordinary usage, in which "credit" is something a person may either give or receive. Others identify "bank credit" or simply "credit" as a form of money, which can be rationalized as the use of credits on the books of banks as a means of payment, but here too it seems preferable to identify bank credit with the debtor-creditor relationship between a bank and its borrowing customers and to speak of a bank's liabilities as its debts or obligations or as claims of others against it.

Part One ═══════════════════

THE FRACTIONAL – RESERVE PRINCIPLE

CHAPTER 1

CREDIT EXPANSION THROUGH
UNSPECIFIED INTERMEDIARIES

1. The Reasons for Intermediation

The growth through history of the share of its financial assets the public chooses to hold through intermediaries, and the proliferation of types of intermediaries, are persuasive evidence that they serve an economic function. Their present importance is not explained by the mere fact that they are powerful engines of credit expansion, for we will see that credit can also be expanded through direct lending and borrowing between principals (see, e.g., section 3 of Chapter 3 below). Rather, the explanation lies in the efficiency with which they can serve the needs of both would-be lenders and would-be borrowers. Specialization and economies of scale are the keys to their success.

Primary lenders and ultimate borrowers, respectively, make the basic decisions to save or to spend. Primary lenders are surplus units, i.e. individuals or groups or enterprises that generate more savings or command more accumulated savings from the past than they can economically use themselves. Ultimate borrowers are deficit units, i.e. individuals or groups or enterprises—typically, entrepreneurs and innovators—that can economically employ more resources than are available to them from their own savings.

Primary lenders and ultimate borrowers obviously have broadly complementary needs, but in a world of imperfect knowledge and incomplete information they need help in finding one another, and modern financial systems have evolved by serving those needs. There are three major components of such systems: the various markets in which financial contracts are bought and sold; brokers, who bring the buyers and sellers in these markets together, but act as agents rather than principals in the transactions they effect; and financial intermediaries, which deal as principals with both lenders and borrowers. Some markets are highly formalized, as organized stock markets; others may be very informal, as over-the-counter markets. There is some overlapping in practice between the functions of brokers and intermediaries, and intermediaries participate directly in some markets without recourse to brokers, but in principle the two functions are distinct.

A simple brokerage function can materially reduce the time, trouble, and expense for both primary lenders and ultimate borrowers in finding opposite numbers who want the same contractual terms and conditions, or in ascertaining the nearest available approximations thereto, but it may leave many other wants rather poorly satisfied. Financial intermediaries can provide greater convenience and larger net returns to many primary lenders by reducing or eliminating the costs, risks, and responsibilities of direct lending, but above all because they offer their own obligations in place of the obligations of a particular ultimate borrower; their obligations are generallly superior to those of their borrowing customers because they are better-known, more readily realizable or marketable, and backed by a more diverse portfolio of assets. At the same time the intermediaries can provide many ultimate borrowers with funds at lower overall costs and greater assurance. They are able to do all this, yet earn an economic return for themselves in the process, largely because they can pool resources from many sources, pool the risks by diversified loans or investments, effect economies of scale, and develop specialized knowledge in their chosen fields. The importance of specialization is obvious in such matters as insurance of various kinds or the administration of annuities or pensions, which involve actuarial considerations, or in trustee services, where legal as well as financial considerations enter. But it is also important in general banking operations: bankers can build up skills in the evaluation of credit risks in general, in the special needs and problems of particular industries or economic functions, and in various ancillary activities.

2. A Simple Model of Financial Intermediation

2.1. The Fractional-Reserve Principle

The key to an understanding of financial intermediation is The Fractional-Reserve Principle: maintaining reserves of less than 100 per cent against obligations, and relying on the ability to recover from third parties for the timely discharge of those obligations. This principle has long been a feature of banking practice and banking theory (not necessarily distinguishing between commercial banks and pure banks as we have defined them), and it applies to other financial intermediaries as well. Just to keep things in perspective, however, it may be useful to take a brief look at some applications that are entirely outside the field of financial intermediation.

Suppose Homemaker A runs short of sugar while baking and borrows a cupful from Homemaker B to complete her (or his) project. Homemaker A definitely has more physical sugar than before, though now embodied in cakes or pies or other baked goods ready for consumption. For her part Homemaker B has less actual sugar than before, by a cupful; but she has a claim on Homemaker A for the difference. She would not likely feel it necessary to add sugar to her next shopping list merely because some of her physical inventory was now replaced by a claim on her neighbour; although for baking purposes she could not use her claim-to-sugar as a substitute for the real thing, she could confidently expect her claim to be honoured promptly in case of need.

The same principles can be applied to loans of commodities among businesses. Steel, oil, and various other staple commodities may be borrowed and lent, even between competitors, with repayment expected in kind rather than in cash. Some of these arrangements may be quite complicated, and may involve repayment in a different part of the world as well as or instead of after a lapse of a period of time, possibly at agreed discounts below or premiums over the original quantity. Evidently commodity loans of this kind could even occur in a barter economy, with claims to repayment in kind replacing actual inventories of commodities (grain, cattle, etc.) to at least a limited extent.

Another example involves stock and bond certificates or, more generally, any type of document that is issued in considerable volume and evidences property rights that are perfect substitutes within their own class or kind. In sophisticated financial markets it is commonplace to borrow and lend securities of various kinds—treasury bills, government and corporate bonds, and equity stocks. The borrower may be a dealer or broker needing a specific security for delivery to a customer, or a speculator who has sold some security short and needs to make delivery, or someone temporarily unable to get possession of securities he owns and wishes to sell. In the case of government securities the lender may be the central bank or some other agency desirous of promoting a broad market in the issues in question, in other cases it may be a financial institution seeking a profit with relatively little risk.

It is clear that any of these borrowing-and-lending arrangements might conceivably generate a volume of claims much greater than any participant realized. Also, any such structure would be quickly immobilized if a sufficient number of creditors suddenly demanded repayment when conditions were such that debtors were unable to repay either out of their own holdings or by alternative borrowing elsewhere: a commodity-credit freeze might occur, closely resembling the financial panics of an earlier day before central-banking techniques had come into general acceptance. Nevertheless these practices have important advantages for all concerned, and share certain common features with financial intermediation.

2.2. A Simple Closed-Economy Model

Let us start with a simple closed-economy model in which the standard money (say, a dinar) is a full-bodied gold coin—just to emphasize that the phenomena we wish to illustrate can and do arise through the straightforward use of the hardest of "hard" monies, and are not dependent on mysterious operations with pen and ink or other tools of legerdemain. The stock of money is limited to 1,000 dinars. So far there have been no financial intermediaries, but now a class of competing and essentially-similar intermediaries becomes established over a period of time. The model says nothing about their structure or operations, nor about the characteristics of the obligations they offer the public, nor about why the public finds these obligations attractive, except that their discharge (or their convertibility into standard money) according to the terms of the contract is assured. The intermediaries are willing to lend the funds so acquired to members of the general public at suitable interest rates, and do not lack for credit-worthy borrowers, but members of the public can not or do not lend to one another directly. Experience establishes a pattern of reserve holdings in standard money by the intermediaries against their obligations, which for convenience we may identify as a fixed minimum ratio to the obligations,[1] and generates confidence that the system is sound as long as this pattern is respected; the profit motive ensures that the lending capacity of the intermediaries is fully used. All transactions are effected in standard money, or could be so effected if the participants wished; if some of the claims on the intermediaries come to be used as money-proper then free convertibility of those claims into standard money on demand is effectively maintained in practice.[2]

As a concrete example, let us say the intermediaries' reserve ratio settles at 20 per cent, and the public comes to hold 40 per cent of its financial portfolio in the form of claims on them. Coining a new term to avoid prejudicial carryovers from traditional banking analysis, we will call this the *acceptance ratio*; it may be measured either in terms of standard money (2:3 in this case) or in terms of total financial assets (0.4 or 40 per cent). We will make the usual assumption that there is no shortage of willing borrowers deemed creditworthy by the intermediaries. The expansionary sequence is illustrated in Table 1.1, through the use of an adaptation of the T-accounts often used in financial analysis to represent a balance sheet at a given point in time. We may call the new presentation "T-square accounts", from their fancied resemblance to a draftsman's T-square; in effect the usual T-accounts are turned on their sides, and successive columns represent a sequence of events over time.

---

[1] All that is really required is that the relationship between reserves and obligations be known and determinate. The relationship may be indirect rather than direct (e.g. expressed as a relationship to assets or stipulated assets); there may be an uncovered or fiduciary tranche, or different requirements for successive tranches; the requirement may be by custom rather than law; the stipulated or observed level may change seasonally or cyclically or secularly. In any of these or other variants the reserve ratio of the model may be identified with the ratio actually observed or followed at the particular point in time or over the particular period under consideration.

[2] Continued convertibility of money-proper is postulated merely to exclude the disruptions of the payments mechanism (financial panics) to which an automatic system is vulnerable if the standard money is (or is itself convertible into) a commodity-money such as gold.

Table 1.1. Schematic Illustration of Credit Expansion in a Closed Economy[1]

Sector assets and liabilities	Time sequence: (1) *	(2) *	(3) *	(4) #	(5) *	(6) #	(7) *	(8) #	(9) * (∞)
General Public									
A Gold Coin	1000	900	950	−320#	630	+286	916	−114.4#	882
Gold claims	—	100	100	+320	420		420	+114.4	588
Total assets	1000	1000	1050		1050	+286	1336		1471
L Debts	—	—	50		50	+286	336		471
Net worth	1000	1000	1000		1000		1000		1000
Intermediaries									
A Gold coin	—	100	50	+320	370	−286	84	+114.4	118
Loans	—	—	50		50	+286#	336		471
L Obligations	—	100	100	+320	420		420	+114.4	588
Total Economy									
A Gold coin	1000	1000	1000		1000		1000		1000
Gold claims	—	100	100	+320	420		420	+114.4	588
Loans	—	—	50		50	+286	336		471
Total assets	1000	1100	1150	+320	1470	+286	1756	+114.4	2059
L Debts of public	—	—	50		50	+286	336		471
Obligations	—	100	100	+320	420		420	+114.4	588
Net worth	1000	1000	1000		1000		1000		1000

[1] Assuming a fixed supply of 1000 dinars of gold coin (standard money) and, after column 3, an acceptance ratio of 40 per cent and a reserve ratio of 20 per cent.

* Balance-sheet position at a given point in time.

\# Changes occurring in a given period of time.

\# Transaction which initiates changes during a given period.

N.B.: In column 9 the final digits are rounded to the nearest whole number, hence detailed figures may not add exactly to totals.

Column 1 of the table represents the situation before the introduction of the intermediaries. In column 2 the public has placed the first 10 per cent of its assets with the intermediaries, and in column 3 the intermediaries have cautiously lent out 50 per cent of their receipts. By column 4 the public is committed to an acceptance ratio of 40 per cent for the intermediaries' obligations, which puts substantial free reserves (i.e. the difference between receipts and the required or customary cash reserves thereon) in the hands of the intermediaries in column 5. By column 6 the intermediaries have settled on the 20 per cent cash reserve ratio, and at each subsequent round they lend their precisely-calculated free reserves. The familiar expansionary sequence can thus go to completion: the public and the intermediaries in turn attempt to restore balance to their portfolios and thereby put the others' out of balance, until the original 1,000 dinars are firmly lodged either as willingly-held balances in the hands of the public or as required reserves in the hands of the intermediaries (column 9). The secondary or induced expansion of financial assets is identical with or "explained by" the credit generated through (or the loans granted by) the intermediaries.

There is of course nothing new or remarkable about this expansion as such. What *is* significant is the assumptions that are *not* necessary for the expansion or "creation" of credit:[3] the intermediaries need not be banks and their obligations need not be money. They might just as well be savings institutions offering non-transferable deposits; or life insurance companies accumulating and investing policy reserves, not because the public consciously chooses to save in this way but because that is a necessary concomitant of the level-premium form of contract; or, with only a slight modification of the model, primary lenders making loans directly to ultimate borrowers. The nature of the intermediaries and the characteristics of their obligations do impose important constraints on the reserve ratios they must maintain and on the acceptance ratios they may hope for, and therefore they do affect the *amount* of credit expansion that can occur through a given type of intermediary in a given context (or rather, as will be made clearer in due course, on the rapidity with which it can occur), but they do not affect the *fact* that credit can be expanded through many types of intermediary.

If we do choose to identify the intermediaries in the model as banks, it should be noted that many variations are possible. They may be publicly or privately owned. Their obligations may be banknotes or currency notes in bearer form, intended as hand-to-hand money, or they may be chequeable deposits or similar book-entries (such as the Giro accounts widely used in

---

[3] "Credit expansion" seems a more accurate term than the commonly-used "credit creation" for describing this phenomenon.

Europe) or other very close substitutes for banknotes. These obligations may be readily convertible into some commodity-money (e.g. gold) or the equivalent (e.g. one or more foreign currencies) at fixed rates, so convertible only with official sanction, convertible (with or without the need for official approval) at fluctuating market rates, convertible at rates that vary according to the nature of the underlying transaction (multiple currency practices), or completely inconvertible except through illegal transactions or black markets; however, for open-economy models we will usually assume that national currencies are freely inter-convertible at approximately-fixed rates. And of course several types of bank may be competing for the public's preferences at the same time.

Specifically, the term "bank" may include a government that issues its own currency notes, in which case the government in its note-issuing capacity should be deemed to lend the proceeds to itself in its fiscal capacity. However, two complications arise in this case. First, a government may force the acceptance of its notes by making them legal tender and supressing alternatives (e.g. it may issue an inconvertible fiat currency). This is especially likely if the government's issue policy reflects its own fiscal needs rather than the perceived needs of the economy. Second, a government note issue (whether direct or through what is described as a Bank of Issue on page 40 below) may easily lead to pyramiding and its attendant complications, as noted in section 3.1 of this chapter.

2.3. Open-Economy Conditions

The principal adjustments necessary to adapt our model to open-economy conditions derive from the fact that some of the ultimate standard money on which the system is based may be attracted abroad in some circumstances ("the external gold drain" of gold-standard days, now more accurately called simply "the external drain"), or may be augmented from abroad under other circumstances. There are two major components of the drain: induced spending on imports ("the import leakage", which may be subdivided into the leakages from spending out of income and from spending borrowed money), and the acquisition of assets located abroad or denominated in foreign currencies. The first is usually of greater practical importance and analytical interest, even though under favourable conditions the external repercussions[4] may ultimately reverse it and restore the domestic situation to something closely approximating closed-economy conditions, as explained in Chapter 8 below. However, there are such important lags and uncertainties in these repercussions that policymakers

---

[4] The term "external repercussions" means the effects that domestic occurrences have on incomes and income-related variables abroad, and the reciprocal effects they imply for the domestic economy.

can not count on an external drain being automatically stemmed in good time. For the most part, therefore, our analysis will disregard the external repercussions.

For the time being we wish to treat the expansion of domestic credit and domestic financial assets in isolation from these complexities; all we need do is acknowledge a determinate relationship between the credit-expansion sequence and the external drain. It will therefore suffice for the present if we identify external claims as a third form in which financial assets may be held, with a distinct acceptance ratio relative to domestic standard money. We may rationalize our procedure in either of two ways. (1) We may look to the long-run general-equilibrium situation, in which all the effects of the induced income-flows (including the external repercussions) have worked themselves out at home and abroad and we are concerned only with the division of the public's residual financial assets between domestic and external holdings. Or, (2) we may look at the situation as one of relatively long-run but partial or incomplete equilibrium, pending the external repercussions, and interpret the acquisition of foreign assets as including the purchase of foreign exchange to buy the foreign goods and services that constitute the import drain; hereafter we will refer to this as the constrained-equilibrium interpretation. If we elect the second option, as we will usually do in Parts One and Two, we may further rationalize our position by noting that the immediate effects on the domestic financial structure are the same regardless of whether the public wishes to retain its external assets more or less permanently or plans to buy imports with them.

At this point it becomes useful to introduce a modification of the terminology we have used so far. When there are two or more financial claims competing for the public's attention, they may compete with one another as much as or more than with standard money. It will usually be preferable, therefore, to speak of the *coefficients of substitution* among financial assets rather than the acceptance ratios of individual claims in terms of standard money.

In adapting our model to open-economy conditions on this basis it will be convenient to make a minor change in our assumptions: instead of envisaging 1,000 gold dinars as the total supply of financial assets in the economy before the introduction of our unspecified intermediaries, let us suppose that a new injection of 1,000 gold dinars occurs in an economy in which the financial intermediaries have already become established, with a given acceptance ratio and a given reserve ratio. Sequence analysis of this type simplifies the presentation, translates easily into a change in the *rate* at which a particular independent variable is changing, and focuses on the marginal changes in all the variables concerned, without requiring us to specify what is happening to their average values over any particular time-period.

Table 1.2. Schematic Illustration of Credit Expansion in an Open Economy[1]

Sector assets and liabilities	Time sequence: (1) *	(2) ±	(3) *	(4) ±	(5) *	(6) ±	(7) *	(8) * (∞)
General Public								
A Gold coin	50	+405	455	−384.75#	70.25	+164.03	234.28 .	84.03
Domestic claims	450		450	+182.25	632.25		632.25 .	756.30
Domestic assets	500	+405	905	−202.50	702.50	+164.03	866.53 .	840.34
External claims	500		500	+202.50	702.50		702.50 .	840.34
Total assets	1000	+405	1405		1405.00	+164.03	1569.03 .	1680.67
L Debts		+405	405		405.00	+164.03	569.03 .	680.67
Net worth	1000		1000		1000.00		1000.00 .	1000.00
Intermediaries								
A Gold coin	450	−405	45	+182.25	227.25	−164.03	63.23 .	75.63
Loans		+405#	405		405.00	+164.03#	569.03 .	680.67
L Obligations	450		450	+182.25	632.25		632.25 .	756.30
Total Economy								
A Gold coin	500		500	−202.50	297.50		297.50 .	159.66
Domestic claims	450		450	+182.25	632.25		632.25 .	756.30
Loans		+405	405		405.00	+164.03	569.03 .	680.67
Domestic assets	950	+405	1355	− 20.25	1334.75	+164.03	1498.78 .	1596.64
External claims	500		500	202.50	702.50		702.50 .	840.34
Total assets	1450	+405	1855	+182.25	2037.25	+164.03	2201.28 .	2436.97
L Debts of public		+405	405		405.00	+164.03	569.03 .	680.67
Obligations	450		450	+182.25	632.25		632.25 .	756.30
Net worth	1000		1000		1000.00		1000.00 .	1000.00

[1]Assuming an increment of 1000 dinars of gold coin (standard money), coefficients of substitution of 1:9:10 among coin, domestic claims, and external claims, and a reserve ratio of 10 per cent for the intermediaries.

* Balance-sheet position at a given point in time.

± Changes occurring in a given period of time.

Transaction which initiates changes during a given period.

N.B.: Final digits are rounded to the nearest whole number, hence detailed figures may not add exactly to totals.

19

Table 1.2 offers a numerical example of a situation in which the intermediaries' cash reserve ratio is 10 per cent, the marginal coefficient of substitution between coin and domestic claims is 1:9, and that between external and domestic assets is 1:1 (or the coefficients are 5 per cent, 45 per cent, and 50 per cent for coin, domestic claims, and external assets).[5] An increase in the supply of gold dinars occurs for some reason—perhaps someone discovers a hoard of coins and puts them into circulation, perhaps new gold production is coined and spent, perhaps there is a net increase in exports paid for in gold or the equivalent, perhaps domestic institutional changes release previously-required reserves. In column 1 the public allocates the increase in its assets according to its preferences, which puts the intermediaries' asset structure out of balance. The resulting sequence of portfolio adjustments through the intermediaries' loans (columns 2 and 6) and the reallocations of the public's cash receipts (column 4) bring an expansion of the economy's financial assets and liabilities until the increment of standard money is fully converted into foreign claims, intermediary reserves, or willingly-held domestic cash balances.

If we focus on the *total* financial assets of the public (including external assets) then, as in the closed-economy case, the credit (or loan) expansion that results from the injection of 1,000 dinars of new standard money is equal to the secondary expansion of financial assets ($680.67 = 1,680.67 - 1,000$). However, if we wish to focus only on *domestic* financial assets, and treat the acquisition of external claims as an external drain, then this simple relationship no longer obtains. Instead, the total credit expansion must be identified with the sum of the secondary expansion of domestic assets and the external drain. In this example it happens that the secondary expansion of domestic financial assets is negative, as it must be unless the coefficient of substitution between foreign and domestic assets is materially less than unity, but the relationship holds nevertheless: $680.67 = (840.34 - 1,000) + 840.34$.

---

[5] The choice of coefficients is of course quite arbitrary and of illustrative significance only, but a brief comment on the coefficient between domestic and external assets may be in order. If the table is interpreted as a long-run model then the external-asset component may be very small, perhaps approaching zero, for a relatively-closed and sound economy with a sophisticated financial structure; but for a relatively small open economy with a limited range of domestic financial assets the coefficient may be a substantial positive integer, especially if the political situation is unstable or if wealth is highly concentrated. (For a discussion of some aspects of this situation see A.N. McLeod, "The Role of Financial Institutions in Developing Countries: A New Perspective", *The Canadian Banker*, Vol. 77, no. 5, September/October 1970, pp. 8–10.) If the table is interpreted as a constrained-equilibrium model, however, then the import drain is likely to be the major component of what are here deemed to be external assets and the coefficient may be of the order of unity even for a relatively closed economy; see section 1.3 of Chapter 11 below.

The basic difference between this open-economy model and the closed-economy model lies in the process by which equilibrium is attained. In the closed-economy model it is attained by expanding domestic financial claims until all standard money is firmly lodged either as required reserves or as willingly-held balances in circulation. In the open-economy model there is a third possibility: the leaching away of standard money through the external drain.

2.4. Alternative Paths to Equilibrium

The equilibrium balance-sheet positions of the public, the intermediaries, and the total economy in Tables 1.1 and 1.2 can be derived directly from the postulated acceptance and reserve ratios, without going through the elaborate sequence analysis there summarized; see the algebraic formulation presented in section 2.5 below. It follows that the public may choose (or we may postulate that the public chooses) to add to its claims against the intermediaries in any fashion whatever, systematic or unsystematic, structured or random, provided the posulated coefficients of substitution among its various financial assets eventually prevail; no pattern of convergence on the equilibrium position is any better than any other, except as it may be represented as offering a more logical reflection of how various members of the public might be expected to act in the real world. Similarly, the lending sequences postulated as being observed by the intermediaries may vary from period to period, perhaps very markedly, provided the postulated reserve ratio ultimately becomes effective.

The standard practice is to assume that the acceptance and the reserve ratios are constant and are rigidly adhered to. This implies that the intermediaries invariably lend their free reserves in each period, no more and no less. The rationale is that one of a large number of competing intermediaries dare not lend more, because it would face a combined currency drain ("the internal gold drain" of gold-standard days) and clearing drain (to its competitors) virtually certain to approximate its entire loan, and would not lend less, because it would thereby sacrifice earnings unnecessarily. In practice this is not entirely realistic, for a variety of reasons, including the probability of significant random gains and losses at the clearinghouse. (In a typical banking system the volume of daily clearings may be of the same order of magnitude as the total of all chequeable deposits, so a relatively small variation in the debits and credits coming against a given bank may be fairly large relative to its cash reserves.) Nevertheless the standard assumption appears to be a reasonable approximation to the actual lending practices of a comparatively small intermediary facing many competitors.

When the obligations of a particular intermediary account for a significant portion of the public's financial assets, however, it may in principle (and sometimes in practice) be able to lend somewhat more than its free reserves. The text-book example of a single bank enjoying a 100-per-cent acceptance ratio in a closed economy presents the most extreme case: upon the receipt of additional reserves in ultimate standard money it can immediately grant loans equal to many times its free reserves, and leap at once to the full equilibrium position. (In an open-economy model, of course, the external drain sharply reduces the potential expansion; thus in Table 1.2 above the equilibrium level of loans is only about 68 per cent above the initial level of free reserves in column 1, whereas in a closed-economy model with otherwise-identical assumptions it would be 426 per cent higher.)

Less-extreme versions do have some application in the real world, however. Suppose the economy is served by just three competing intermediaries, each presumably operating many branches throughout the economy and all offering equivalent services; Intermediary A does 50 per cent of the business, Intermediary B 30 per cent, and Intermediary C 20 per cent, but there is no collusion or consultation; the acceptance ratio for their obligations is 90 per cent, and their cash reserve ratio is 10 per cent; and current conditions closely resemble a closed-economy model, perhaps for the reasons outlined on page 4 above. Now suppose that free reserves appear in the system, without specifying how or why they arise. How rapidly will they be able to expand credit? What assumptions can we reasonably make about how their managers will respond?

If any one intermediary gains free reserves as a result of what its managers see as a temporary fluctuation in the flow of clearing balances, they will presumably react cautiously if at all. If they believe that the gain is shared by their competitors, i.e. that there is a net increase in free reserves for the whole system, and if they believe their competitors have the same perception, they might conceivably act as a monopoly intermediary might do and expand their loans by about five times their free reserves, confident that their competitors would do likewise. If they are sure the gain is more than a temporary swing of the clearings but are not sure it is shared by their competitors (perhaps it is even at their expense) then the managers of Intermediary A might lend about 168 per cent of its free reserves, Intermediary B about 132 per cent, and Intermediary C about 119 per cent. In the case of Intermediary A, for example, the reasoning would be that 10 per cent of any loan would be lost to a currency drain, 45 per cent would be lost to a clearing drain in favour of its competitors, and 45 per cent would be redeposited in its own offices and would thus convert 4.5 per cent of its free reserves to required reserves; hence it could lend $1/0.595$ times its free reserves. For Intermediaries B and C the figures in the denominator would be 0.757 and 0.838 respectively.[6]

---

[6] In addition to the notation used in section 2.5 immediately below, let us use w ($0 \leq w \leq 1$) for a given intermediary's share of the market and F for its free

Table 1.3. Schematic Illustration of Credit Expansion Through a Few Intermediaries in a Closed Economy[1]

Sector assets and liabilities	Time sequence:							
	(1) *	(2) ±	(3) ±	(4) *	(5) ±	(6) ±	(7) *	(8) * (∞)
General Public								
A Gold Coin		+ 59	+ 88	148	+ 37	+ 65	249 ...	526
Claims on A		+ 264	+400	664	+ 166	+292	1122 ...	2368
Claims on B		+ 158	+240	398	+ 99	+175	673 ...	1421
Claims on C		+ 106	+160	266	+ 66	+117	449 ...	947
(Total claims)		(+ 528)	(+800)	(1328)	(+331)	(+585)	(2244) ...	(4737)
L Debts		+1475		1475	+1018		2493 ...	5263
Intermediary A								
A Reserves–Required		+ 38	+ 29	66	+ 19	+ 26	112 ...	237
–Free	{ 500	− 840	+ 257	257	− 432	+ 237	237 ...}	—
		+ 340			+ 175		...}	
Loans[2]		+ 840		840	+ 432		1273 ...	2632
L Obligations	{	+ 378	(+178B	664	+ 194	+156B	1122 ...}	2368
			(+107C			+108C	}	
Intermediary B								
A Reserves–Required		+ 12	+ 29	40	+ 9	+ 18	69 ...	143
–Free	{ 300	− 396	+262	262	− 346	+163	163 ...}	—
		+ 96			+ 84		...}	
Loans[2]		+ 396		396	+ 346		743 ...	1579
L Obligations	{	+ 107	(+227A	398	+ 94	+117A	673 ...}	1421
			(+ 64C			+ 65C	}	
Intermediary C								
A Reserves–Required		+ 4	+ 22	27	+ 4	+ 14	45 ...	95
–Free	{ 200	− 239	+200	200	− 239	+126	126 ...}	—
		+ 39			+ 39		...}	
Loans[2]		∣ 239		239	+ 239		478 ...	1053
L Obligations	{	+ 43	(+151A	266	+ 43	+ 78A	449 ...}	947
			(+ 71B			+ 62B	...}	

[1] Assuming the injection of 1000 dinars of free reserves in an unspecified manner, divided proportionately among the intermediaries; an acceptance ratio of 90 per cent, of which A:B:C = 5:3:2; and a reserve ratio of 10 per cent.

[2] Intermediary A expects its free reserves to be depleted by 59.5 per cent of its loans (10 per cent to a currency drain, 45 per cent to a clearing drain to its competitors, 4.5 per cent as required reserves on redeposits), hence lends 1/0.595 times its free reserves. For Intermediary B the denominator becomes 0.10 +0.63 +0.027 = 0.757, and for Intermediary C 0.10 + 0.72 + 0.018 = 0.838.

* Cumulative totals at a given point in time. The change in assets exceeds the change in liabilities by the amount of the free reserves in column 1.

± Changes occurring in a given period of time.

N.B.: Final digits are rounded to the nearest whole number, hence detailed figures may not add exactly to totals.

The resulting expansion is summarized in Table 1.3. Column 1 shows only the net free reserves of each intermediary, without specifying how they arose.[7] Each stage is arbitrarily divided into two parts, in order to show both (a) the results each intermediary expects (which we suppose are fully realized) and (b) the additional effects of their actions on one another. In column 2 Intermediary A lends about 168 per cent of its free reserves, not being sure how the others are situated; the borrowers withdraw their loans, which promptly reappear as redeposits of 378 dinars in the lending institution and a like sum in its competitors, just exhausting its initial free reserves. Had its gain of reserves been at the expense of the others (i.e. had Intermediaries B and C actually been under-reserved by 300 and 200 dinars respectively in column 1) this would still have left them under-reserved and they would have had to call some of their loans; that in itself would have had adverse effects on Intermediary A's reserves, but the implication would be that the public's coefficients of substitution had shifted in favour of Intermediary A and against Intermediaries B and C, hence lending 168 per cent of its free reserves would nevertheless have been a reasonable policy. But we are postulating that both competitors (unknown to Intermediary A) have gained reserves in the same proportion; Intermediary B is in the process of lending about 132 per cent of its free reserves, and Intermediary B about 119 per cent, which exhaust their initial free reserves also. Simultaneously, however, each intermediary benefits from the redeposit of a portion of its competitors' loans, which it had not counted on, thus creating new free reserves of about 720 dinars in column 3. These are lent in the same pattern in columns 5 and 6, and the process is repeated until all the free reserves are absorbed either as additions to the coin in circulation or as required reserves in the hands of the intermediaries.

---

reserves. A loan of L will cause a currency drain of $(1-a)L$, a clearing drain of $a(1-w)L$, and an increase of awL in its own reserve requirements. Equating the sum of these absorptions of reserves with F, we get $(1-a)L+a(1-w)L+awL=F$; solving for L, we get $L=F/[1-aw(1-r)]$. Since we are postulating that $a=0.9$ and $r=0.1$, setting $w=0.5$ makes the denominator 0.595; setting $w=0.3$ makes it 0.757; and setting $w=0.2$ makes it 0.838.

[7] Postulating that they are the result of a new injection of standard money into the economy implies that the amount was about 1,234 dinars, of which the public allotted 123 to coin in circulation and 1,111 to claims on the intermediaries; these figures plus a net worth of 1,234 must be added into columns 1, 4, 7, and 8. Alternatively, we may postulate that the free reserves arose because the required or customary reserve ratio was reduced from some higher figure to 10 per cent; in that case we must insert -500, -300, and -200 in column 1 for the required reserves of Intermediaries A, B, and C respectively, and deduct these sums from the corresponding figures in columns 4, 7, and 8.

The resulting loan sequence of approximately

$$1{,}475 + 1{,}018 + 765 + 539 + \ldots\ldots$$

is not a simple geometric progression, because of the asymmetric lending patterns postulated for the three intermediaries, but it nevertheless converges on the same equilibrium value (about 5,263 dinars) as the more usual sequence

$$1{,}000 + 810 + 729 + 656 + \ldots\ldots \quad .$$

Initially the largest intermediary gets a disproportionate share of the loans, but the cumulative total for each competitor gradually approaches its equilibrium share. The other sequences are also somewhat irregular, for the same reason, but all approach the expected equilibrium values. Note, however, that the balance-sheet columns (4, 7, and 8) all show an excess of assets over liabilities equal to the initial injection of free reserves from sources that are unexplained.

2.5. Algebraic Formulation

An algebraic formulation of the simple one-intermediary model can be expressed in terms of the following symbols representing the variables and parameters indicated:

G: An increment of standard money (alternatively, ultimate standard money) made available to the public in some way. In principle it is an exogenously determined variable, but it will be treated as an arbitrarily chosen constant; i.e., $G = \bar{G}$. By hypothesis $G = Gd + Gk + Gp$, subject to the constraint that $0 \leq Gd, Gk, Gp \leq G$.

Gd: The external drain, i.e. the portion of G that will be used to acquire foreign financial claims or to purchase imports. As a temporary expedient to permit the treatment of open-enonomy conditions without raising the income implications, it is assumed for now that $Gd = Af$.

Gk: The portion of G that is retained by the intermediaries as reserves for the claims the public holds against them. By hypothesis $Gk = r.K$.

Gp: The portion of G that the public chooses to retain directly. By hypothesis $Gp = (1-a)Ad$.

K: The total claims the public acquires against the intermediaries by the process of placing successive amounts of standard money $(G_1, G_2, \ldots)$ with them in exchange for specific claims. By hypothesis $K = a.Ad$. Subject to the constraint that $0 \leq K \leq Ad$.

L: The loans made (or credit granted) by the intermediaries. By hypothesis $L = (1-r)K$.

Ad: The public's domestic financial assets. By hypothesis $Ad = Gp + K$.

Af: The public's foreign financial assets. By hypothesis $Af = d.Ad$, and it is temporarily assumed that $Af = Gd$.

25

At: The public's total assets. By hypothesis $At = Ad+Af = Ad(1+d)$.

a: The public's acceptance ratio for claims; i.e., $a = K/Ad$. Subject to the constraint that $0 \le a \le 1$.

d: The coefficient of substitution between domestic and foreign claims; i.e., $d = Af/Ad$. In the closed-economy version of the model $d = 0$.

r: The reserve ratio of the intermediaries; i.e., $r = Gk/K$. Subject to the constraint that $0 \le r \le 1$.

The expansionary sequence begins when G dinars or their equivalent value are received by the public, which allocates $d.G / (1+d)$ to Af, $(1-a)G / (1+d)$ to Gp, and $a.G / (1+d)$ to K. The intermediaries now retain $ar.G/(1+d)$ as reserves and lend $a(1-r)G/(1+d)$, thus returning a like sum to circulation, which the public reallocates as before. The various sequences may be summed by the usual formula for converging geometric series, the common ratio being $a(1-r) / (1+d)$.

Alternatively, the equilibrium relationships among the public's gross assets (and its debts to the intermediaries) can be found by identifying the equilibrium distribution of standard money (G). Thus

$$G = Gd+Gk+Gp = d.Ad+ar.Ad+(1-a)Ad$$

$$\therefore Ad = G/[1+d-a(1-r)] \dots\dots\dots\dots\dots (1.1)$$
$$Af = d.G/[1+d-a(1-r)]\dots\dots\dots\dots (1.2)$$
$$At = (1+d)G/[1+d-a(1-r)]\dots\dots\dots (1.3)$$
$$Gd = d.G/[1+d-a(1-r)]\dots\dots\dots\dots (1.4)$$
$$Gk = ar.G/[1+d-a(1-r)]\dots\dots\dots\dots (1.5)$$
$$Gp = (1-a)G/[1+d-a(1-r)]\dots\dots\dots (1.6)$$
$$K = a.G/[1+d-a(1-r)]\dots\dots\dots\dots (1.7)$$
$$L = a(1-r)G/[1+d-a(1-r)]\dots\dots\dots (1.8).$$

The secondary expansion of total financial assets is $At-G$ or (from equation 1.3) $(1+d) G/[1+d-a(1-r)] -G$, which reduces to $a(1-r)G/[1+d-a(1-r)]$—i.e. it is identical to the credit expansion as given by equation 1.8. However, if Af is treated as simply an external drain and attention is focused entirely on domestic financial assets, the secondary expansion thereof is $Ad-G$; substituting for Ad from equation 1.1 and simplifying, we get $[a(1-r)-d] G/[1+d-a(1-r)]$. (Note that this expression will be negative unless $d \le a(1-r)$.) Adding the external drain as given in equation 1.4 to the secondary expansion of Ad we get $a(1-r) G/[1+d-a(1-r)]$, which we can identify from equation 1.8 as the credit expansion; that is, the credit expansion is equal to the sum of the secondary expansion of domestic financial assets and the external drain.

A useful modification of this general presentation is to set $G = 1$ in equations 1.1 to 1.8, thereby deriving a family of multipliers that can be applied to any given marginal injection of new standard money into the economy in order to derive the resultant increase in total financial assets or any component thereof. The figures in the final columns of Tables 1.1, 1.2, and 1.3 can be converted into such families of multipliers by moving the decimal point three digits to the left.

In the constrained-equilibrium interpretation of the open-economy case, the public's initial allocation of G may be rationalized by supposing that G is the net saving out of some previous income-expanding sequence and therefore has already been divided betweeen Af and Ad in the ratio of the marginal propensities to import (m) and to save (s); hence $d = m/s$. Given the appropriate values for the other parameters, we can solve equations 1.1 to 1.8 independently of any income-generating sequences associated with them, a long as we know or are prepared to postulate the *relative* values of m and s.

If we know or wish to postulate the *absolute* values of the two propensities, however, we can substitute m/s for d in equation 1.1. Subject to the constraint that $0 \leq m, s, (m+s) \leq 1$, we thus derive

$$Ad = sG / [(m+s) - as(1-r)] \quad \dots \dots \dots \dots \dots \dots \dots (1.9)$$

and corresponding modifications of equations 1.2 to 1.8. These relationships are treated further in section 3.3 of Chapter 5 below, including the income implications. (Equation 5.6 below reduces to equation 1.1 by setting $m = z = 0$ and $n = 1$, and to equation 1.9 by setting $d = z = 0$ and $n = 1$.)

If G represents a net receipt of ultimate standard money by the nation (say, from the mining and minting of gold or from net export earnings) and *either* (a) the monetary system responds automatically *or* (b) monetary policy is neutral, then external reserves increase by the equivalent of $Gk + Gp$. However, if G is not a net receipt of new income, but originates from a freeing of or "economizing on" ultimate standard money (e.g., by an increase in a, or a decrease in r) or from central-bank open-market purchases, then the resultant credit expansion will reduce external reserves by Gd.

2.6. The Leakage Principles

Expansionary sequences of the kind here used have two important properties, which we may call The Leakage Principles: (1) the absolute sum of the leakages will equal the sum of the multiplicands that initiate the sequence, and (2) if there are two or more leakages their absolute values will be proportional to their respective marginal increments during the sequence (or, more correctly, their average rates of change over the relevant span). Thus in section 2.5 immediately above the initial injection is G, the leakages are $Gd, Gk,$ and Gp, and the equilibrating condition is that G be fully absorbed by the leakages in the ratio $d:ar:(1-a)$. The same is true of the sequences often used to illustrate the various income-multipliers and their com-

27

ponents,[8] and of the combined credit-and-income sequences introduced in Chapter 4 below.

3. More Elaborate Models

3.1. A Complex Financial Structure

There are two major ways in which the simple model here introduced can be made more realistic, i.e. more meaningful for application in the real world: by introducing the income-implications of the spending of borrowed money, and by postulating a more complex financial system than the single class of intermediary so far considered. Part Two of this book is addressed to the first of these elaborations, and we strongly recommend that you take at least a preliminary look at Chapters 4 and 5 before proceeding with Chapters 2 and 3. The short-run dynamics of this approach are particularly significant. However, many of the institutional aspects of credit expansion can be analyzed in isolation from the income implications, as has indeed been done for several generations, thereby considerably simplifying the presentation. The rest of this chapter and the next two chapters are therefore addressed to the second way in which our simple model can be elaborated, from what is primarily a long-run viewpoint.

We may replace our single type of intermediary by many different types, each type offering a different range of services and obligations in order to attract customers: pure banks (which may be banks of issue or banks of deposit or both) and commerical banks, savings banks, building societies, savings and loan associations, trust companies, insurance companies, investment funds, pension funds, and so on. We may suppose that there are several competing intermediaries of each type, and that all operate on the same general principles with respect to cash reserves and portfolio management, although the typical reserve ratio and the preferred loan or investment choices may differ greatly because of the differing natures and maturity-patterns of their obligations. We may also incorporate direct lending and borrowing between individuals and other principals (business firms, associations, etc.) as well as through intermediaries, and a variety of markets in which securities and other financial contracts may be traded.

The fact that different types of financial intermediary may have different reserve ratios has important implications for credit expansion. The essential import of the process illustrated in Tables 1.1 and 1.2 is that a difference in the *form* in which the public chooses to hold its financial assets

---

[8] Cf. para. 2 (p. 637) of the Technical Notes to A.N. McLeod, "Credit Expansion in an Open Economy", *The Economic Journal*, Vol. LXXII, September 1962, pp. 611–640.

may bring about a change in the *total amount* of them, and provoke a credit expansion in the process. We may now generalize further and say that any change in coefficients of substitution that favours intermediaries with relatively low reserve ratios, or any other change that economizes on reserves, will bring additional credit expansion. The possibility of such shifts is enhanced as new types of intermediary become established, or as existing intermediaries find new ways of serving public wants.

A particularly important change occurs if one type of intermediary succeeds in getting its obligations accepted as money-proper. The full significance of the change can be better explained in terms of short-run dynamics, as in Part Two, but even in terms of long-run analysis it makes a very material difference: the new form of money (which must be identified as a credit-based money) may come to serve as well as or better than the ultimate standard money as the cash reserves of other financial intermediaries. This leads to what may be called the pyramiding of credit expansion, or "pyramiding" for short, because the credit structure comes to resemble an inverted pyramid based on a relatively small amount of standard (or ultimate standard) money. We will examine this phenomenon in greater detail in Chapter 2.

3.2. A Credit-Based Standard Money

A special case of pyramiding occurs if a single bank of issue achieves a high acceptance ratio for its obligations. Historically this has usually occurred as a result of the government granting a monopoly or virtual monopoly of the note-issue privilege to a particular bank, whether for good, bad, or indifferent reasons, and the acceptance of its obligations may have been enhanced by some accident or mischance that drove the ultimate standard money out of general circulation (e.g., a period of inconvertibility due to the exigencies of war, financial mismanagement, or some other *force majeure*). Nowadays the typical case is the establishment of a central bank and the centralization of external reserves either in its hands or in the hands of some government agency. However it arises, such a situation permits two important reinterpretations of the model we have been discussing so far.

First, whereas so far we have usually spoken as if the standard money is identical with the ultimate standard money (a full-bodied gold coin or the equivalent), the analysis can be readily adapted to a credit-based standard money. The closed-economy version can be so reinterpreted without modification; nothing would be changed by substituting a credit-based currency, or even a fiat currency,[9] for the gold dinar. However, the open-

---

[9] A fiat currency may be viewed as simply a special case of a credit-based currency; in effect the notes so issued are non-interest-bearing perpetual-debt vouchers.

economy version applies in its full rigour only if the domestic money is allowed to respond automatically and proportionately to changes in the supply of ultimate standard money. If the ultimate standard money is a commodity (e.g. gold) then this implies fixed or virtually-fixed exchange rates with any other country using the same ultimate standard money (as under various versions of the gold standard); if it is a given foreign currency then it implies a fixed exchange-rate with that currency; if it is foreign exchange in general then it implies a system of fixed rates or a reasonable approximation thereto. Nevertheless the model can also be applied to fluctuating or flexible exchange-rate systems with credit-based standard monies. Freely fluctuating rates (a "clean float", with no change in external reserves) makes the domestic financial system respond precisely as it would in a closed economy; any use of external reserves to manage the rate or to cushion changes in it means that the open-economy version applies *pro tanto*, in that the surrender of reserves to domestic purchasers implies the extinction of an equivalent amount of the credit-based standard money in exchange.

The second important reinterpretation of the model is the possibility of introducing discretionary monetary policies. So far we have tacitly assumed that the financial system operates mechanically or automatically under a given set of rules and preferences in response to stipulated "disturbances" or departures from equilibrium. It is true that the existence of rules implies that they might be changed from time to time in response to changing circumstances, but there has been no suggestion of a recognized authority continuously responsible for discretionary day-to-day decisions about credit policy. Automatically-controlled systems of this kind have a historical basis in most parts of the world, and automatic responses are still important even in these days of managed currencies: money-managers operate primarily by manipulating the parameters to which the system responds, rather than by suppressing or replacing the responses themselves.

Thus we may interpret the standard money in our model as the monetary obligations of a modern central bank or some other discretionary monetary authority. In this case we may identify the new injection of standard money in our model as the result of a policy decision by the monetary authority (say, an open-market purchase of securities); in the open-economy version this brings about a loss of ultimate standard money, but presumably the authorities will have anticipated it and will be willing to tolerate it in pursuit of other policy objectives, otherwise they would not have undertaken the expansion.

Discretionary monetary policies mean, of course, that the authorities may choose to offset the contractionary effects of an external drain by open-market purchases or some other policy action, or on the other hand to reinforce the drain by restrictive policies. The role of ultimate standard money as a regulator of the domestic financial system is thereby reduced to the vanishing point. In itself this may not mean any material weakening of the balance-of-payments discipline, even in a flexible-exchange-rate system, for external reserves may still be desirable as a protection against economic misfortunes and either an undervalued or an overvalued currency brings its own retribution. It is no more than the obverse of the fact that the very essence of a discretionary system is the right of the authorities to run down the external reserves, even to zero (or, by borrowing abroad, below zero), for what they deem to be good reason.

3.3. The Simple Model Refurbished

In Chapter 2 below we will look in some detail at credit pyramiding, and consider some of the complications encountered in a more elaborate model of the financial system. We will find that from a long-run-equilibrium point of view the main effect is to greatly increase the amount of credit expansion that can occur on a given base, i.e. to economize on standard money or ultimate standard money. We can therefore reinterpret our simple one-intermediary model as an accounting consolidation of all the various financial intermediaries operating in the economy, in which inter-institutional claims (such as the deposits an insurance company or near-bank may maintain with a bank) are netted out. On this interpretation the acceptance ratio and the reserve ratio of the model become the weighted averages of the acceptance and reserve ratios of all the individual intermediaries in the economy.

4. Three Technicalities

Some doubt may be voiced about the practical significance of the sequence analysis of credit expansion illustrated in Tables 1.1 and 1.2 on pages 15 and 19 above, on the ground that a sequence of that kind can not go to completion in any finite time period. It appears, however, that the problem is largely a creation of the restrictive and mechanistic assumptions of our simple model and of models like it. We tacitly assume that the public instantly reallocates its financial resources according to fixed coefficients of substitution, and that disturbances to equilibrium are allowed to occur (and work themselves out) one at a time, whereas in the real world there are likely to be significant leads and lags in various responses and there is likely to be a series of disturbances of varying magnitudes, some positive and some negative, operating simultaneously. Furthermore the process of credit expansion is intimately bound up with the flow of money payments in the economy and the generation of income through the operation of the spending stream, even though it is possible to analyze the two processes separately. We will make a beginning at an integrated sequence in Chapter

4, but the essentials are simple enough: the spending of borrowed money generates new income and thus produces a series of income-related developments.

Two aspects are immediately relevant for our sequence analysis: as income rises we may expect (a) import demand to rise (the import leakage) and (b) the demand for hand-to-hand currency to rise (the currency drain). We will treat the import leakage in somewhat greater detail in Chapters 4 and 5 below, and will adduce reasons for believing that the resultant drain on external reserves will operate with an appreciable lag. There are independent but parallel reasons for believing that the currency drain will also lag somewhat behind the increase in money income; this was the basis of much work on the monetary aspects of the business cycle before World War II by Hawtrey[10] and others. Between them these two lags suggest that in the initial stages of an expansion the financial system would temporarily retain more reserves of standard money than would prove compatible with ultimate equilibrium conditions and would therefore tend to overexpand credit, thus quickly bringing the financial structure to or above the theoretical equilibrium level. If we also allow for the operation of a number of independent disturbances, differing in magnitude and direction, the fairly prompt realization of the relationships postulated by sequence analysis seems quite reasonable.

A second problem arises from the fact that we are also working under the temporary constraint that all coefficients of substitution are constants. This implies that the stock of every type of financial asset, and the total stock of all financial assets, must cease to grow if any one of them ceases to grow. From this it would follow, for example, that net saving out of income must become zero in order that a given stock of money-proper might come into equilibrium with a given flow of money-income. This paradox is easily resolved, of course, by reinterpreting the coefficients of substitution as variables instead of constants. Nevertheless the assumption of fixed values is a useful simplification; they may be interpreted as the marginal rates applying at a particular point in time.

A third objection that can be made against the sequence analysis here used is that it seems more appropriate to near-banks than to banks of deposit. Thus in Tables 1.1, 1.2, and 1.3 all loans from and all redeposits (as we may as well call them for brevity) in the intermediary are in gold coin, and the implication is that gold coin is used in the meantime to effect whatever transactions occur.

There is no problem if the intermediaries are deemed to consist of or to

[10] R.G. Hawtrey, *Good and Bad Trade*, London, Constable & Co. Ltd., 1913; *Currency and Credit*, London and New York, Longmans Green, 1919; and *Capital and Employment*, London and New York, Longmans Green and Co., 1937.

Table 1.4. Bank Expansion in a Closed Economy: Cheqeuable-Deposit Banking

Sector assets and liabilities	Time sequence: (1)	(2)	(3)	(4)	(5)	(6)	(7)	(8) (∞)
General Public								
A Standard money	+ 1000	− 900		+ 81		+ 66		
		(+ 100)		(+ 181)		(+ 247)		...(+ 526)
Cheques for encashment			+ 810	− 810	+ 656	− 656	+ 531	... (−)
Deposit money		+ 900		+ 729		+ 590		
				+ 1629		(+ 2219)		(+ 4737)
Total	+ 1000		+ 810		+ 656		+ 531	
		(+ 1000)	(+ 1810)	(+ 1810)	(+ 2466)	(+ 2466)	(+ 2997)	...(+ 5263)
L Debts			+ 810		+ 656		+ 531	
					(+ 1466)		(+ 1997)	...(+ 4263)
Net Worth	+ 1000							
			(+ 1000)		(+ 1000)		(+ 1000)	...(+ 1000)

Banking System

Bank A / Bank C

	(1)	(2)	(3)	(4)	(5)	(6)	(7)	(8) (∞)
A Reserves—Required		+ 90				+ 59		
						(+ 222)		
—Free		+ 810		− 810		+ 531		...
Loans			+ 810				+ 531	
							(+ 1997)	...
L Deposits		+ 900	+ 810	− 810		+ 590	+ 531	
			(+ 1710)	(+ 900)		(+ 2219)	(+ 2750)	...

Bank B

	(1)	(2)	(3)	(4)	(5)	(6)	(7)	(8) (∞)
A Reserves—Required				+ 73				
				(+ 163)				...(+ 474)
—Free				+ 656		− 656		... (−)
Loans					+ 656			
					(+ 1466)			...(+ 4263)
L Deposits				+ 729	+ 656	− 656		
				(+ 1629)	(+ 2285)	(+ 1629)		...(+ 4737)

Note: Figures in parenthesis are cumulative totals. The public's acceptance ratio for bank deposits is 0.9, and is re-established in the cumulative totals in each even-numbered column; the banks' cash-reserve ratio is 0.1, and their total free reserves are "written up" in the borrower's deposit account in the odd-numbered columns then chequed against in the even-numbered columns.

include banks of issue: the public's claims on them will consist of or include banknotes, which by hypothesis are acceptable substitutes for gold coin for transactions purposes. However, if we wish to interpret our intermediaries as chequeable-deposit banks, we can easily modify or reinterpret the tables in a way that preserves the full monetary use of their obligations yet maintains the 1:9 ratio between standard money and chequeable deposits at all times. This is done in Table 1.4, which retains essentially the same presentation as Table 1.3 on page 23, but with three modifications. First, a third asset, "cheques for encashment", is added to the public's T-square accounts; in effect, the first line of Table 1.3 is divided into two distinct parts. Second, we revert to the customary assumptions that "new" money is first received by the general public, that each bank lends only its free reserves, and that each redeposit is made in one individual bank. (Note that, alternatively, the banking system may be deemed to consist of a large number of small banks A, B, C, D, . . . , instead of only three banks.) Third, to economize on space, interim balance-sheet positions are omitted and the representations of the individual banks are staggered in two tiers.

In column 1 1,000 dinars of "new" money (say, newly mined and minted gold coin) is put into circulation, and in column 2 the public deposits 900 dinars in Bank A in order to restore its desired ratio between standard money and chequeable deposits, thus generating 810 dinars of free reserves. In column 3 the bank makes a loan to a customer by "writing up" a credit of 810 dinars in his chequing account and recording his promissory note as an offsetting asset; the borrower immediately writes a cheque for the full amount in favour of a supplier or creditor, who is deemed to have received it but not yet encashed it.[11] In column 4 the payee deposits the cheque in Bank B but immediately withdraws 81 dinars in cash, so the money supply has increased by 1,810 dinars, of which 181 dinars is in standard money and 1,629 dinars is in chequeable deposits.[12] Bank B now

---

[11] Technically, a cheque is neither standard money nor deposit money, it is merely a claim to money until it is cleared to and honoured by the payer's bank, but in practice it is usually treated as a cash item. For our purposes "cheques for encashment" may be deemed to be claims to standard money and chequeable deposits in the ratio 1:9—especially since by hypothesis the cheques are good and will be honoured on presentation.

[12] In Bank B's hands the cheque becomes "cash in transit" or "debit float" until it can be cleared to Bank A and payment obtained in standard money or its equivalent (e.g., by offsetting it against other claims that Bank A may have on Bank B). A bank may give immediate credit to the depositor, or may defer credit until the funds have been recovered through the clearing mechanism or for some standard period deemed equal to the average clearing time. These technicalities are of considerable practical importance in day-to-day banking operations, but need not complicate our presentation of the basic principles; you may think of column 4 as including both the actual negotiation of the cheque at Bank B and the clearing of it to Bank A.

has free reserves of 656 dinars, and the sequence of loans and redeposits continues to the same ultimate equilibrium position as before.

Three brief comments may be added, in the interests of realism. First, instead of a single borrower at each round, we should be thinking in terms of many borrowers and many depositors. Second, these depositors will not make their deposits in a single bank in the system but will distribute them among all banks in a pattern determined by the preferences of each depositor, the geographic location of each bank, and other considerations. Third, the "new" deposits will not necessarily stay with the bank in which they are first made but will be absorbed into the dynamic flow of the total stock of deposits through the financial system. This dynamic flow of funds may very well reallocate resources from one bank to another, so that the accident of which bank first receives a given inflow of funds may have little to do with whether that bank grows and prospers more than others.

This third question—the appropriateness of interpreting our intermediaries as banks—will arise even more forcefully in sections 1 and 3 of Chapter 4 below, where redeposits are identified with savings out of income. The full resolution of the difficulty lies in separately identifying money-to-hold and money-to-spend, as is done in section 2 of Chapter 5. The justification for the procedure used in Tables 1.1, 1.2, and 1.3 is that it simplifies the presentation without prejudicing the conclusions. At this stage we are primarily interested in the long-run equilibrium position, and the stock of money-proper must become money-to-hold if it is to be in equilibrium with the rate of flow of money-income; the dynamics of the conversion of money-to-spend into money-to-hold can wait until later.

5. The Controlling Factors

5.1. Public Acceptance

In each of the sequences we have discussed there are two necessary conditions for a credit-based expansion of the public's liquid assets: (1) the general public must be willing to accept alternatives to standard money for some portion of its portfolio of liquid assets, and (2) the issuers of acceptable alternatives must maintain reserves of less than 100 per cent in standard money against those obligations.

At the risk of becoming embroiled in a deep philosophical argument over whether one necessary condition can be "more necessary" than another, we may suggest that the most fundamental controlling factor in any expansionary sequence is the general public's willingness to accept a particular financial claim as a substitute for standard money. No credit expansions can take place without this acceptability of the substitute, and the potential credit expansion therefrom is limited to the amount of substitutes the public is willing to accept in lieu of standard money.

The potential expansion is much greater where the public is willing or can be led to accept something approaching 100 per cent substitution of the new instrument for standard money, as in the case of transferrable claims (banknotes and chequeable deposits), and may then approach infinity in a closed-economy model in the absence of a stipulated minimum reserve requirement; in other cases even zero reserves would leave potential credit expansion finite, because the new instrument could not (or not completely) replace standard money for transactions purposes. But how close the actual acceptance of any particular instrument comes to its potential acceptance depends primarily on the preferences of the public.

5.2. The Primary Reserve Ratio
Confidence that a particular financial intermediary or type of intermediary is maintaining cash reserves adequate to its liquidity needs is presumably a factor in the public's willingness to accept the obligations of that intermediary or type of intermediary. As a controlling factor in credit expansion, however, the role of the primary (cash) reserve ratio that any issuer of claims is constrained to keep against his liabilities, whether in a closed or an open economy, and whether dictated by law or by prudence or whatever, is strictly subordinate to the acceptability of the claims he issues as a substitute for standard money for transactions purposes, for asset purposes, or for both. Unless an issuer can persuade someone to accept his obligations for one or both of these purposes, his reserve ratio will be inoperative. Even when a given type of institution does get an appreciable acceptance as a repository for a portion of the public's savings, a sharp reduction in the reserve ratio leaves the potential credit expansion distinctly limited.

5.3. International Transferability of Claims
A third controlling factor operates to limit credit expansion in an open economy: the fact that the ownership of liquid assets can be transferred from one country to another, through the foreign exchange markets and in other ways. These transfers of title may consist of the exchange of one liquid asset for another (purely financial-capital transactions), or they may arise in settlement of the well-known exchange leakages arising out of income-expansion sequences either in the domestic economy itself or in the rest of the world. In either case the immediate effect is a loss of foreign-exchange reserves (an external drain) for one country and a corresponding gain for another. Generalizing somewhat from the simple model we have used so far, we may say that, if the domestic credit structure is directly or indirectly based in a more-or-less-determinate way on the volume of foreign-exchange reserves, even a relatively moderate marginal propensity to import or marginal propensity to acquire foreign assets will sharply

reduce the potential credit expansion compared to closed-economy conditions. Even a fully-managed monetary system operates under severe constraints in this respect.

CHAPTER 2

PYRAMIDING

1. Preliminaries

The pyramiding of credit expansion, or pyramiding for short, arises when the obligations of some type or types of financial intermediary become acceptable by some or all other intermediaries for at least a part of their cash-reserve needs. By hypothesis the obligations of or claims on all intermediaries are supported by cash reserves of less then 100 per cent, hence they are substantially credit-based. Typically, but not necessarily, the standard money itself will be a credit-based money. Typically, but not necessarily, a commodity-money or the equivalent will serve as the ultimate standard money.

This chapter will deal exclusively with the institutional aspects of pyramiding, i.e. the growth of loans by and claims against intermediaries, but you should keep clearly in mind the implication that there is an associated expansion of income and savings as well.

2. Simple Pyramiding

2.1. Definition
Let us define simple pyramiding as a situation in which one and only one particular issue of credit money comes to be used as cash reserves by other financial intermediaries as a substitute in whole or in part for an intrinsically valuable standard money such as a gold coin; and, for greater certainty, in this definition we will specifically include the limiting case in which this particular issue of credit money is an inconvertible paper currency. This will cover situations in which the financial claim in question is only a partial substitute for standard money for cash-reserve purposes, in which it is the effective standard money in practice though not so recognized at law, and in which its status as standard money is enshrined in law as well as in practice. Practical considerations suggest that no financial claim issued by one intermediary will be used as cash reserves by other intermediaries unless it is widely accepted by the general public as an effective substitute for standard money for all purposes including transactions purposes, and that any financial claim that does in fact achieve the degree of hegemony over other claims that our definition postulates has at least the potential of displacing whatever has previously been standard money and itself becoming the standard money.

The typical case of simple pyramiding is that noted on pages 29ff above, in which an officially-recognized bank of issue or central bank becomes established and is given a monopoly of the note issue, or in some other way achieves a high acceptance ratio for its obligations. Let us use the term Bank of Issue for this privileged intermediary, differentiating it from a central bank primarily by the postulate that it does not attempt to carry out a discretionary monetary policy and merely responds mechanically to external stimuli. For simplicity we will speak as if all other intermediaries in the model are banks of deposit as rigorously defined on page 6 above, though if you wish you may think of a combined system of banks and all other financial intermediaries (sometimes called "non-bank financial intermediaries", or "non-banks" for short) as long as you respect the stipulation that claims against the Bank of Issue are the only form of credit-money that is eligible as cash reserves.[1] We will also speak as if banknotes are the only obligations of the Bank of Issue, though in practice deposit balances placed with it by the deposit banks may substitute for note holdings in some uses.

2.2. Standard Money in Transition

Let us now envisage the establishment of a Bank of Issue in a hypothetical closed economy in which a gold franc is the standard money and until now full-bodied gold coin has been the only form of hand-to-hand currency, though banks of deposit operate and offer chequeable deposit accounts; they enjoy a 90 per cent deposit-acceptance ratio, and maintain cash reserves of 10 per cent. Obviously the new note-issue is a good candidate to supplement or supplant gold coins as the standard money of the economy, if only it can win sufficient acceptance by the public. Where the unadorned term "standard money" would otherwise be ambiguous we will refer to gold coin (or the equivalent) as the "ultimate" standard money and the note issue as the "new" or "potential" standard money. We will use the term "composite standard money" to mean whatever combination of ultimate standard money and notes is accepted in practice by the public as hand-to-hand currency and the deposit banks as reserves. Also, we will define the public's acceptance ratio for the new notes in terms of the ultimate standard money. However, we will now define the public's deposit-acceptance ratio in terms of the composite standard money actually in use at any given time, on the supposition that the significant relationship is between deposits and hand-to-hand currency rather than between deposits and the ultimate standard money.

---

[1] You may also observe that the model applies equally well to a system in which the other banks are banks of issue rather than banks of deposit, but use the notes of the Bank of Issue wholly or partly for their cash reserves. Historical examples of such systems are well known.

First, suppose that public opinion gradually accepts a representative full-bodied convertible franc, that is a paper currency against which the Bank of Issue is obliged to keep 100 per cent reserves in gold coin or gold bullion and which it is obliged to issue for or redeem in gold on demand, in order to get the convenience of a paper currency without any risk of inflation. Clearly there is no change in the credit-expanding potential of the financial system; the total volume of the composite standard money available to the public and the banks (i.e. the note issue plus such gold as is not held as reserves for these notes) is exactly the same as the total supply of ultimate standard money no matter whether the public's note-acceptance ratio is zero or 100 per cent or anything in between, and no matter whether the banks of deposit hold their reserves in coin or in notes.

Next, suppose the Bank of Issue is permitted to reduce its reserve ratio below 100 per cent, and the public comes to accept the revised note issue for a material portion of its hand-to-hand currency requirements. A single intermediary like our privileged Bank of Issue will soon observe (a) that it has material market power in dealing with its borrowers and (b) that the reduction in its reserves in ultimate standard money (the internal gold drain) associated with a given loan will be appreciably less than the loan. In the real world the first of these points leads away from the automatic responses we are here postulating and towards the establishment of a discretionary central bank, but that does not concern us now. The second point merely means that the credit-expansion process associated with its activities may proceed much more rapidly than the step-by-step sequence associated with competitive banking, as noted in section 1.4 of Chapter 1 above; this, too, is largely irrelevant for our present purposes.

Table 2.1 gives some numerical illustrations of the establishment of a new standard money and the introduction of simple pyramiding. Column 1 represents the situation before the establishment of the Bank of Issue, and column 2 represents the introduction and complete acceptance of the Bank of Issue's notes as representative paper money; there is no expansion of credit or of domestic financial assets in column 2 compared to column 1, nor would there be for any intermediate note-acceptance ratio between zero and 100 per cent on the part of either the public or the deposit banks. Column 3 represents the further expansion of the system that will occur if the Bank of Issue's reserve ratio is reduced to 10 per cent (the same as the deposit banks) and if the public accepts its notes for all hand-to-hand currency requirements. On these assumptions the volume of credit and of the public's financial assets will be unaffected by a change in the deposit-acceptance ratio, and without pyramiding the only possibility of further expansion from the position shown in column 3 would be to reduce the reserve ratio for notes or deposits or both.

Table 2.1. The Start of Simple Pyramiding in a Closed Economy[1]

Sector assets and liabilities	$A=B=0,$ $0\leq R\leq1$ (1)	$A=B=1,$ $R=1$ (2)	$A=1, R=0.1$ $B=0$ (3)	$B=0.5$ (4)	$B=1$ (5)	$R=0.1,$ $A=B=145/190$ (6)
General Public						
A Gold coin	526	–	–	–	–	398
Banknotes	–	526	1,000	1,681	5,263	1,283
Bank deposits	4,737	4,737	9,000	15,126	47,368	15,126
Domestic assets	5,263	5,263	10,000	16,807	52,632	16,807
L Debts	4,263	4,263	9,000	15,807	51,632	15,807
Net worth	1,000	1,000	1,000	1,000	1,000	1,000
Deposit Banks						
A Gold coin	474	–	900	756	–	358
Banknotes	–	474	–	756	4,737	1,154
Loans	4,263	4,263	8,100	13,613	42,632	13,613
L Deposits	4,737	4,737	9,000	15,126	47,368	15,126
Bank of Issue						
A Gold coin	–	1,000	100	244	1,000	244
Loans	–	–	900	2,193	9,000	2,193
L Note issue	–	1,000	1,000	2,437	10,000	2,437
Held by public	–	526	1,000	1,681	5,263	1,283
Held by banks	–	474	–	756	4,737	1,154
Memoranda:						
Standard money[2]	1,000	1,000	1,900	3,193	10,000	3,193
Basic gold ratio[3]	19%	19%	10%	5.95%	1.9%	5.95%

[1] A numerical example, assuming a public deposit-acceptance ratio of 90 per cent and a deposit-bank reserve ratio of 10 per cent in composite standard money. Subject to the constraint that $0\leq A,B,R\leq1$, A is the public's and B is the deposit-banks' note-acceptance ratio and R is the Bank of Issue's reserve ratio, in gold coin. The figures are derived from the algebraic formulation given in section 2.6 below, rounded to the nearest whole number.

[2] Gold coin and banknotes held outside the Bank of Issue.

[3] The ratio of gold retained in the economy (= net worth) to the public's domestic financial assets.

Now let simple pyramiding begin—that is, let the deposit banks begin to accept notes for some portion of their reserve requirements. Column 4 shows that a 50 per cent note-acceptance ratio by the deposit banks brings a 68 per cent increase in domestic financial assets compared to the no-pyramiding situation in column 3 on the assumptions here made, and an increase of over 75 per cent in credit. In the limiting case (column 5) in which the deposit banks' note-acceptance ratio reaches 100 per cent, like that of the public, pyramiding brings a more-than-five-fold increase in domestic financial assets. Column 6 is essentially a variant of column 4; it has been added to bring out a subsidiary point, which will be discussed shortly.

In column 1 there is one and only one standard money, the gold franc. In columns 2 and 5 the notes of the Bank of Issue have replaced gold coin as the sole standard money. In columns 3,4, and 6 there is a composite standard money: the new standard money plus any ultimate standard money held outside the Bank of Issue. (Alternatively you may say that it consists of the ultimate standard money plus the secondary expansion of the Bank of Issue's notes; the main thing is to avoid double counting of the ultimate standard money held as reserves against the new standard money.)

The fact that the public and the deposit banks may have different note-acceptance ratios, as in columns 3 and 4, is immaterial; what matters is the weighted average of their note-acceptance ratios. This is brought out in column 6, where the note-acceptance ratio of both the public and the banks is equal to their weighted-average value in column 4, i.e. about 76.3 per cent; any other combination of note-acceptance ratios with the same weighted-average value would produce the same balance-sheet totals for all three sectors, as you may verify by experiment.

Of course, the numerical results given in the table have very limited meaning in themselves. The analytically significant point is that simple pyramiding can bring an appreciable increase in the expansion of domestic financial assets and credit on a given base of ultimate standard money. Alternatively, you may say pyramiding reduces the ratio of ultimate standard money to domestic financial assets, shown as the "basic gold ratio" in the table. This is not a commonly-used ratio, and indeed it holds little practical or theoretical interest under modern conditions, but it graphically illustrates the effects of pyramiding in economizing on external reserves.

2.3. A Double Money-Multiplier
In this closed-economy model the domestic money-multiplier (or financial-asset multiplier) can be cleanly divided into two segments. Since there is no external drain to complicate matters, the supply of composite

standard money can be derived independently of the expansion of deposit money that may be associated with it; then the deposit-bank expansion can be determined in the usual way from the supply of composite standard money.

The techniques developed in Chapter 1 above can easily be adapted to this purpose. First, we may identify the unspecified intermediary as the Bank of Issue and replace "general public" by "general public and deposit banks". Substituting the weighted average of the public's and the deposit banks' note-acceptance ratios (their combined holdings of banknotes divided by their combined holdings of notes and coin) for the public's deposit-acceptance ratio, setting $d=0$, and using the Bank of Issue's reserve ratio, equation 1.1 on page 26 above will give the values for the composite standard money shown in Table 2.1. Second, we can then apply the techniques of Chapter 1 once more, and generate a further multiple expansion of domestic financial assets and credit from this supply of composite standard money. Thus in all the columns of Table 2.1 the figure for total financial assets is the same multiple of the composite standard money, and so is the credit expansion *generated by the deposit banks*, because the public's deposit-acceptance ratio and the deposit banks' reserve ratio are unchanged. However, the *total* credit generated is a progressively larger multiple of the standard-money supply in columns 3 to 5 inclusive because of the additional credit expansion associated with the credit-based portion of the composite standard money.

2.4. The Process of Expansion

As a practical matter, however, it is more realistic to envisage pyramided credit expansion as a single integrated process. Table 2.2 sets it out schematically. The note-acceptance ratio of the public and the deposit banks is assumed to be 80 per cent and the Bank of Issue's reserve ratio 40 per cent in ultimate standard money; the public's deposit-acceptance ratio is 90 per cent and the deposit banks' reserve ratio 10 per cent in composite standard money. The Bank of Issue's reserve ratio has been chosen with an eye to typical practices under classic gold-standard conditions,[2] but even so has merely illustrative significance, and the other parameters have been chosen primarily for arithmetic convenience.

---

[2] See A.I. Bloomfield, *Monetary Policy under the International Gold Standard: 1880–1914,* New York, Federal Reserve Bank of New York, 1959, pp. 29–34. Legal reserve requirements usually applied only to note issues, and were not necessarily proportional; for example, the Bank of England was required to maintain a reserve of 100 per cent of its note issue in excess of a set fiduciary figure (which was changed from time to time). However, Bloomfield uses the ratio of all external assets to all sight liabilities (notes and deposits) of central banks, which is essentially what is intended by the "gold coin" and "notes" of our Bank of Issue.

Table 2.2. The Simple-Pyramiding Process in a Closed Economy[1]

Sector Assets and Liabilities	(1) *	(2) #	(3) #	(4) *	(5) #	(6) #	(7) *	(8) * (∞)
General Public								
A Gold coin	20		+ 25.8	46		+ 25.5	71 ...	202
Banknotes	80	+ 480	− 376.8	183	+ 230.4	− 128.4	285 ...	810
Bank deposits	900	+ 810	+ 351.0	2,061	+ 1,044.9	+ 102.9	3,209 ...	9,109
Domestic assets	1,000	+ 1,290		2,290	+ 1,275.3		3,565 ...	10,121
L Debts	−	+ 1,290		1,290	+ 1,275.3		2,565 ...	9,121
Net worth	1,000			1,000			1,000 ...	1,000
Deposit Banks								
A Gold coin	180		+ 70.2	250		+ 20.6	271 ...	182
Banknotes	720		+ 280.8	1,001		+ 82.3	1,083 ...	729
Loans	−	+ 810		810	+ 1,044.9		1,855 ...	8,198
L Deposits	900	+ 810	+ 351.0	2,061	+ 1,044.9	+ 102.9	3,209 ...	9,109
Bank of Issue								
A Gold coin	820		− 96.0	704		− 46.1	658 ...	615
Loans	−	+ 480		480	+ 230.4		710 ...	923
L Note Issue	800	+ 480	− 96.0	1,184	+ 230.4	− 46.1	1,368 ...	1,538
Held by public	80	+ 480	− 376.8	183	+ 230.4	− 128.4	285 ...	810
Held by banks	720		+ 280.8	1,001		+ 82.3	1,083 ...	729
Memoranda:								
Standard money[2]	1,000			1,480			1,710	1,923
Basic gold ratio[3]	100%			44%			28%	10%

[1] A numerical example. The note-acceptance ratio for the public and the deposit banks is 80 per cent in gold coin, the public's deposit-acceptance ratio is 90 per cent and the deposit banks' reserve ratio is 10 per cent in terms of the composite standard money, and the note-reserve ratio is 40 per cent in terms of gold coin. Final digits are rounded to the nearest whole number.

[2] Gold and banknotes held outside the Bank of Issue.

[3] The ratio of gold held in the economy (= net worth) to the public's domestic financial assets.

* Balance-sheet positions at given points in time.

Changes occurring in a given period of time.

45

The presentation starts (column 1) at the point where the public has received an increase of 1,000 francs in ultimate standard money, perhaps through the minting of new gold production, and has arranged its financial-asset portfolio in accordance with its coefficients of substitution among coin, notes, and deposits, namely 1:4:45, by retaining 20 francs in coin, acquiring 80 francs in notes from the Bank of Issue either directly or through the deposit banks, and depositing the balance. The deposit banks in turn have tendered 720 francs in gold to the Bank of Issue in exchange for notes, thus dividing their reserve-holdings between notes and coin in the accepted ratio in anticipation of net withdrawals by the public or growing reserve requirements. In column 2 the intermediaries make loans equal to their free reserves. Under closed-economy conditions the Bank of Issue might have decided to lend much more than this initially, but we may as well anticipate the limitations imposed when we move to open-economy conditions, in which case the Bank of Issue will face an external drain approximating the amount of its loans. We have represented these as being made in the form of an increase in its note issue, though if you wish you may think of it as making loans to or buying securities from individuals and paying by cashier's cheques on itself, which will in due course be deposited with the deposit banks; for its notes, its deposit liabilities, and its cashier's cheques alike are nothing more than its own IOU's. Similarly, we have shown the deposit banks as making loans by "writing up" their own deposits. In column 3 the public re-establishes its desired asset mix, and the deposit banks restore the accepted ratio of coins to notes in their reserve holdings. By column 4 the Bank of Issue and the deposit banks find themselves with new lending capacity, and thus the expansion continues until their free reserves are eliminated.

The equilibrium position is most easily found from the final allocation of ultimate standard money in the usual way. The increments of the Bank of Issue's loans and outstanding notes constitute simple geometric progressions with a common ratio of 0.48 and thus can be easily summed. The increments of the deposit banks' assets and liabilities, however, follow a more complex pattern. The second increase of their loans (column 5) is 29 per cent higher than the first (column 2), because the initial loans by the Bank of Issue are over 59 per cent of the initial loans of the deposit banking system, and the redeposit of these loans adds more to the reserves of the deposit banks than they lose through the currency drain. The third increase in the deposit-banks' loans (not shown in the table) is just short of 1,033 francs, and subsequent increments decline further. While not a simple geometric progression, the sequence can be summed by standard algebraic techniques.

2.5. Open-Economy Conditions

In adapting the model to open-economy conditions let us use the same constrained-equilibrium interpretation as before, and let us start with an initial net receipt of 1,000 francs in gold coin or the equivalent (perhaps from new export earnings) which the public decides to add to its domestic financial assets. We may again use d to indicate the link between domestic credit expansion and the external gold drain, as in section 2.5 of Chapter 1 above, but we need not specify whether the drain represents the acquisition of external assets, an import leakage out of income or out of the spending of borrowed money, or some combination of the three.

Table 2.3 illustrates how simple pyramiding affects credit expansion in an open economy. The public's note-acceptance ratio is assumed to be 100 per cent, partly for simplicity but partly in recognition of the fact that nowadays virtually no country permits the circulation of full-bodied coins or the equivalent;[3] the deposit-acceptance ratio again has been set at 90 per cent, the deposit-reserve ratio at 10 per cent, and the note-reserve ratio at 40 per cent. Columns 1 to 3 inclusive are the appropriate non-pyramiding reference points for comparative purposes. Comparing column 4 with column 1, the introduction to simple pyramiding on the terms indicated (raising the deposit banks' note-acceptance ratio from zero to 100 per cent) adds 71 per cent to the domestic-financial-asset multiplier (column 4 compared to column 1), and a reduction in the Bank of Issue's reserve ratio toward zero (not shown in the table) would raise that multiplier astronomically. Now contrast this with the $d=1$ case in columns 2, 5, and 7. The change in the deposit-banks' note-acceptance ratio from zero to 100 per cent raises the domestic-financial-asset multiplier only 5 per cent, and reducing the Bank of Issue's reserve ratio to zero brings a total increase of only 13 per cent from the no-pyramiding level (column 2). In the $d=10$ case the increases are even smaller: the total in column 6 is only 0.5 per cent above column 3, and in column 8 only 1.3 per cent.

The case of a zero basic gold ratio (columns 7 and 8) can easily be reconciled with the real-world conditions for a financial system managed by an efficient central bank, which may choose to allow its external reserves to fall to (or below) zero, as noted on page 31 above. A reconciliation with an automatically-operating system is also possible, if we interpret the example as involving marginal increments of deposits to an established structure. We might postulate that the Bank of Issue is required to maintain a fixed total reserve up to some maximum note liability; or that a change of conditions has led to a relaxation of required or customary reserves, thus permitting an expansion of the financial structure on the same base of ultimate standard money.

---

[3] The exceptions include a declining number of small countries in which the currency of another country is used as the local standard money.

Table 2.3. Simple Pyramiding in an Open Economy[1]

Sector assets and liabilities	R=0.4, A=1, B=0			R=0.4, A=B=1			R=0, A=B=1	
	d=0	d=1	d=10	d=0	d=1	d=10	d=1	d=10
	(1)	(2)	(3)	(4)	(5)	(6)	(7)	(8)
General Public								
A Banknotes	769	88.5	9.87	1,316	92.94	9.92	100	10
Bank deposits	6,923	796.5	88.85	11,842	836.43	89.32	900	90
Domestic assets	7,692	885.0	98.72	13,158	929.37	99.25	1,000	100
L Debts	6,692	769.9	85.88	12,158	858.74	91.70	1,000	100
Net worth	1,000	115.0	12.83	1,000	70.63	7.54	—	—
Deposit Banks								
A Gold coin	692	79.6	8.88	—	—	—	—	—
Banknotes	—	—	—	1,184	83.64	8.93	90	9
Loans	6,231	716.8	79.96	10,658	752.79	80.39	810	81
L Deposits	6,923	796.5	88.85	11,842	836.43	89.32	900	90
Bank of Issue								
A Gold coin	308	35.4	3.95	1,000	70.63	7.54	—	—
Loans	462	53.1	5.92	1,500	105.95	11.31	190	19
L Note issue	769	88.5	9.87	2,500	176.58	18.86	190	19
Held by public	769	88.5	9.87	1,316	92.94	9.92	100	10
Held by banks	—	—	—	1,184	83.64	8.93	90	9
External Drain	—	885.0	987.17	—	929.37	992.46	1,000	1,000
Memoranda:								
Standard money[2]	1,462	168.1	18.76	2,500	176.58	18.86	190	19
Basic gold ratio[3]	13%	13%	13%	7.6%	7.6%	7.6%	0%	0%

[1] Numerical examples, assuming a public deposit-acceptance ratio of 90 per cent and a deposit-bank reserve ratio of 10 per cent in composite standard money. Subject to the constraint that $0 \leq A, B, R, \leq 1$, A is the public's and B is the deposit-banks' note-acceptance ratio, and R is the Bank of Issue's reserve ratio, in gold coin, and d is the ratio of the external drain to domestic liquid assets. The figures are derived from the algebraic formulation given in section 2.6 below, rounded to the nearest whole number.

[2] Gold coin and banknotes held outside the Bank of Issue.

[3] The ratio of gold retained in the economy (= net worth) to the public's domestic financial assets.

2.6. Algebraic Formulation

In order to analyze the simple-pyramiding case algebraically we need to introduce several new variables in addition to those used in section 2.5 of Chapter 1 above, and some previously-used variables must be redefined:

Gk: Now subdivided into Gb and Gi, the portions held by the deposit banks and the Bank of Issue respectively as all or part of their cash reserves. By hypothesis $Gk=Gi+Gb$.

N: The notes issued by the Bank of Issue. By hypothesis they are held either by the public (Np) as part of Ad or by the deposit banks (Nb) as part of their cash reserves; i.e. $N=Np + Nb$.

K: Now subdivided into claims against the Bank of Issue (Np) and claims against the deposit banks (Dp) respectively. By hypothesis $K=Np+Dp$.

L: Now subdivided into loans granted by the Bank of Issue (Li) and loans granted by the deposit banks (Lb) respectively. By hypothesis $L=Li+Lb$.

Ad: In the present context $Ad=Gp+Np+Dp$.

A: The public's acceptance ratio for Np in terms of coin; i.e. $A=Np/(Gp + Np)$. Subject to the constraint that $0 \leq A \leq 1$.

B: The deposit banks' acceptance ratio for Nb in terms of coin; i.e. $B-Nb/(Gb + Nb)$. Subject to the constraint that $0 \leq B \leq 1$.

Su: The ultimate standard money of the economy. By hypothesis $Su-G - Gd$.

Sc: The composite standard money of the economy. By hypothesis $Sc = N+Gp+Gb$; but $Gi = RN$ and $G = Gp+Gb+Gi+Gd$, hence $Sc = N(1-R)+Gp+Gb+Gi = N(1-R)+G-Gd$.

$S'c$: A partial-equilibrium value of Sc, explained below and defined as $N(1-R)+G$.

R: The reserve ratio maintained by the Bank of Issue in terms of coin; i.e. $R = Gi/N$. Subject to the constraint that $0 \leq R \leq 1$.

a: The public's acceptance ratio for Dp in terms of its combined holdings of notes and coins; i.e. $a = Dp/Ad = Dp/(Gp+Np+Dp)$.

r: The reserve ratio of the deposit banks in terms of their combined holdings of notes and coins; i.e. $r = (Gb+Nb)/Dp$.

As in previous cases, the equilibrium position is most easily obtained by focusing on the allocation of G. The amount of hand-to-hand currency

49

associated with the equilibrium value of Ad will be $(1-a).Ad$, of which $(1-A)(1-a).Ad$ will be in gold $(=Gp)$ and $A(1-a).Ad$ will be in notes $(=Np)$. Deposit-bank reserves will be $r.aAd$, of which $(1-B).arAd$ will be in gold $(=Gb)$ and $B.arAd$ will be in notes $(=Nb)$. Since $N=Np+Nb$ and $Gi=NR$, $Gi=R[A(1-a)+arB]Ad$. By hypothesis the external drain is dAd $(=Gp)$ and $G=Gp+Gb+Gi+Gd$, hence $G=[(1-A)(1-a)+ar(1-B)+AR(1-a)+arBR+d]Ad$; solving for Ad and simplifying, we get:

$$Ad = G/W \dots\dots\dots\dots\dots\dots\dots\dots\dots\dots\dots\dots \quad (2.1)$$

where $W=d+(1-a)[1-A(1-R)]+ar[1-B(1-R)]$.

Note that Ad will be less than G, and therefore the secondary expansion of domestic assets will be negative, if the denominator of the right-hand member of the equation is greater than unity. That is, $Ad-G<0$ if various parameters, the highest value of d for which $Ad-G \geq 0$ is unity. This in turn requires either (a) that $r=0$ and $a=1$, or (b) that $R=0$ and (i) $A=B=1$ or (ii) $a=0$ and $A=1$ or (iii) $a=B=1$—i.e. that some form or combination of forms of domestic credit-based money that requires no reserves in ultimate standard money enjoys 100 per cent acceptance. (These of course are conditions that would lead to an unlimited expansion in a closed economy.)

The equilibrium values of all the other variables may be determined from Ad by applying the appropriate coefficients. However, it will be useful to identify those of the note issue (N) and the composite standard money (Sc) specifically:

$$N = [A(1-a)+arB] G/W \dots\dots\dots\dots\dots\dots\dots\dots\dots (2.2)$$
$$Sc = [1-a(1-r)] G/W \dots\dots\dots\dots\dots\dots\dots\dots\dots\dots (2.3).$$

If you wish to separate the open-economy expansionary process into an initial expansion of composite standard money and a subsequent expansion of domestic financial assets on that base, analagous to the closed-economy case in section 2.3 above, it will not do to divide equation 2.3 by G to obtain the first multiplier and equation 2.1 by equation 2.3 to obtain the second, even though $Sc/G \times Ad/Sc = Ad/G$; Ad/Sc is not a true multiplier in this case, but merely a ratio between the equilibrium values of the two variables on the assumptions made,[4] and Sc/G is the wrong mulitplier for the first purpose. We want a preliminary partial-equilibrium value of Sc (call it $S'c$) to which we can apply equation 1.1 on page 26 above to derive the equilibrium value of Ad, and which will reduce to Sc after the external drain. The required value is $S'c = G+N(1-R)$, i.e. the

---

[4] See section 2.2 of Chapter 4 below, including footnote 5.

initial injection of ultimate standard money plus the equilibrium value of $Li.$[5] Hence:

$$S'c=[1+d-a(1-r)] \, G/W \dots\dots\dots\dots (2.4).$$

Now we can convert equation 1.1 into a multiplier, $1 / [d+1-a(1-r)]$, apply it to $S'c$, and derive Ad; or, alternatively, we can convert both equation 2.4 and equation 1.1 into multipliers and apply them simultaneously to G to derive Ad.

A number of special cases merit brief mention:
(1) If $d = 0$ (the closed-economy case) then $S'c = Sc$; the expansion of composite standard money and the expansion of deposit-money are independent, as in section 2.3 above.
(2) If $A = B$ (i.e. if the public and the deposit banks maintain the same mix of coin and notes in their holdings) then the denominators in equations 2.1 to 2.4 reduce to $d+[1-a(1-r)][1-A(1-R)]$. If in addition $d = 0$ (the closed-economy case) then the first-stage multiplier becomes $1 / [1-A(1-R)]$ and the second $1 / [1-a(1-r)]$; not only can they be calculated independently, but also they contain no parameters in common.
(3) If $A = B = 1$ (100 per cent acceptance of notes in lieu of coin) the denominators reduce to $d+R[1-a(1-r)]$.
(4) If $A = B = 0$ or if $R = 1$ then equation 2.1 reduces to equation 1.1 on page 26 above.

The step-by-step expansion in algebraic terms is simple in principle but complicated in practice by the rapidly-rising number of terms to be accommodated. The starting-point is the net receipt of G francs after any increase of foreign assets (Af) that happens to be associated therewith, which the public treats as a net addition to domestic financial assets (Ad); the public retains $(1-A)(1-a).G$ francs in coin, exchanges $A(1-a).G$ francs at the Bank of Issue for notes, and places $a.G$ francs with the deposit banks. In their turn the deposit banks retain $(1-B).aG$ francs in coin and exchange $B.aG$ francs for notes; their free reserves are $a(1-r).G$ francs, which they lend. The Bank of Issue receives a total of $[A(1-a)+aB].G$ francs in coin from the public and the deposit banks in exchange for its notes, and lends $(1-R)[A(1-a)+aB].G$ francs. These loans are made by crediting the borrowers' deposit accounts and by new note issues, respectively, thus raising the public's total domestic financial assets (Ad) by the same amount. By hypothesis the public divides these funds between an external drain and a net increase of domestic financial assets in the ratio of

---

[5] We may rationalize the Bank of Issue's action by supposing that past experience permits it to estimate the values of the various parameters fairly accurately, and thereby determine (a) the approximate net receipt of ultimate standard money by the economy as a whole from the initial increase in its own note issue and (b) the amount of loans it can safely issue on that basis.

d:1, and apportions its accumulated domestic financial assets as before, thus providing the deposit banks and the Bank of Issue anew with free reserves; and so on.

3. Cross Pyramiding

3.1. Definition

A different type of pyramiding may exist if similar financial institutions are able to count claims on one another as part of their cash reserves; we may call this "cross pyramiding". Well-known examples of the practice are to be found throughout the banking history of the U.S.A., and in other countries as well. It offers material advantages to local or regional banks in a multi-bank system, because they must carry deposit balances with banking correspondents in major financial centres for clearing and other purposes regardless of whether they count as part of their required reserves. In the days of banknote banking it might have involved notes issued by other banks, deposit balances with other banks, or both. Examples are still to be found today, as when a bank counts balances with its correspondents as part of its required or customary reserves.

3.2. Cross Pyramiding with Competing Banknote Issues

Some versions of cross pyramiding involve situations in which all banks are banks of issue, or are combined banks of issue and deposit. The need for till money to meet daily fluctuations in cash demands is much less for a bank of issue and deposit than for a bank of deposit only, because its own stock of unissued notes (just so much stationery until issued, albeit expensive stationery) will normally be acceptable to members of the public who wish to convert their deposits into currency; combining the two functions in a single institution may therefore permit it to operate with a lower reserve ratio. In order to isolate the direct effects of cross pyramiding, however, we will assume that the reserve ratio is unchanged. Furthermore the required or customary ratio and other constraints on the note issue may differ from those on deposits, so we may as well treat the two functions as if they were performed by separate banks.

One of the simpler versions of cross pyramiding gives results that are virtually identical with simple pyramiding. Let us interpret Tables 2.1 to 2.3 above as representing the establishment of a number of competing banks of issue in an economy where competing banks of deposit are already operating.[6] Provided that on the average their reserve ratios are the same

---

[6] As a matter of historical record, competing banks of issue preceded or were at first more important than banks of deposit in many jurisdictions; however, that is irrelevant for our purposes.

and the public's acceptance ratio for their notes is the same as for the Bank of Issue, exactly the same volume of money, monetary components, loans, exchange drain, etc., will obtain as under simple pyramiding. We will not be able to identify their note issues as a component of a new composite standard money, because their diversity is a contradiction of the concept of standard, but they are clearly close substitutes for standard money.[7]

In a system of competing banks of issue or combined banks of issue and deposit there is of course an advantage for each bank in paying out its own notes whenever possible, countered by the public's tendency to return notes in repayment of loans, for deposit, or for redemption in coin. If cross pyramiding does not occur then the 'homing instinct' of banknotes will be strongly reinforced, because any bank receiving the notes of competing banks in the course of business will want to present them promptly through the clearinghouse or otherwise for redemption in standard money, exactly like cheques on other banks; the expansion will be the same as in columns 1 to 3 of Table 2.3 for the parameters there assumed. If notes of other banks are acceptable as part of a bank's customary or required reserve, however, this homing instinct is greatly diminished, because the notes then become as good a substitute for standard money for the banks as for the general public; the expansion will be the same as in columns 4 to 6. The prohibition against holding their own notes as part of their reserves will not hamper the expansion unless one bank becomes so much larger than the others that their total note issues are insufficient to meet its reserve requirements (in which case the large bank of issue may be on the way to becoming a *de facto* Bank of Issue, thus changing the situation entirely).

If cross pyramiding is allowed, however, the rules need not preclude the use of the notes of other banks as part of the reserves behind a given bank's own note issue as well as its deposits. This leads to a more general approach to the subject in the following section.

3.3. The General Case

Banks of deposit and banks of issue may conceivably count claims on other banks of deposit for reserve purposes, claims on other banks of issue, or a combination of the two. Reserves may be divided in various proportions among standard money, notes, and deposits, and the proportions for banks of deposit may differ from those for banks of issue. The reserve ratio for

---

[7] In fact it must be acknowledged that "standard money", though a useful analytical concept, is of limited practical significance. Like "legal tender", it is prone to popular misunderstanding. What matters for most purposes is that a given object or claim be a *commonly acceptable tender*; whether it is also standard money is mainly a matter of semantics, and whether it is a legal tender becomes relevant only in very unusual disputes about whether a valid settlement of a specific debt was made or offered to be made by the debtor.

banknotes may differ from that for deposits, and the reserve ratio for inter-bank deposits may be different from (presumably more severe than) that for the general public. In order to give reasonable coverage of these multi-tudinous possibilities within a manageable compass we will look primarily at limiting or extreme cases, though we will generally try to avoid "extremely extreme" cases such as unlimited expansions, which are usually rather uninteresting analytically because infinity is a very intract-able statistic. We will also suppose that inter-bank deposits are subject to the same reserve requirements as other deposits; this considerably simp-lifies the presentation without compromising the basic relationships.

The first three columns of Table 2.4 illustrate some of the principal possibilities in terms of a closed-economy model in which the public's note-acceptance ratio is 80 per cent in ultimate standard money and its deposit-acceptance ratio is 90 per cent in the composite standard money; the reserve ratio for notes is 40 per cent and for deposits 10 per cent, but the composition of these reserves varies. In column 1 the deposit banks' note-acceptance ratio is 80 per cent, like the public's, while the banks of issue keep their reserves wholly in ultimate standard money; the results are identical with the final equilibrium of Table 2.2, except that we now interpret the case as one of cross pyramiding instead of simple pyramiding.

Now let the banks of issue also accept the notes of other banks for 80 per cent of their reserves, as represented in column 2: domestic financial assets rise 77 per cent on the assumptions here made, and credit expansion somewhat more (85 per cent). If both types of bank keep 80 per cent of their reserves in deposits at other banks instead of in notes and the balance in ultimate standard money, as in column 3, domestic financial assets rise to more than double the level of column 1. However, the difference between columns 2 and 3 is due solely to the assumed difference in reserve ratios between banks of deposit and banks of issue, and therefore is not ana-lytically significant: any shift from relatively high-reserve to relatively low-reserve assets would produce similar results.

Columns 1 and 3 mark out the range of possible variations in the public's domestic financial assets if the public's coefficients of substitution and the banks' reserve ratios are unchanged and if the banks do not accept claims on other banks (whether notes or deposits or any combination of the two) for more than 80 per cent of their reserves. The remaining columns relax these constraints; however, the presentation shifts to the $d = 1$ open-economy case in order to avoid trying to compare unlimited expansions. Column 4 is a reference column, comparable to simple pyramiding, in which the banks of issue keep their reserves in gold and the banks of deposit keep theirs in banknotes. The limiting position will be a public acceptance ratio of 100 per cent for bank claims in lieu of coin combined with either an

Table 2.4. Schematic Illustrations of Cross Pyramiding in a Closed Economy[1]

Sector assets and liabilities	A=0.8, d=0			A=d=1			
	g=0.8 e=f=h=0	e=g=0.8 f=h=0	f=h=0.8 e=g=0	g=1 e=f=h=0	e=g=1 f=h=0	f=h=1 e=g=0	R=r=0
	(1)	(2)	(3)	(4)	(5)	(6)	(7)
General Public							
A Gold coin	202	358	430	—	—	—	—
Banknotes	810	1,432	1,720	92.94	100	100	100
Bank deposits	9,109	16,105	19,346	836.43	900	900	900
Domestic assets	10,121	17,895	21,495	929.37	1,000	1,000	1,000
L Debts	9,121	16,895	20,495	858.74	1,000	1,000	1,000
Net worth	1,000	1,000	1,000	70.63	—	—	—
Deposit Banks							
A Gold coin	182	322	433	—	—	—	—
Banknotes	729	1,288	—	83.64	90	—	—
Bank deposits	—	—	1,730	—	—	104	—
Loans	8,198	14,495	19,464	752.79	810	940	900
L Deposits	9,109	16,105	21,626	836.43	900	1,044	900
Held by public	9,109	16,105	19,346	836.43	900	900	900
Deposit banks	—	—	1,730	—	—	104	—
Banks of issue	—	—	550	—	—	40	—
Banks of Issue							
A Gold coin	615	320	138	70.63	—	—	—
Banknotes	—	1,280	—	—	127	—	—
Bank deposits	—	—	550	—	—	40	—
Loans	923	2,400	1,032	105.95	190	60	100
L Note issue	1,538	4,000	1,720	176.58	317	100	100
Held by public	810	1,432	1,720	92.94	100	100	100
Deposit banks	729	1,288	—	83.64	90	—	—
Banks of issue	—	1,280	—	—	127	—	—
External Drain	—	—	—	929.37	1,000	1,000	1,000
Memorandum:							
Basic gold ratio[2]	9.88%	5.59%	4.65%	7.6%	0%	0%	0%

[1] Assuming a public deposit-acceptance ratio of 90 per cent, a deposit-reserve ratio of 10 per cent, and a note-reserve ratio of 40 per cent, except as indicated. Subject to the constraint that $0 \le A, e, f, g, h, r, R,$ $(e+f), (g+h) \le 1, A$ is the public's note-acceptance ratio in gold coin, e and f are the fractions of the note-reserve and g and h are the fractions of the deposit-reserve ratios held in notes and in deposits respectively, r is the deposit-reserve ratio, R is the note-reserve ratio, and d is the ratio of the external drain to domestic liquid assets. The figures are derived from the algebraic presentation given in section 3.4 below, rounded to the nearest whole number.

[2] The ratio of the gold retained in the economy (=net worth) to the public's domestic financial assets.

55

overt reduction of both reserve ratios to zero in ultimate standard money (as in column 7) or the covert accomplishment of the same thing by accepting inter-bank claims for 100 per cent of all reserves (as in columns 5 and 6).[8] The public's asset portfolio is identical in all three columns, and so is the *consolidated* balance sheet of all financial intermediaries; but their *combined* balance sheet (merely adding like assets and liabilities) is not.

3.4. Algebraic Formulation

The principal variants of cross pyramiding can be accommodated by a few additions to the variables and parameters used in section 2.6 above. Let Dt be total bank deposits including inter-bank deposits. Also let banks of issue apportion their reserves among coin, notes, and deposits in the ratio of $(1-e-f):e:f$, and banks of deposit in the ratio of $(1-g-h):g:h$, subject to the constraint that $0 \leq e, f, g, h, (e+f), (g+h) \leq 1$. The reserve ratios for inter-bank deposits might be r', but setting $r' = r$ simplifies the presentation without compromising any matter of principle.[9]

The equilibrium distribution of the public's portfolio among coin, notes, deposits, and external assets (or the external drain) will be unchanged from section 2.6 above. The liabilities of the banks of issue will consist of notes held by the public, by other banks of issue, and by other banks of deposit; those of the deposit banks will consist of the deposits of the public and of other banks. That is:

$$N = A(1-a).Ad+eR.N+gr.Dt \quad \dots\dots\dots\dots\dots\dots \text{(2.5)}$$
$$Dt = a.Ad+fR.N+hr.Dt \quad \dots\dots\dots\dots\dots\dots \text{(2.6)}.$$

Solving for N and Dt in terms of Ad we derive:

$$N = [A(1-a)(1-hr)+agr] \; Ad \; / \; [(1-eR)(1-hr)-fgrR] \quad \dots\dots \text{(2.7)}$$
$$Dt = [a(1-eR)+fAR(1-a)] \; Ad \; / \; [(1-eR)(1-hr)-fgrR] \quad \dots \text{(2.8)}.$$

The equilibrium distribution of the initial injection of ultimate standard money ($= G$) is $(1-a)(1-A).Ad+R(1-e-f).N+r(1-g-h).Dt+d.Ad.$

---

[8] More specifically, and in the notation used in Table 2.4 and in section 3.4 immediately below, umlimited expansion in a closed-economy model or a 100 per cent external drain in an open-economy model will occur if either $R=0$ or $e+f=1$ *and* either $r = 0$ or $g+h = 1$.

[9] It may be noted that the reserve ratio may also differ for different classes of deposits of the general public, and therefore in the preceding presentations r should be interpreted as the weighted average of the various applicable ratios. We may now further reinterpret r as the weighted average of the ratios applicable to the public's deposits and inter-bank deposits.

Substituting from equations 2.7 and 2.8 we derive:

$$Ad=[(1-eR)(1-hr)-fgrR] \, G \, / \, V \quad\dotsfill\quad 2.9$$

where $V=[1+d-a-A(1-a)]$ $[(1-eR)(1-hr)-fgrR]+R(1-e-f)$ $[A$
$(1-a)(1-hr)+agr]+r(1-g-h)[a(1-eR)+fAR(1-a)]$.

4. Compound Pyramiding

4.1. Definition
Compound pyramiding may be defined as double or multiple strata of
simple pyramiding; that is, a situation in which a second type of financial
intermediary uses the obligations of the first type as its cash reserves, a
third type uses the obligations of the second as its cash reserves, and
(conceivably at least) further tiers of intermediaries use the obligations of
the preceding tiers as their cash reserves. Some three-tier compounding
certainly occurs in the real world, as when insurance companies, savings
banks, and other intermediaries use deposits at commercial banks as part
of their cash reserves, though in most cases they need to hold at least some
portion in composite standard money as well. Some cross pyramiding may
occur at the second-tier level, in that some banks may be able to count
inter-bank deposits as part of their cash reserves. It could also conceivably
occur at third and higher tiers, but it is difficult to find examples of such a
situation in practice; credit transactions do occur among various financial
intermediaries for a wide variety of reasons, but the debts so arising are not
usually treated as cash reserves by the creditors.

4.2. Credit Substitution by Non-Banks
The principles of compound pyramiding can be illustrated by a schematic
arrangement in which a Bank of Issue and two other types of financial
intermediary operate. Initially let there be just a Bank of Issue that maintains a reserve of 40 per cent in gold or the equivalent against its note issue,
which enjoys a 100 per cent acceptance ratio and is therefore the domestic
standard money, and a system of deposit banks which enjoy a deposit-
acceptance ratio of 90 per cent and hold 10 per cent reserves in notes,
under closed-economy conditions. Now let a new type of intermediary be
introduced—say, savings and loan associations—to represent all other
financial intermediaries (or non-banks). They issue "shares" that are
redeemable at par on demand or according to stipulated conditions and pay
a positive rate of interest, hence are attractive to savers. The new intermediaries win 20 per cent of the public's financial assets, and keep the
same 10 per cent reserves as the banks. Their shares are not transferable,

however, and therefore are not substitutes for either notes or deposits for transactions purposes, hence we will assume that the public wishes to hold notes and deposits in the same ratio as before the appearance of the savings and loan associations.

Column 1 of Table 2.5 represents the credit structure per 1,000-franc increment of ultimate standard money in the initial position before the savings and loan associations are introduced. Column 2 is a second reference column, involving only simply pyramiding; it shows that on the assumptions here made there will be some further expansion of credit and of domestic financial assets even if the savings and loan associations keep their reserves in the same form as the banks. The reason is simple enough, of course: since the public now holds 20 per cent of its domestic portfolio in shares and maintains the former ratio of 1:9 between notes and deposits, the relative share of note holdings (which are subject to a higher reserve ratio) declines and the reserves thus released now support more deposits and shares.

Now in column 3 we introduce compound pyramiding. In order to simplify our comparisons let us continue to assume that the savings and loan associations' reserve ratio is the same as that of deposit banks, but that some or all of these reserves are held as bank deposits. We may as well go all the way and have the savings and loan associations hold all their reserves as bank deposits; in practice, of course, they would presumably have to hold some banknotes as well, so the situation would lie somewhere between columns 2 and 3. As it is, we find that compound pyramiding on these assumptions adds 11.7 per cent to domestic financial assets compared to column 2, though it adds 12.6 per cent to the credit expansion.

As far as the mechanics of the calculations are concerned, we could let the share-acceptance ratio approach unity and let the deposit-acceptance ratio approach zero. This possibility is examined in the next section, where it results in a 154 per cent increase in domestic financial assets compared to column 2. On the present assumptions, however, savings and loan shares can not entirely displace money-proper, hence the expansion must terminate at some intermediate point. On the other hand reducing their reserve ratio to zero, as in column 4, brings an increase of only 13 per cent in the public's domestic financial assets from column 2, or 1.3 per cent from column 3.

By hypothesis the introduction of the savings and loan associations reduces the *relative share* of deposits and notes in the public's financial assets, but in the closed-economy case illustrated in column 3 their *absolute amount* is very little less than in column 1, and the total assets and liabilities of the deposit banks actually increase a little.[10] In the open-

---

[10] The required reserves are the key to this increase. A shift from deposits to shares means an absorption of deposits by the savings and loan associations for reserve

Table 2.5. Schematic Illustrations of Compound Pyramiding in a Closed Economy[1]

Sector assets and liabilities	a=0.9 b=0	a=0.72 b=0.2 *	a=0.72 b=0.2	a=0.72 b=0.2 #	a=0.7 b=0.2	a=0 b=0.9	a=0 b=1
	(1)	(2)	(3)	(4)	(5)	(6)	(7)
General Public							
A Banknotes	1,316	1,163	1,299	1,316	1,453	2,294	—
Bank deposits	11,842	10,465	11,688	11,842	10,174	—	—
S & L shares	—	2,907	3,246	3,289	2,907	20,642	250,000
Domestic assets	13,158	14,535	16,234	16,447	14,535	22,936	250,000
L Debts	12,158	13,535	15,234	15,447	13,535	21,936	249,000
Net worth	1,000	1,000	1,000	1,000	1,000	1,000	1,000
S & L Associations							
A Banknotes	—	291		—	—	—	—
Bank deposits	—	—	325	—	291	2,064	25,000
Loans	—	2,616	2,922	3,289	2,616	18,578	225,000
L Shares	—	2,907	3,246	3,289	2,907	20,642	250,000
Deposit Banks							
A Banknotes	1,184	1,047	1,201	1,184	1,047	206	2,500
Loans	10,658	9,419	10,812	10,658	9,419	1,858	22,500
L Deposits	11,842	10,465	12,013	11,842	10,465	2,064	25,000
Held by public	11,842	10,465	11,688	11,842	10,174	—	—
Held by S & L's	—	—	325	—	291	2,064	25,000
Bank of Issue							
A Gold coin	1,000	1,000	1,000	1,000	1,000	1,000	1,000
Loans	1,500	1,500	1,500	1,500	1,500	1,500	1,500
L Note issue	2,500	2,500	2,500	2,500	2,500	2,500	2,500
Held by public	1,316	1,163	1,299	1,316	1,453	2,294	—
Held by S & L's	—	291	—	—	—	—	—
Held by banks	1,184	1,047	1,201	1,184	1,047	206	2,500
Memoranda:							
Basic gold ratio[2]	7.6%	6.88%	6.16%	6.08%	6.88%	4.36%	0.4%
Open-economy totals:[3]							
Domestic assets	929	936	942	943	936	958	996
Total note issue	177	161	145	143	161	104	10
Total deposits	836	674	697	679	674	86	100
Total S & L shares	—	187	188	189	187	862	996

[1] Assuming a note-acceptance ratio of 100 per cent in gold coin for all sectors except the Bank of Issue, a note-reserve ratio of 40 per cent in gold coin, and (except as indicated) a reserve ratio of 10 per cent in notes for the deposit banks and in bank deposits for the S&L's. Subject to the constraint that $0 \le a, b$, $(a+b) \le 1$, a and b are the fractions of its domestic financial assets the public wishes to hold in deposits and shares respectively. The figures are derived from the algebraic presentation given in section 4.4 below, rounded to the nearest whole number.

[2] The ratio of the gold retained in the economy (= net worth) to the public's domestic financial assets.

[3] The $d = 1$ case, i.e. the external drain equals the increase in the public's domestic financial assets.

* The savings and loan associations' reserves are in banknotes.

\# The savings and loan associations' reserves are reduced to zero.

economy case, however, there are absolute reductions in the assets and liabilities of both the deposit banks and the Bank of Issue, because the external drain rises and further depletes the supply of ultimate standard money—the expansion through the savings and loan associations is partly at the expense of the banking system.[11] See the memorandum items at the foot of Table 2.5; the open-economy items not shown will bear the same ratio to their closed-economy counterparts as those shown.

4.3. Credit Substitution by New Banks

In the real world some institutions not formally classed as banks in a particular economy, and therefore not subject to the same legal and other constraints, offer transferable claims which the public can and does use to effect payments.[12] They may be subject to alternative forms of supervision and regulation, including required or customary cash reserve ratios, that may be comparable to officially-recognized banks in most respects except one very important one: they are not required (and perhaps are not permitted) to keep reserves in the form of deposits with the central bank or other monetary authority; normally they hold at least a portion of them in the form of deposits with officially-recognized banks. Such institutions are intended to be included in the strict definition of a bank offered on page 6 above, but their status and their potential evolution require explicit recognition.

We can incorporate such institutions into our model by identifying them as a second tier of banks in a compound-pyramiding credit structure. Let us call them "new" banks, because we can identify them with the "new" intermediaries we have just introduced, even though in the real world some of them have a long history. In section 1.2 of Chapter 11 below we will

---

purposes, thus reducing the supply available to the public; but by hypothesis the public's note holdings fall proportionately, and the notes thus released permit some expansion of deposits. In column 4, where the savings and loan associations' reserve ratio is reduced to zero, the public's holdings of deposits and notes are unchanged from column 1, as are the deposit banks' assets and liabilities.

[11] Cf. A.N. McLeod, "Credit Expansion in an Open Economy", *The Economic Journal*, Vol. LXXXII, September 1962, para. 28, p. 621.

[12] Many European countries have so-called Giro systems, often operated by the post office; these are credit-transfer systems that effect payments in essentially the same way as chequeing systems (which may be described as debit-transfer systems). In Britain some trusteed savings banks offer chequeing privileges or the equivalent, and in Canada a considerable variety of institutions do the same. In the U.S.A. similar practices were largely ended by the banking reforms of 1933, but recently negotiable orders of withdrawal (NOW accounts) have reintroduced them; in addition the so-called dual banking system (some banks are subject to state controls only, some are regulated by national legislation) introduces further complexities. The instruments in question do not always qualify as cheques under the applicable legal definition, but their practical functioning is virtually identical.

consider whether a discretionary central bank can regulate or control a system of such new banks, and if so how, but for the present we will be solely concerned with how the system will work under automatic responses to an injection of new standard money under the revised assumptions.

We can reinterpret Table 2.5 as showing the relationships among the Bank of Issue, the old banks, and the new banks, disregarding the existence of non-bank financial intermediaries in the same way as we have done previously when focussing primarily on the banking system. (Alternatively, you may think of the new banks as an accounting consolidation of the banking functions of all intermediaries not officially recognized as banks with all intermediary functions not covered by our strict definition of banking.) Suppose that an existing type of savings institution converts its obligations to transferable form, finds some way of effectively clearing cheques with the officially-recognized banks, and gets acceptance for holding and servicing a part of the public's transactions balances; or suppose that an entirely new type of institution sets up in business and accomplishes the same things. By hypothesis the new banks' liabilities (let us still call them "shares", to distinguish them from the "deposits" of the old banks) are good substitutes for deposits, not for notes, so *ceteris paribus* the ratio of notes to total domestic financial assets will remain unchanged. Column 1, not column 2, therefore becomes the appropriate starting point: if the new banks were to keep all their reserves in notes, then any gain in the acceptance of shares would be matched franc for franc by a reduction in deposits, so there would be no net change in domestic liquid assets.

If on the assumptions here made the new banks now win 20 per cent of the public's portfolio and hold their reserves with the old banks, as in column 5, there is an increase of 10.5 per cent in domestic financial assets over column 1. By coincidence all sector balance-sheet totals are identical with column 2, though their composition is different. In this case, however, there is nothing to stop the new banks substituting their shares for all publicly-held deposits, if they can offer the general public sufficiently attractive terms. Column 6 represents the limiting position on these assumptions: an increase of 74 per cent in domestic financial assets from column 1, but a reduction of the role of the old banks to that of custodians of the new banks' reserves. Reducing the new banks' reserve ratio to zero (not shown in the table) would raise total domestic financial assets to 25,000 francs per 1,000 francs of initial injection of standard money, 90 per cent above column 1, but would reduce the old banks' deposits to zero and leave the Bank of Issue's notes to serve only the public's need for hand-to-hand currency.

All very hypothetical, of course. However, remember that we are talking of a purely automatic system in which domestic monetary policy plays no part. Even in closed-economy conditions the amount of credit expansion here envisaged is not all that great; if the change were spread over a considerable period of time it need not imply inflationary price rises, so the authorities might see no reason to change the rules, and indeed it might well be that the expansion was no more rapid than necessary to prevent deflation. Furthermore, the new banks may have important competitive advantages under the assumed conditions. First, whereas the monopoly position of the Bank of Issue may permit it to refuse to pay interest to its creditors, competition among the old banks may lead them to pay interest on the deposits (i.e. the reserves) of the new banks. Second, we have assumed that the new banks observe the same reserve ratio as the old banks, albeit in a different medium; they may find they can operate on a smaller ratio. Third, the supply of reserves may be far more elastic for the new banks than for the old, as long as the public continues to hold an appreciable volume of deposits as well as shares. By hypothesis, shares are good substitutes for deposits in the hands of the public, hence the new banks can "buy" additional reserves by offering lower service costs or higher interest rates on their shares than the old banks offer on deposits; but the old banks' reserves are limited to a portion of the available supply of notes. Fourth, the new banks may have evolved new techniques which the old banks do not or (perhaps due to legal constraints) can not copy. The fact that nothing like this has yet happened in any country does not prove it could not happen.

However, for a really spectacular expansion we can still move in on the use of hand-to-hand currency. Suppose that technical innovations—such as the cashless banking by the use of computer cards and point-of-sale terminals now being talked about—greatly expand the scope for the use of deposit-money (or share-money) for even small payments like bus fares and the purchase of newspapers, so the acceptance ratio for deposits and shares rises towards unity. If the new banks have competitive advantages in using these techniques and are able to move towards 100 per cent acceptance for their shares the limiting position will be 250,000 francs for domestic financial assets, all in shares, as in column 6 of Table 2.5. If they can now reduce their reserve ratio to zero (not shown in the table) then in the closed-economy model there will be an unlimited inflation; in the $d = 1$ open-economy model domestic financial assets will rise to 1,000 francs per 1,000 francs initial injection of ultimate standard money, all held with the new banks, and the external drain will absorb the entire 1,000 francs of ultimate standard money.

4.4. Algebraic Formulation

Only minor modifications of the notation used in section 2.6 above are here required. Assuming a 100 per cent note-acceptance ratio by the public and by all intermediaries except the Bank of Issue, let the public allocate its domestic financial assets (Ad) among notes, deposits, and shares in the ratio of $(1-a-b) : a : b$, and let the reserve ratio of the second-tier intermediaries be a multiple cr of that of the deposit banks $(= r)$, of which $cr(1-p)$ is in notes of the Bank of Issue and crp is in claims on the deposit banks, subject to the constraint that $0 \leq a, b, cr, p, (1-a-b) \leq 1$. The share liabilities of the new intermediaries (Sp) will be $b.Ad$; total deposits (Dt) become $(a+bcpr) . Ad$, i.e. the sum of the claims of the public and the new intermediaries on the deposit banks; and the note issue (N) becomes $[(1-a-b)+bcr(1-p)+r(a+bcpr)] . Ad$, i.e. the sum of the holdings of the public, the new intermediaries, and the deposit banks. The Bank of Issue holds all the ultimate standard money retained by the economy, hence $G = R.N+Gd$, from which we derive:

$$Ad = G / \overline{R\,[(1-a-b)+bcr(1-p)+r(a+bcpr)]+d} \dots \dots \quad (2.10).$$

The values of Ad and the other variables are of course materially affected by the coefficients of substitution among notes, deposits, and shares. One possibility is to set the public's note holdings at ka, where k is an arbitrary constant subject to the constraints that $0 \leq k \leq 1$ and $(ka+a+b) = 1$; i.e., to make the coefficients $ka:a:b$. This would be appropriate, for example, if shares are deemed not to be substitutes for money-proper, and if it is further assumed that the composition of money-proper is not altered by the introduction of the new intermediary. Another possibility is to let the ratio be $k:a:b$, subject to the constraints that $0 \leq a, b, k \leq 1$ and $(k+a+b) = 1$; this assumes that shares are substitutes for deposits but not for notes. Other possibilities are limited only by your ingenuity. For example, even if shares are deemed to be non-transferable you might postulate that notes and deposits are differently affected; say, that precautionary and speculative balances tend to be held as deposits rather than notes before the change, and tend to be transferred into shares thereafter, so the coefficients of substitution change from $k:a:0$ to $k':a':b$.

5. Economizing on Ultimate Standard Money

The various types of pyramiding may be looked on as devices for diluting the net reserves or "backing" for domestic financial assets in the form of ultimate standard money (gold or the equivalent), thereby raising the various credit and other multipliers; or, if you prefer, as a means of *economizing on* ultimate standard money. Whether this is deemed to be desirable or undesirable is another matter, of course. If inflationary pressures are evident then presumably most people will agree that the results are undesirable, the potentially pejorative term "dilution" will seem appropriate, and "economizing" will be considered a mere euphemism;

but if the money supply is not growing fast enough to meet the needs of trade and deflationary pressures are evident then presumably most people will agree that techniques such as pyramiding are desirable ways of economizing on ultimate reserves.

Pyramiding is not the only way of economizing on ultimate standard money: that is an important feature of every technique of credit expansion examined in this book, and of virtually every financial innovation through the ages in the real world, though in most cases it was an accidental byproduct rather than an explicit objective. If we look only at the mechanical linkages between reserves in ultimate standard money and the structure of domestic financial assets and credit, it would appear that we could retain the direct convertibility of all claims into (say) gold and yet, by manipulating the acceptance and reserve ratios, duplicate any degree of economizing on the use of gold that can be accomplished by pyramiding. However, very low cash-reserve ratios introduce practical problems in an automatic system. In part these problems are psychological: if reserves fall below some ill-defined level the public may lose confidence in the banking structure, and the deposit-acceptance ratio may fall abruptly. But there are also more objective reasons for scepticism of low-reserve systems. This scepticism may be rationalized in purely metallist terms, though there is a sound practical basis for it that is equally valid in purely cartalist terms.[13] In the real world a fairly substantial reserve in standard money is necessary for a bank (and a relatively smaller cash reserve for other intermediaries) simply to meet normal daily fluctuations in cash inflows and outflows, and in an automatic system further precautionary reserve is necessary to meet (or to cushion the intermediary's reaction to) unanticipated cash demands.

Modern central banking appears to have evolved naturally out of simple pyramiding. The economic implications of the special privileges that were intentionally or unintentionally given the Sveriges Riksbank (established in 1668), the Bank of England (1694), and officially-recognized Banks of Issue in other countries were slow to be understood,[14] but in retrospect it is

---

[13] Cf. J.A. Schumpeter, *History of Economic Analysis*, New York, Oxford University Press, 1954, pp. 288ff. Schumpeter defines *theoretical* metallism as "the *theory* that it is logically essential for money to consist of, or to be 'covered' by, some commodity", and theoretical cartalism as the denial of this proposition. He then identifies *practical* metallism as the belief that, as a principle of *policy* that might well be accepted even by a theoretical cartalist, "the monetary unit 'should' be firmly linked to, and freely interchangeable with, a given quantity of some commodity". (Commodity-monies are commonly called "metallist" monies, since metals offer important advantages as monetary commodities.)

[14] The first classical treatment of central banking was of course Walter Bagehot's *Lombard Street*, London, Henry S. King, 1873. A second and much-less-well-

clear that these privileges and the centralization of external reserves that went with them yielded unexpected fruit. Whether privately or publicly owned, they gradually came to accept the responsibilities the logic of their special status demanded. Pretty much the same sequence of events occurred more or less independently in a number of countries, but the British case is particularly well-known because of the dominance London came to exercise over the world's financial structure by the end of the 19th century. In the 20th century these examples were followed more and more widely, and fully-fledged central banks were established *de novo* in many countries, so a central bank is now an all-but-universal feature of national financial systems.

In principle cross-pyramiding techniques can economize on reserves of ultimate standard money and provide ample credit-based money for all domestic purposes. In practice, howver, they suffer from serious weaknesses that were well illustrated in certain historical examples, especially in the U.S.A. prior to the establishment of the Federal Reserve System in 1913. There was no dominant Bank of Issue, except during the relatively short lives of the First and the Second Banks of the United States, and convertibility into full-bodied coin was the main protection of the public against irresponsible banking practices. Cross pyramiding did permit commercial banks to economize on specie reserves, but it left these reserves uncertain in amount and location, thereby contributing to the instability of the banking system. The worst features were eliminated or reduced after 1863 by the establishment of the National Banking System and the ending of note issues by state banks, yet problems remained: the issues of bank-notes by the National Banks were inelastic, especially downward, and seasonal changes in circulation drew reserves from the deposit banks in one period and created an influx of free reserves in another. Unlike simple pyramiding under a Bank of Issue, cross pyramiding does not evolve naturally into money-management.

An alternative banking structure permits a relatively small number of competing banks of issue and deposit to operate through networks of branches under rules than make no distinction between notes and deposits so far as reserves are concerned.[15] The immediate results are closely

known classic is A.F.W. Plumptre's *Central Banking in the British Dominions*, Toronto, The University of Toronto Press, 1940; it is not too much to say that this volume transformed the theory of central banking from "doing what the Bank of England does" into a rational set of principles.

[15] Such an arrangement has certain practical advantages if, as is usually the case, there are seasonal fluctuations in the public's demand for notes relative to deposits. In an automatic pyramided-credit system the peak seasonal demand for notes withdraws reserves from the banks and causes a seasonal credit stringency, and in a managed-

parallel to those of simple pyramiding. Essentially-automatic systems of this kind operated very successfully until recent times in a number of countries, and fulfilled all that was expected of a monetary system before the adoption of modern money-management techniques, to which they do not lend themselves.

Finally, it should be noted that the various possible ways of economizing on external reserves are essentially alternatives to one another. Manipulating acceptance and reserve ratios and various types of pyramiding may supplement or reinforce one another up to some rather indefinite point, but if one technique or combination of techniques has reduced external reserves to the lowest level public opinion will tolerate then resort to a different technique can promote no further credit expansion (or reduction of reserves) unless it leads the public to tolerate a lower overall reserve ratio.

---

money system the central bank or other monetary authority must consciously act to offset any such tendency. In a system (whether automatic or discretionary) in which notes and deposits are obligations of the same institutions and are subject to the same reserve requirement there are no such effects.

CHAPTER 3
A COMPLEX FINANCIAL STRUCTURE

1. The Functional Approach

The analysis of the institutional aspects of financial intermediation presented in Chapters 1 and 2 is essentially an elaboration of the view of money and banking that became prevalent in the first third of the twentieth century, differing from that view primarily in that it extends the analysis to other intermediaries besides banks and to other financial assets besides money-proper. It may be described as the "mechanistic" approach, because it is mainly concerned with the mechanism by which the volume of financial assets is increased and the expansion of credit is brought about.

While it can hardly be said that there is now a new consensus paralleling that of say the 1920's, there is considerable common ground among economists of various shades of opinion concerning what may be called the "functional" approach to money (and, by extension, to financial assets in general)—that is, the approach through the functions money performs, why it is held, and so on. This approach stems ultimately from the Cambridge cash-balances view of money, and, more immediately, from Keynes's liquidity-preference concept; but it has been materially influenced and improved by monetarist and other criticisms of Keynesian analysis. In its crudest form liquidity-preference was expressed in terms of only two assets, money and bonds, but quite early there developed the idea of a schedule of alternative asset-forms arranged in order of decreasing liquidity: money-proper, close substitutes for money, remoter substitutes, through successively less-liquid claims, to various physical assets differing markedly in the ease with which they can be turned into money-proper and in the possible range of prices at which the conversion might be expected to be made.

Differences in liquidity have several dimensions. First, there is the time dimension; short-dated assets tend to be more liquid than longer-dated assets. Then there is a dimension according to the issuer of the claims; government debt is typically more liquid than most private debt with the same term to run,[1] and the debts of various private issuers can be arrayed in a sequence of decreasing liquidity (realizeability). Third, there is a dimension which relates to the nature of the assets themselves. Financial claims are usually more liquid than physical assets, and commonly trade at rela-

---

[1] This is no more than a general rule, of course; even in the major developed countries today some private claims are considered more liquid than some claims on issuers that are included in the government sector.

tively narrow spreads between bid and asked prices on either institutionalized or informal (over-the-counter) exchanges. However, mortgages tend to be relatively illiquid and difficult to trade for technical reasons, and bonds issued by some private and government issuers may be difficult to dispose of even though they are nominally in negotiable form. Indeed, it appears that in some Middle Eastern centres office buildings and other income-producing properties are traded by wealthy oil sheiks more readily than government bonds, and hence must be considered more liquid.

The functional approach is not antithetical to the mechanistic approach; on the contrary, in an important sense it is complementary to it. Whereas the mechanistic approach is primarily a discussion of the supply of money and takes the demand for granted, the functional approach is primarily a discussion of the demand for money and takes the supply as given or controllable. It is commonly couched in mathematical or quasi-mathematical terminology, in that the demand for money is said to be a function of a number of more-or-less-specifically-listed variables. Among other things this means that it lends itself to empirical testing by the application of quantitive analytic techniques, and much work of this kind has been generated, some of it more productive than others. Nevertheless its usefulness is not confined to econometric applications; the quasi-mathematical formulation of the various demand functions has also proven a useful way of setting out the basic relationships for didactic and expository purposes without requiring recourse to actual mathematical techniques.

2. Alternative Vehicles for the Employment of Savings

2.1. The Demand for Money-to-Hold
The functional approach to the theory of money here presented is couched specifically in terms of money-to-hold, not money-to-spend. It is fairly obvious that precautionary and speculative balances are money-to-hold, for theirs is a reserve or "holding" function. But even transactions balances must be held at any given moment, for the purpose of meeting some transactions need in the future or because of inevitable lags between the receipt of funds and their application for some desired purpose. The demand for transactions balances in the sense here used is therefore quite distinct from the demand for money-to-spend, which in essence means the demand for access to resources for either productive or consumption purposes, not the demand for money as such.

2.2. The Demand for Assets in General
The demand for money-to-hold is simply a special case of the demand for assets in general. Money is only one of the forms in which wealth can be

held; an individual may hold as little or as much of it as he wishes, except that his holdings can not exceed his total assets (gross wealth), but his desire to hold money at any given time must bear some logical relationship to his desire to hold other assets.

A community's wealth or total assets may be computed in various ways, depending on the nature of the analysis. In real terms gross total assets consist of the accumulated gross real savings out of past income, and may be identified with a stock of physical assets; net total assets consist of gross total assets less accrued losses through wearing out or depletion or the like, or an accounting allowance therefor; and both gross and net totals may be valued in money terms at either historical cost or current market values.[2] If we include all claims to physical assets in the term "financial" then financial assets gross or net include all real assets but may also include financial claims that have no physical counterpart, such as the accumulated current deficits of governments (sometimes called "honourary investments" in deflation-ridden days). However, the term "total" or "gross" assets as applied to the community may also be used in an even fuller sense, meaning the sum of the individual gross assets of all natural and juridical persons without deduction for offsetting liabilities, rather like the combined as distinct from the consolidated balance sheet of a group of related business firms. The demand for money is part of the total demand for assets in this broad sense, because much of the money-supply nowadays is credit-based and any attempt to compare it with total assets on a consolidated basis would require eliminating the credit-based portion and would therefore reduce the concept of "money" to a meaningless residual.[3]

The stock of real or financial assets in any of these senses, valued at historical costs, is directly related to the flow of real income or money-income (as the case may be) in ways that may be precisely interpreted in terms of integral calculus but are easily illustrated in a simple two-dimensional diagram. Let the vertical axis represent the values (in terms of current money or other suitable numeraire) of income (Y), consumption (C), and savings (S), and let the horizontal axis represent historical time. Any given ordinate of the Y-curve will be the sum of the corresponding C-curve and S-curve ordinates, and the slopes of the curves at those points will represent their rates of change; the slopes of the C-curve and the S-curve may also be interpreted as the community's marginal propensities to

---

[2] Some of the relationships between the values of assets at historical cost and at market prices will be noted in section 2.4 below.

[3] Ideally one might wish to limit total assets (in the broad sense) to those of all *natural* persons, i.e. to consolidate all of each individual's holdings in or through corporations and other juridical persons with his direct holdings, as being a more meaningful aggregate; see section 2.4 of Chapter 11 below.

consume and to save respectively. The curves thus represent the *flows* of income, consumption, and savings, and the areas under each curve between any two points in time are *stock* concepts: the total income produced (or earned) in the period, the total consumed, and the total saved.[4]

Our present interest focuses on the flow of savings, which can be subdivided into a variety of component flows subject to the incentives, aspirations, preferences, and whims of individual savers, and each of these subsidiary flows of savings implies a continuous process of adding to a particular category of asset. The public will allocate its increments of savings among these alternative assets according to its composite assessment of the relative advantages to be obtained from each, and in principle should carry the allocation to the point at which it is a matter of indifference where a marginal increment of savings is placed. Clearly, therefore, these alternative vehicles are in competition with one another for a share in the savings being generated out of income.

Thus the demand for real assets is a function of real income, expectations about the future of the economy (particularly the real rate of growth), the real rate of saving, the real rate of return on assets in general, and probably other factors less easily identifiable. The demand for financial assets is a function of all these plus the current level of prices and expectations about the direction and rate of change in them over the foreseeable future. The demand for any particular asset, including money-proper, is in addition a function of the characteristics and the supplies of all other assets currently available and the rates of return thereon (the spectrum of interest rates, yields on equity stocks, rents and quasi-rents on land and other physical assets, including possible capital gains or losses); a function of expectations, confidence, convenience, custom, etc., as these relate to the holding of these particular asset forms; and so on.

The demand for all these types of assets can be further subdivided into various components. We can subdivide the demand for money into the demand for coin, for banknotes, for particular denominations of coin and banknotes, for chequeable deposits of various types or at specific banks, and so on. We may also subdivide the demand for near-bank deposits into various types at specific institutions, etc; the demand for bonds into various categories (by term, by issuer, etc.); and so on for mortgages, equity stocks, etc.

Then of course there may be feed-back effects on income itself, and on

---

[4] If savings are identified as additions to financial assets only, as in most of the discussion in this book, then the *C*-curve must be identified with all expenditure not financed by borrowing (including the direct acquisition of capital goods out of income). For application to open-economy situations, the *C*-curve must also be deemed to include net spending on imported goods and services.

the public's allocation of its income between consumption and saving. The rate of saving reacts on the rate of capital formation, which in turn has implications for future income. The expected rate of return on new capital formation has a bearing on the rate of return or the expected rate of return on savings in general and on each particular savings vehicle. The expected rate of return on savings may affect the public's allocation of income between consumption and saving. And so on.

In sum, all these variables are interrelated in a system of general equilibrium in which the value of each affects and is affected by the value of each of the others. In mathematical terminology they are all implicit functions of one another. The general rate of saving, and the allocation of new savings among the various alternative vehicles, are functions of income, wealth, the composite attraction of expected rates of return on savings in general, the relative attractiveness of particular savings vehicles, and presumably a wide range of other factors that may influence income and its allocation between consumption and saving. But income itself is in part a function of accumulated wealth and the rate of saving (through their influence on the supply of capital facilities), just as wealth and saving are in part a function of income.

2.3. Coefficients of Substitution

In Chapter 1 we introduced the term "coefficients of substitution" as a shorthand expression for the determinants of the public's allocation of its liquid assets among various alternatives. As a first approximation we have usually assumed so far that all coefficients are given or exogenously-determined ratios, but of course they are really complex functions of many variables, most of which have been identified in the immediately preceding section. Even if we confine our attention to the coefficients of substitution among financial assets, as we will usually continue to do, we must recognize that they will be affected by returns or hoped-for returns on physical assets, by psychological factors, and probably by other unspecified influences. For the construction of a relatively simple model we may think of a single representative interest rate, a single representative yield on equities, a single representative rental rate, and so on, but in reality there are complex structures of interest rates, of equity yields, and of rentals, the components of each structure being closely interrelated and each structure being interrelated with the other two structures and with other coefficients of substitution as well.

As a second approximation we may suppose that the public's coefficients of substitution are linear functions of a relatively small number of parameters, and that their marginal values are constants. If the net rate of saving is positive the various components of wealth (categories of assets) will be growing at constant rates, and each will share proportionately in the increase of savings per unit of time (which must be deemed to include additions to various types of directly-held physical assets as well as to financial claims). Contrariwise, if the rate of saving is negative, each will share proportionately in the decreases. In other words the marginal rates of growth of each type of asset will be constant and proportionate. However, the average rates of growth of each type of asset will not necessarily be either constant or proportionate; for example, a given type of asset A may have been known and accepted in the historical past long before a second type of asset B became available and gained its present degree of acceptance.

Now suppose that the marginal coefficients of substitution change— there is a change in profit expectations, a sudden doubt about the solvency of a major intermediary, an awakening to the existence and significance of inflationary pressures, or the like. Obviously, the public may sharply change its allocation of income between saving and consumption, and its allocation of savings among various components of total wealth. Whether total saving increases or decreases, the shift in the flow of savings is likely to be favourable to certain types of assets and unfavourable to others, which will require important adaptations on the part of various financial intermediaries and financial markets. In addition, however, there will presumably be a shift (or an attempt to shift) out of some types of existing assets into others—that is, an attempt to change the form in which the accumulated savings of the past are held, quite separate and distinct from the change in the allocation of new savings. Furthermore, since the annual addition to accumulated savings is probably small relative to total wealth accumulated in the past, this effect of the change in the marginal coefficients of substitution may quite overwhelm the shift in the flow of current saving so far as the effect on particular institutions and markets is concerned.[5] Consideration of the adjustments thus made necessary leads to the links between the historical costs and the market values of various assets.

2.4. The Revaluation Effect

We may note an important difference between more or less "open end" claims like claims on banks and other depositories, and more or less "closed end" claims like specific issues of bonds or equities. Depository-type institutions can quickly expand their liabilities by buying existing claims from private holders if the public's coefficients of substitution move

---

[5] The classic example, of course, is a "run" on the reserves of a particular bank, or of the banking system in general. The resulting liquidity crisis may ruin even the soundest bank if the standard money is an inelastic commodity-money, but can be effectively neutralized if it is an elastic credit-based money under the control of an efficient central bank or similar authority.

in their favour, the immediate effect being to change the nature but not the amount of the public's liquid claims.[6] In addition, of course, depository expansion may occur through the granting of new loans which are spent for capital-formation or consumption purposes, with the usual income-expanding effects; and, in an expansionary climate, the proceeds of either new or existing securities sold to other members of the public or to financial intermediaries by the public are likely to be similarly used. Banks have an obvious advantage in the process, because their liabilities are readily acceptable by everyone, except in extreme inflation, but other depositories participate *pro tanto*: as a rule they have no reason to reject any deposit tendered them, because they can quickly put the funds to work by way of security purchases even if suitable loan opportunities do not present themselves at once.

In sharp contrast, if the public's coefficients of substitution move in favour of bonds (especially corporate bonds or junior government bonds, but even central government bonds) or equities, the supply is likely to be very inelastic in the short run because the issuers are not likely to be able to make effective use of the funds on short notice, and in any case would need anything from a few weeks to many months to comply with regulatory requirements, to arrange for the management and the underwriting of the issue, and to market it successfully; and, contrariwise, once issued it is difficult to retire them on short notice. As for physical assets (land, capital goods, etc.), the supply is even less elastic in the short run.

If the general public wishes to shift an appreciable portion of past accumulated savings from claims on one type of financial intermediary to another, as distinct from altering the flow of new savings, the solution is relatively simple in principle: the institution losing deposits sells assets, the one gaining deposits buys assets. For example, the central bank may buy assets from the commercial banks in exchange for central-bank notes to meet claims for withdrawals of deposits or to permit an expansion of deposits, and the commercial banks can provide deposit claims against themselves (and access to central-bank claims) to other intermediaries by buying assets from them; the major problem is that the assets offered by the one institution may not be identical with those desired by the other. In the case of a shift involving bonds, equities, and physical assets, however, it may be virtually impossible to alter the available supply in the short run. In a money-and-market economy, the obvious answer is that the current market values of these various assets carried over from the past must change until they again become competitive at the margin with alternative asset forms, including newly-issued claims offered on terms designed to

[6] See the penultimate paragraph of section 4 below, on p. 87.

attract current savings at the new values of coefficients of substitution.

The adjustment of the capital value of any given asset (or of the capital values of any group of assets, including the sum total of past accumulated wealth) as a result of some change in the coefficients of substitution may be called The Revaluation Effect. Any asset is subject to a revaluation effect, up or down, if the public revises its opinions about the future returns to be expected from that asset, whether the return is expressed as an interest rate, an operating profit, a capital gain, a rental, or whatever. A more general revaluation effect occurs for all assets yielding a more-or-less-fixed return (or a fixed expected return) in monetary terms if the general level of interest rates changes.

A change in the public's expectations about the future behaviour of the general price level, or about the future health of the economy, may have important differential valuation effects on various types of assets, and these effects may be both direct and indirect. For example, the effects on fixed-interest securities would be different from those on equities, and the effects on a highly leveraged equity (e.g., shares in a corporation with a high ratio of debt to share capital) would be different from those on a low-leveraged equity; and indirect effects, via the implications for changes in interest rates, might modify the direct effects expected to apply to a given financial asset as a result of changes in the general price level or the economic climate.

Important instances of The Revaluation Effect occur with national currencies that are not freely convertible into a commodity-money such as gold or foreign exchange. This includes particular currencies that are either inconvertible or subject to effective exchange controls in a predominantly fixed-exchange-rate free-convertibility system, and to individual credit-based currencies that are floating more-or-less-freely in terms of one another. By hypothesis there can be neither an external nor an internal drain, except as the authorities may choose to allow their external reserves to be drawn down for some policy reason or other (e.g. to permit "essential" imports or to keep the exchange rate within bounds deemed desirable), hence our closed-economy models will apply with little or no modification. The value of foreign exchange in general, or of foreign currencies individually, and the values of assets denominated therein, will be determined by the willingness of non-residents to sell their currencies and the willingness of residents to buy them at market-clearing prices.

2.5. The Wealth Effect
At any given level of income an increase or decrease in wealth may be expected to affect the demand for money, and perhaps also to alter the marginal propensities to save and to spend, all of which may have re-percussions on income, saving, consumption, investment, interest rates, and so on. This appears to be equally true regardless of whether the

increase or decrease in wealth is due to the flow of new saving out of income or to revaluation effects of the type just discussed or to some other cause.

3. A Model of the Financial System

3.1. A Typical System

In a sophisticated modern financial system the range of financial inter-mediaries to which the fractional-reserve principle can be applied is ex-tremely wide. Typically it includes a central bank or other standard-money-issuing authority, a group of commercial banks which accept not only chequeable deposits but also other types of deposits, a number of other types of institutions that compete with commercial banks in accepting deposits offering more or less parallel advantages (near-banks), contractual savings institutions like life-insurance companies and pension funds, issuers of casualty insurance of various kinds (which do not build up policy reserves as do most kinds of life insurance, but do accumulate contingency reserves and pre-paid premiums), closed-end and open-end investment trusts, specialized lenders such as factoring companies, mortgage com-panies, consumer-finance companies, and sometimes still other types of specialized institutions (like discount houses and acceptance houses) that do not fit neatly into any simple description. Typically, near-banks may include savings banks, trust companies, mortgage loan companies, building societies, savings and loan associations, credit unions, and the like, which accept short-term deposits or sell relatively short-dated bonds or deben-tures or other obligations. Some of them may accept deposits transferable by cheque or similar instrument, even though they are not officially recognized as "banks" under the applicable legal definition.

Such a system also includes the issuance of various financial contracts by various natural and juridical persons, partnerships, associations, governmental bodies, and so on which do not carry on a primarily financial business but which may be brought within the compass of the fractional-reserve principle by an extension of the argument presented in section 2.2 of Chapter 1 above. These issues should specifically be deemed to include common equities as well as fixed-interest securities, and various inter-mediate types such as different classes of voting and non-voting shares, preferred shares, convertible bonds and debentures, and the sometimes-complex combinations thereof.[7] Then there are the various formal and

---

[7] An equity claim may be thought of as simply a form of debtor-creditor contract in which no formal repayment date is specified and in which the *quid pro quo* is a share in residual profits or hoped-for profits both currently and in the event of dissolution of the enterprise.

informal markets on which such issues may be traded; while not themselves generators of credit as such, they certainly facilitate credit contracts between principals. Finally, there are the brokers and dealers in those markets. Technically they too merely facilitate debtor-creditor transactions between principals, but in practice they may "take a position" in securities (either long or short) and for this purpose may make use of funds or securities left with them by customers; to the extent that they do so they too are acting as financial intermediaries.

It should be noted that financial markets are direct competitors of financial intermediaries as a means of channelling funds from primary lenders to ultimate borrowers, yet also provide invaluable assistance to them in employing their (or their creditors') funds with maximum efficiency. It is a useful first approximation to assume that intermediaries can immediately lend their free reserves in full to willing borrowers, as we have done and will continue to do in our numerical examples, but reality is rather different. Loans are commonly granted in the form of lines of credit which the borrowers may draw down at their convenience over a period of time, perhaps with the option of repaying in whole or in part and drawing down again to meet needs that may fluctuate for seasonal or other reasons. In earlier days, when financial markets in most countries were poorly developed and central banking was unknown or rudimentary, banks and other financial intermediaries might find themselves with redundant cash reserves at certain seasons even though at other seasons their resources were fully employed; indeed, this still occurs in some countries. In a modern economy with well-developed financial markets and an efficient central bank or other lender of last resort, however, this is no longer necessary: free reserves not immediately drawn down by borrowing customers can be safely invested in marketable securities. In addition to their "primary" (cash) reserves, banks and other financial intermediaries usually hold "secondary" reserves in the form of short-dated liquid securities that can be quickly turned into cash with little risk of capital loss. In addition they may hold a portfolio of other marketable securities with a somewhat longer range of maturity dates, which can be gradually sold off if necessary to honour their commitments to borrowing customers. We will introduce examples of this procedure in sections 3.2 and 3.3 of this chapter, next below, and will have more to say about it in section 4.

3.2. The Model
The operation of a complex modern financial system may be illustrated by a model in which there is a central bank, a system of deposit banks in the strict sense defined on page 6 above (including the chequeable-deposit activities of both "recognized" commercial banks and their near-bank

competitors if any), a group of other financial intermediaries (non-banks) deemed to be a consolidation of both near-banks (including the non-chequeable-deposit activities of the commercial banks) and "far-banks", a government sector, and a private sector which includes business enterprises (whether incorporated or not), consumers, and various non-business associations. Rather than have separate lending and borrowing sectors (surplus and deficit spending-units respectively) we will let private lending and borrowing appear in the reduced form of claims on the private sector and debts of the private sector in that sector's T-square accounts without offsetting one against the other, purely as a space-saving device; but we will permit the public sector to be a net lender to the government. The business component of the private sector may issue equity shares as well as fixed-interest securities, and other components and the government sector may issue fixed-interest securities of various kinds. The general public divides its portfolio of financial claims equally among private claims, government securities, claims on the non-banks (non-monies), and money-proper (of which one quarter is in notes and three quarters in chequeable deposits). Its net worth is overstated by the amount of its ultimate liability to repay the government's debt out of taxes, which it does not take into account when drawing up its balance sheet.

At this stage we will be interested in the automatic responses the system makes in the absence of discretionary intervention by the central bank, so we will assume that monetary policy is strictly neutral. Let us also postulate a closed-economy model, in order to focus on the domestic aspects of the analysis. We will assume that there are adequate financial markets on which a suitable range of financial assets, at least some of which are more or less commonly held by all sectors and intermediaries, can be traded effectively. The central bank keeps a reserve of 25 per cent in gold. The deposit banks keep a minimum primary reserve of 10 per cent entirely in notes of and deposits with the central bank. The non-banks on the average keep minimum primary reserves of 5 per cent, of which one-fifth is in notes of the central bank (though in principle there is no reason why they could not hold a portion of it as deposits with the central bank as the deposit banks do) and four-fifths as deposits with the deposit banks. The general public holds no gold, only financial claims (money and non-monies) and holdings of real physical assets, and the government sector holds neither gold nor financial assets; but, as in our earlier analysis, we will ignore the physical assets[8] and focus exclusively on the financial assets. Equilibrium in the

---

[8] You may consider physical assets as being deducted in the process of deriving net financial worth in the public's T-square accounts; or, if it seems more meaningful to you, you may think of the public's assets being greater than shown by the value of its holding of physical assets and its net worth being increased by the same amount.

distribution of the public's assets includes equilibrium in the level and structure of interest rates and in the values of all other parameters that affect the coefficients of substitution among the public's asset holdings.

Table 3.1 presents a schematic illustration of the model based on the familiar assumption that the basic reserve is 1,000 units of gold—say, marks. The government sector has borrowed 20,000 marks to finance its own past deficits; the counter-entry is shown as a negative net worth, which must be construed to mean that the government looks to the taxpaying members of the public to eventually repay the lending members. It should be noted that column 6, "the banking system", is technically a consolidation of the deposit banks and the central bank (columns 4 and 5) and not just the summation of the various entries in the two columns; that is to say, the note and deposit claims that the deposit banks hold against the central bank have been deducted from the latter's obligations to arrive at the net note-and-deposit obligations of the system as a whole to the non-banks and the general public. Column 7 similarly consolidates the assets and liabilities of the non-banks with the banking system, and thus in principle shows only the net claims and obligations of primary lenders and ultimate borrowers whether directly or indirectly (through financial intermediaries). Complete consolidation has not been effected in the assets and liabilities of the general public, on the assumption that the remaining lenders and borrowers are all natural persons; we may postulate that the positions of corporations or other juridical entities have already been consolidated with those of their shareholders or other natural persons.

It is often convenient to use a consolidation of the banking system along these lines in analytical work where the minutiae of the methods by which a central bank or other monetary authority influences the financial structure are not at issue or can be taken for granted—e.g., in analyzing the success with which the authorities have managed to contain expansionary pressures within the banking system or to what extent credit expansion should be attributed to the private sector or the government sector. The reason why a similar consolidation of the entire financial structure, or even of all major financial intermediaries, is seldom if ever attempted, even by those who fully accept the substitutability of alternative sources of credit, is primarily because data on these other sources are not available in anything like the same detail or with nearly the promptness as banking data.

Evidently the same final pattern will be reached regardless of the order in which new institutions or new lending procedures are introduced into the model, and in this sense the final complex model can be built up by the consolidation of various components as illustrated in Table 3.1: the governing factor will be the equilibrium values of the public's coefficients

Table 3.1. Schematic Illustration of a Complex Financial System in a Closed Economy[1]

Assets and Liabilities	General public	Govern-ment	Non-banks	Deposit banks	Central bank	(Banking system[2])	Con-solidated total[3]
	(1)	(2)	(3)	(4)	(5)	(6)	(7)
A Gold coin	—	—	—	—	1,000	(1,000)	1,000
Notes	2,950	—	118	466	—	(—)	2,950
Chequeable deposits	8,850	—	472	466	—	(—)	8,850
Non-monies	11,799	—	—	—	—	(—)	11,799
Government securities	11,799	—	4,200	1,000	3,000	(4,000)	20,000
Private claims	11,799	—	7,009	7,389	—	(7,389)	26,198
Total	47,198	—	11,799	9,322	4,000	(12,389)	70,796
L Notes	—	—	—	—	3,534	(3,068)	2,950
Chequeable deposits	—	—	—	9,322	466	(9,322)	8,850
Non-monies	—	—	11,799	—	—	(—)	11,799
Government debt	—	20,000	—	—	—	(—)	20,000
Private debt	26,198	—	—	—	—	(—)	26,198
Net worth	21,000	−20,000	—	—	—	(—)	1,000

[1] Assuming that the public's coefficients of substitution among coin, notes, chequeable deposits, non-monies, government securities, and private claims are in the ratio of 0 : 0625 : 0.1875 : 0.25 : 0.25 : 0.25 ; that the non-banks on average keep reserves of 5 per cent, one-fifth in notes and four-fifths in chequeable deposits at the deposit banks; that the deposit banks keep reserves of 10 per cent, half in notes and half in deposits at the central bank; that the central bank keeps reserves of 25 per cent in gold; that the government holds no financial assets; and that the borrowing members of the general public hold no financial assets as specific offsets to their own debts. Final digits are rounded to the nearest whole number.

[2] Consolidation of columns 4 and 5, netting out deposit-bank claims on the central bank.

[3] Columns 1 plus 2 plus the consolidation of columns 3 and 6, netting out non-bank claims on the banking system.

of substitution among the various types of financial assets available.[9] However, these equilibrium values may change over time even if they are approximately constant at a given point in time, not only because of changes in public attitudes and the introduction of new types of financial intermediaries but also because of evolutionary changes and adaptations in the nature of existing types of claims.[10] As we will see, particular interest attaches to changes in the coefficients that link standard money to money-proper and money-proper to all other financial claims.

3.3. Induced Changes in the Coefficients of Substitution

By now we have gotten about all the use we can hope for out of the assumption, as a first approximation, that the coefficients of substitution are constants, and we must be prepared to look on them as functions of many variables whose values are determined as part of the equilibrating process in a general-equilibrium matrix that encompasses all economic variables. However, we suggested on page 71 above that, as an interim measure or a second approximation, we may look on them as linear functions of a relatively small number of parameters whose values we may take as given or arbitrarily assignable. These parameters would certainly include the rate of interest, or the various components of the structure of interest rates and other rates of return, but they might also include psychological factors such as convenience, habits, recollections of past favourable or unfavourable experiences with a particular type of claim (perhaps for reasons that are no longer valid), moral or ethical judgements

[9] The sequence in which the components are added may nevertheless result in interim positions in which both the absolute level of a particular asset and its ratio to the other financial assets already introduced into the model may exceed their final equilibrium levels. For example, the introduction of Intermediary A whose obligations are good substitutes for gold coin for some purposes may result in a given credit expansion and a given configuration of financial assets as A lends or invests the funds it attracts; but if Intermediary B is then introduced, whose obligations are even better substitutes for gold coin for certain purposes, the relative position of A may deteriorate and it may even suffer an absolute decline in the funds at its disposal. The explanation is that the coefficients of substitution among financial assets are interrelated and the introduction of a new type involves not only the establishment of new coefficients between the new financial asset and each of the previously introduced financial assets but also the readjustment of all the pre-existing coefficients.

[10] For example, the great expansion in the use of chequeable deposits instead of banknotes or currency notes in Britain, North America, and elsewhere during the 19th century was in part due to changing public attitudes that made chequeing accounts more acceptable to both payees and payors, but it was undoubtedly also attributable in part to the development of more efficient banking techniques and to the gradual clarification of certain questions of commercial law relating to cheques and other bills of exchange in those jurisdictions.

(e.g., support for cooperative associations rather than profit-oriented institutions), and so on. In terms of the theory of portfolio choice, however, we may subsume these various considerations in the balance between (1) a high rate of return and (2) liquidity, especially if we are prepared to countenance the inclusion of psychical as well as financial returns in the calculus.

Table 3.2 illustrates some of the possibilities. Since we are here interested in the automatic responses of the financial system rather than what the central bank must do to cope with them, we will assume that monetary policy is passive throughout and therefore in a closed-economy model the money supply is invariant, but we need not specify whether this is because the central bank is following *laissez-faire* principles or because it believes the changes that are occuring are appropriate to the circumstances, nor whether the economy is below, at, or striving to exceed the full-employment level. Column 1 is identical with the situation depicted in Table 3.1, except that we have used the consolidated position of the banking system (i.e. the central bank and the deposit banks) since we are not particularly interested in the minutiae of their relationships, and this in turn permits us to deal largely in round numbers. The principal casualty in this treatment is that we ignore the (relatively small) effect that changes in the total obligations of non-banks will have on the level of bank deposits through absorbing standard money for or releasing it from reserve requirements. Presumably the interest rate (or the various rates of interest) and the other parameters which affect the coefficients of substitution are in equilibrium at the margin of substitution among the various assets, otherwise there would be changes in one or more of the parameters, the coefficients, and the various assets until equilibrium was attained.

In column 2 we assume that there is a new 5,000-mark issue of government securities to finance some project or other without any change in the institutional parameters. Presumably there will be some increase in the level and perhaps also a change in the structure of interest rates in order to induce the public to absorb the new issue either directly or through the non-banks. The effect on the parameters that determine the public's demand for private claims will be more uncertain, because they include equities as well as fixed-interest securities; the public's demand for equities will tend to suffer if interest rates rise materially, but on the other hand may benefit from increased profit expectations associated directly or indirectly with whatever government spending program is financed by the issue. The net increase in total assets may range from zero[11] to something substantially

---

[11] It is quite conceivable that the net effect on the public's total assets might be negative; e.g., the public might fear (whether rationally or irrationally) that the new issue presaged irresponsible government intervention in the economy and its liquidity-

Table 3.2. Schematic Illustration of Changing Coefficients of Substitution in a Closed Economy[1]

	(1)	(2)	(3)	(4)	(5)	(6)
General Public						
A Notes	3,000	2,980	2,965 (	2,965)	2,625	—
Chequeable deposits	9,000	8,920	8,860 (	8,860)	7,875	35,088
Money-proper (M–1)	12,000	11,900	11,825 (	11,825)	10,500	35,088
Non-monies	12,000	14,000	15,500 (	15,500)	42,000	35,088
M–2	24,000	25,900	27,325 (	27,325)	52,500	70,175
Government securities	12,000	14,500	13,200 (	11,900)	12,000	35,088
Private claims	12,000	12,500	12,475 (	16,650)	12,000	35,088
Total	48,000	52,900	53,000 (	55,875)	76,500	140,351
L Debt	27,000	26,900	32,000 (	36,175)	41,250	69,675
Net worth	21,000	26,000	21,000 (	19,700)	35,250	70,675
Government						
L Debt	20,000	25,000	20,000 (	18,325)	34,250	69,675
Net worth	−20,000	−25,000	−20,000 (	−18,325)	−34,250	− 69,675
Non-Banks						
A Notes	120	140	155 (	155)	420	351
Bank deposits	480	560	620 (	620)	1,680	1,404
Government securities	4,000	6,500	3,800 (	3,425)	18,250	16,667
Private claims	7,400	6,800	10,925 (	10,925)	21,650	16,667
L Non-monies	12,000	14,000	15,500 (	15,500)	42,000	35,088
Net worth	—	—	— (	− 375)	—	—
Banking System						
A Gold coin	1,000	1,000	1,000 (	1,000)	1,000	1,000
Government securities	4,000	4,000	3,000 (	3,000)	4,000	17,921
Private claims	7,600	7,600	8,600 (	8,600)	7,600	17,921
Total	12,600	12,600	12,600 (	12,600)	12,600	36,842
L Notes	3,120	3,120	3,120 (	3,120)	3,120	351
Chequeable deposits	9,480	9,480	9,480 (	9,480)	9,480	36,491
Consolidated totals[2]	72,000	78,800	80,325 (	82,825)	129,000	210,526

[1] Column 1 is identical with Table 3.1, except for rounding off (and it may be inferred that the reserve ratio of the deposit banks is a little under 10 per cent). Columns 2 and 3 represent induced changes in the public's coefficients of substitution in response to a new government issue and new private issues respectively. Column 4 represents the market valuation of the items in column 3; all other columns are in terms of historical costs. Columns 5 and 6 represent exogenous changes in the public's coefficients of substitution; column 6 is calculated in the same way as Table 3.1, and final digits are rounded to the nearest whole number.

[2] Netting out claims by financial intermediaries on one another.

greater than the amount of the new government issue. There will be no increase at all if the public refuses to add to its portfolio at the going rates of interest (perhaps because they are in a range approximating liquidity-trap conditions), or if the resulting increase in interest rates is so great as to drive enough private borrowing out of the market to accomodate the new government issue; the increase will exceed the new government issue if the private sector is stimulated to offer new issues of its own as well, at rates of return the public is willing to accept. The illustrative figures used assume that half the new issue is absorbed by the public directly and half through the non-banks; that some private claims are shifted from the non-banks to the general public, but some private claims are driven out of the market entirely; and that the increase in interest rates is sufficient to induce the public to hold somewhat less money-proper (to accommodate the reserve needs of the non-banks) despite the increase in its total portfolio (i.e. in its wealth).[12] However, these assumptions are quite arbitrary, since it would be difficult to incorporate any specific pattern of changes in interest rates and other parameters in this simple illustrative model.

Column 3 (which should be compared with column 1 rather than column 2) represents a situation in which it is the private sector that takes the initiative in the face of unchanged institutional parameters. New fixed-interest securities, new equities, or both totalling 5,000 marks will be issued to finance capital formation where new profit opportunities have been perceived, and business entities will draw on their unused lines of credit at banks and non-banks. The banks must sell off an equal amount of marketable (probably government) securities to honour their loan commitments; the non-banks may have to do likewise, though they should be able to finance a considerable increase in private loans from the increase in their obligations (which in this model include the non-chequeable deposits of the commercial banks). Accordingly the general public must absorb some of the outstanding government (and possibly private) issues initially held by financial intermediaries. Clearly interest rates must rise on these issues, and probably on non-bank claims and other debt contracts as well; as

---

preference might be materially increased as a consequence, which would effectively reduce the acceptance ratio for all or most substitutes for money. However, if we assume that the public approves the government's fiscal policies then a net decrease in its total financial assets can presumably be ruled out.

[12] In practice some private borrowers would draw down a substantial portion of their unused lines of credit at the banks (and at the non-banks as well, which in this model include some of the activities of commercial banks), thereby forcing the banks to sell off marketable securities in order to honour their loan commitments; this would reduce or eliminate the contraction in private credit, and would require a greater absorption of marketable (presumably largely government) securities by the general public either directly or through the non-banks.

before, this should permit the non-banks to attract the reserve funds they need out of the public's holdings of money-proper.

Column 4 illustrates the possible market value of the various assets and liabilities at the same point in time as column 3 (where all values are expressed in terms of their historical cost), on the assumption that the private credit expansion has been accompanied by a strong speculative increase in equity prices; in other words it illustrates The Revaluation Effect in such a situation. The amount of the various assumed revaluations is of course quite arbitrary, but it has been supposed that the average value of privately-held private claims (presumably equities in large part) has risen about 33 per cent, and that the average value of government securities held by the public and by the non-banks has fallen about 10 per cent (being principally relatively long-dated debt which would depreciate in value as holders tried to switch into equities). Presumably the government securities held by the banking system, on the other hand, would be short-dated and would not depreciate materially.

Note that the general public expects to receive the full face value (historical cost) of its claims against the non-banks (15,500 marks), whereas liquidation of their portfolios would yield total proceeds of no more than 15,125 marks even if the attempted realization did not drive the market value still lower; the shareholders (whom we may think of as simply a special class of depositors) would apparently suffer a capital loss of 375 marks or more if these intermediaries were wound up. (In practice, of course, they would have set aside contingency reserves out of earnings, not shown in their T-square accounts, to meet such eventualities.) Also, note that the public's T-square accounts show a decline of 1,300 marks between columns 3 and 4, or 1,675 marks if we correct for the potential loss on non-monies, whereas The Revaluation Effect is a zero-sum game in which one man's gain is another's loss. The explanation is that the public's T-square accounts ignore the implicit obligation of the taxpaying members of the public to retire the government's debt to the government-security-holding members. The amount required to buy back the government's outstanding debt falls *pari passu* with the depreciation in value of government securities, hence the true net worth of the public in column 4, as in all other columns, is 1000 marks—i.e. the value of the real assets (gold) in the system.

Still considering column 4, it is clear that any individual could redeem his obligations ahead of time by buying them back at the market price if he chose to do so, or could sell off his other asset holdings and replace them with money-proper, presumably with negligible effects on the price structure of assets in general or any given asset in particular. Obviously, however, if the public in general were to attempt to cash in on whatever paper profits it had, or to take its losses and convert into a more liquid position, the net effect would be to mark down all values until the residual holders were no longer willing to accept the losses they would incur by resale at the now-lower levels—in other words there would be a new revaluation effect, this time a negative one.

3.4. Independent Changes in the Coefficients of Substitution

To complete the illustration of a complex financial system we need to take a brief look at the effects of independent or exogenous changes in the public's coefficients of substitution.

In column 5 of Table 3.2 we suppose that the coefficient of substitution between non-monies and money-proper becomes 4:1 instead of 1:1 as in column 1—not from a desire to show a dramatic change, but merely because that is the lowest ratio at which the arithmetic generates simple round figures. There is a moderate contraction in the volume of money-proper in the hands of the public, because some will be bid away by the non-banks for reserve purposes, but we have assumed that the public's appetite for government and private security-issues is unchanged. The net effect is a credit expansion of 28,500 marks compared to column 1, which we have arbitrarily divided equally between the government and the private sectors.

In column 6 we alter the assumptions rather more: we suppose that changing payment practices and techniques greatly reduce the demand for hand-to-hand currency. (Say, the increasing use of credit cards replaces many small cash payments by a single monthly cheque, and electronic transfers through point-of-sale computer terminals not only tend to replace cheques but also become feasible for quite small purchases formerly made in cash.) The limiting position is illustrated, in which the demand for hand-to-hand currency is reduced to zero and all the central bank's obligations are absorbed as required reserves by the banks and non-banks. Further expansion could of course occur if the various institutional reserve-ratios were reduced, and the expansion would be unlimited in a closed-economy model if either the reserve-ratio of the central bank or the reserve-ratios of all other intermediaries were reduced to zero.

3.5. Algebraic Formulation

The notation used in section 4.4 of Chapter 2 above needs little modification in order to represent a complex financial structure. As before the note-acceptance ratio is assumed to be 100 per cent for the public, the banks, and the near-banks alike, but we have added two new types of assets in the public's portfolio; we may therefore specify that the public allocates its domestic financial assets (Ad) among notes, deposits, non-bank claims, government securities, and private claims in the ratio of $(1-a-b-i-j)$: $a:b:i:j$, and we have as additional constraints that $0 \le i, j$, $(1-a-b-i-j)$ ≤ 1. In Table 3.1 it is assumed that the government holds no financial assets, not even chequeable deposits, which is a little unrealistic but simplifies the presentation; it is also tacitly assumed that borrowers in the private sector hold no cash balances attributable directly to their obligations as debtors (i.e. no more than they would hold in any case).[13] In addition the table is limited to the closed-economy case ($d = 0$) but it is just as easy to derive the open-economy case for the algebraic formulation; the same procedure as on page 63 above will apply, except that the public's note holdings will be $(1-a-b-i-j)$. Ad in this case, so domestic financial assets will be given by the equation

$$Ad = G \, / \, \overline{R \, [(1-a-b-i-j)+bcr(1-p)+r(a+bcpr)]+d} \, \ldots \, (3.1).$$

Column 6 of Table 3.2 may also be derived from this equation, by the use of the fixed coefficients of substitution and the reserve ratios indicated in the text. In columns 1 to 5 inclusive, however, the coefficients cease to be constants and become unspecified functions of interest rates and other parameters; instead of deriving the public's total portfolio from the given coefficients and reserve-ratios, the *average* values of the coefficients may be derived from the given reserve-ratios and the postulated portfolio composition.

4. Disintermediation

Although financial intermediaries deal as principals with both primary lenders and ultimate borrowers, the fact remains that the net effect of their activities is *mediation* between these two independent groups. That leaves it open for the primary lenders and the ultimate borrowers they normally serve to find other ways of getting together. We introduced some examples of this in Section 3.3 of this chapter.

Credit contractions instead of expansions are of course possible, as history testifies, by a reversal of the processes we have described. In principle this may involve the non-renewal of maturing loans or the calling of demand loans. However, such actions may be painful not only for the borrowers (who may suffer losses or bankruptcy due to having to terminate their projects prematurely) but also for the lender (who may incur losses through the forced sale of collateral security or through the bankruptcy of his debtor). Usually, therefore, financial intermediaries are loath to call their loans or to curtail lines of credit once they are granted; they normally prefer to sell off a portion of their portfolios of marketable securities, either

---

[13] Alternatively the government sector (and perhaps private borrowers as well) might be treated as an additional class (or additional classes) of financial intermediaries, and their cash holdings treated like the cash reserves of the non-banks.

as an alternative to or as a means of delaying the calling of loans.

The process by which an intermediary sells off some of its marketable securities (claims on ultimate borrowers) to its own creditors (primary lenders) in exchange for the extinction of their claims against it has become known as *disintermediation*. In its pure form it involves no change in the public's total assets and no change in the total volume of credit outstanding in the community, merely an exchange of lenders' claims on the intermediary for direct claims on ultimate borrowers. (Presumably there is also some net release of standard money from the cash reserves of the intermediary into general circulation.)

In common usage, however, the term "disintermediation" is applied to the sale of marketable government or private claims by financial intermediaries (usually but not necessarily commercial banks) to the general public and their simultaneous replacement by newly-expanded loans, with no reduction in the intermediaries' reserves. This may be identified as disintermediation in the pure sense accompanied by an equal re-expansion of the assets and the liabilities of the intermediaries concerned; it is one of the ways in which credit expansion can continue, for a time at least, even though the central bank may be preventing any further increase of bank credit. It is often spoken of as a technique of credit restraint, despite the fact that it involves a net *increase* (equal to the amount of securities bought by the public) in the total volume of credit generated by the financial system; any credit restraint that occurs is the result of the upward pressure on interest rates and yields necessary to induce the public to expand its holdings of non-monies, not to the disintermediation (in this loose sense) as such.

The opposite of disintermediation, which might logically be called "intermediation" though that is not common usage, is included in the well-known term "monetizing the public debt". However, monetizing the public debt includes both the purchase by the banking system of existing public debt held by the general public and the purchase of newly-issued public debt, e.g. in support of a policy of deficit spending to stimulate the economy. What we may call the pure form, i.e. the purchase of existing debt from the public without any increase in the public's total financial assets and without any stimulating effect on the economy, is a well-known feature of economic models of an economy in deep depression; with interest rates at something approximating liquidity-trap levels the public may be willing to sell bonds at relatively high prices (low yields) with no intention of spending the proceeds but merely to hold them in the more liquid form of bank deposits, and may be relatively indifferent about holding balances of money-proper or relatively-low-yielding balances of near-money. Under these conditions it implies no difference in the spending stream whether ultimate lenders hold claims on ultimate borrowers directly as principals or indirectly through financial intermediaries.

Even with no more monetary expansion than necessary to produce an appreciable easing of interest rates in slack times, commercial banks (and other intermediaries) will add significantly to their portfolios of marketable securities, especially in the short-maturity range, in order to keep their funds fully employed when loan demand is soft. They know from experience that they can sell off these securities to third parties (i.e. to members of the general public) when they need funds; they may have to take some capital losses in so doing, because security prices will be down (yields will be up), but their losses on short-dated securities will normally amount to no more than a modest reduction in the net returns they will receive over the period in which they hold the issues, and will be offset by the expectations of higher returns from the rising volume of business and personal loans.

Part Two ═══════════════

THE MACROECONOMICS OF CREDIT EXPANSION

CHAPTER 4

CREDIT-AND-INCOME EXPANSION

1. Vining's Sequence Analysis

1.1. Basic Elements

Long-run equilibrium analysis can explain certain aspects of financial intermediation, but other important aspects require consideration of the short-run dynamic process by which "disturbances" or departures from equilibrium work themselves out. A useful approach to these dynamics can be derived from an integration of the generally-accepted theory of bank credit expansion (or "creation") and the then-novel income-multiplier theory to be found in a pioneering article written by Rutledge Vining many years ago,[1] though Vining himself does not develop this aspect of it at all. Rather, he employs a long-run-equilibrium approach closely parallel to that used in the institutional analysis of Chapter 1 above. His presentation is therefore not without shortcomings for the purposes we want to pursue, but some of these shortcomings are themselves instructive, so we will begin with an adaption of his model. The dynamic implications will be examined in Chapter 6 below.

Vining's presentation focuses attention on the process by which new equilibrium rates of flow of income and its components are achieved when new bank reserves are injected into the system. However, we will replace his term "bank" by our more neutral term "intermediary". We will also present it as if it were a question of a single injection of new reserves, as in section 2.3 of Chapter 1 above.

1.2. A Numerical Example

The presentation is best thought of as if all savings take the form of claims against a representative intermediary. Vining himself repeatedly emphasizes the limitations imposed by the rigidity of his assumptions—particularly that the propensity to consume is constant, that the bank reserve-ratio is constant, and that all unspent money is deposited in banks. Furthermore, he deals with a closed-economy model. We will also assume explicitly, as Vining does implicitly, that there is no lack of willing creditworthy borrowers and that all borrowed money is spent.

We can easily adapt the model we used in Chapter 1 to Vining's assumptions by setting the acceptance ratio at 100 per cent and the reserve

---

[1] "A Process Analysis of Bank Credit Expansion", *The Quarterly Journal of Economics,* Vol. LIV, no. 4, August 1940, pp. 599–623.

Table 4.1. A Numerical Illustration of Vining's Expansionary Sequence [1]

Period	New Claims	New Reserves	New Loans [7]	New Income Total		Spent [3]	Saved [4]
	(1)	(2)	(3)	(4)		(5)	(6)
1	1,000.00	100.00	900.00		900.00	810.00	90.00
				81.00			
2	90.00	9.00	81.00	810.00	891.00	801.90	89.10
				80.19			
3	89.10	8.91	80.19	801.90	882.09	793.88	88.21
				79.39			
4	88.21	8.82	79.39	793.88	873.27	785.94	87.33
.	.	.	.	.	.	.	.
.	.	.	.	.	.	.	.
.	.	.	.	.	.	.	.
Σ_1^∞	10,000.00	1,000.00	9,000.00		90,000.00	81,000.00	9,000.00

[1] Assuming an acceptance ratio of 100 per cent, a reserve ratio of 10 per cent, and a marginal propensity to save of 10 per cent.
[2] Is spent and becomes income in the same period.
[3] Becomes income in the next period.
[4] Placed with the intermediary in the next period.

ratio at 10 per cent; but, just for variety, let's call the currency a crown instead of a dinar (as in Chapter 1) or a dollar (as Vining does). Although it is not part of his presentation, it will do no violence to his argument if as already indicated we interpret our model as the injection of a new supply of 1,000 crowns of a gold coin after the obligations of the intermediary have effectively achieved 100 per cent acceptance. Following Vining's income-expansion assumptions, we will suppose that the intermediary promptly lends its free reserves and that the money is at once spent and creates income in the same period.

Table 4.1 illustrates how the combined credit-and-income expansion would work out. In Period 1 the public places its 1,000 crowns with the intermediary, which lends 900 crowns; the borrowed money is spent and produces 900 crowns of income, of which 810 is to be spent and 90 saved. In Period 2 the 810 crowns to be spent from the previous period appear as income; but the 90 crowns saved in the previous period are placed with the intermediary in this period, and 81 crowns are lent out and spent, thus raising the total increase of income to 891 crowns. Of this sum, 801.90 crowns is spent and 89.10 saved; in Period 3, therefore, additional income of 882.09 crowns is created. The entries for subsequent periods are determined in the same way. The totals of the various columns may be found from the formula for the summation of a converging geometric progression; the common ratio is 0.99 in columns 1, 2, and 3 from Period 2 on, and in columns 4, 5, and 6 from Period 1 on.

Note that total new savings out of income are equal to, or rather are identical with, the secondary expansion of domestic claims. This relationship survives the transition to open-economy conditions (as in Table 4.3 below) and to the more sophisticated versions presented in Chapter 5 below (as in Tables 5.1 and 5.3). Thus it is clear that all "created" credit-based claims must ultimately be saved out of income; money is no different from other financial claims in this respect. (It is true that *in Table 4.1* the secondary expansion of domestic claims is also equal to total loans granted by the intermediary, as it is in Table 1.1 above; but this relationship does not survive the transition to open-economy conditions, either in Table 1.2 above or in Tables 4.3 and 5.3 below, thanks to the operation of The Leakage Principles.)

The substantial step-down in the redeposit sequence between Period 1 and Period 2 in Table 4.1 is a departure from the traditional version of bank-credit expansion. The reason for the difference is simple enough: traditionally it is assumed that with no currency drain (100 per cent acceptance ratio) the entire amount of each loan will be redeposited in the next period, whereas Vining assumes that only the increment of savings generated in the same period[2] by the spending of the borrowed money is redeposited. (In terms of the algebraic formulation given in section 1.3 below, these redeposits are L and $s.L$ respectively.) For the time being we are focusing primarily on the long-run implications and therefore we are not particularly concerned with the differences between alternative paths to equilibrium.

Instead of tracing Vining's sequence period by period we can directly compute total claims and total loans by reference to the equilibrium distribution of standard money in the system, and then derive the totals for the income and income-related columns by a separate calculation. In this case we note that all standard money becomes available to the intermediary as reserves, hence a reserve ratio of 10 per cent gives total claims of 10,000 crowns and loans of 9,000 crowns. Here it becomes important to note that on Vining's assumptions the initial injection of 1,000 crowns is not

---

[2] It may be noted that the "periods" used in the two sequences need not be the same. In the traditional version of bank-credit expansion (and in Chapter 1 above) the period is identified with the lending and redeposit of funds, but now it is identified with the time in which income is spent and becomes income again. But each of these periods is primarily a didactive device; neither is "right" or "wrong" in itself, and there is no logical reason to suppose they are of equal length or are related in any rigid way.

new income, it is merely the conversion of one form of existing financial assets into another; only the spending of borrowed money generates new income. That being so, and since the marginal propensity to save of 10 per cent means a standard income-multiplier of 10, loans of 9,000 crowns eventually generate new income of 90,000 crowns.

It may be noted that these figures can be disaggregated into the components of a series of simple income-expansion sequences based on the standard income-multiplier. Thus the initial loan of 900 crowns generates new income of 900 crowns in Period 1, 810 crowns in Period 2, 729 crowns in Period 3, and so on; the first two terms of this sequence are easily identified in the table, but subsequent terms are included with terms of other series. Similarly, the 90 crowns saved in Period 1 result in loans of 81 crowns in Period 2 and generate income of a like sum in that period, 72.90 crowns in Period 3, 65.61 crowns in Period 4, and so on; the 81 crowns is clearly visible in the table but not the subsequent terms. The figure of 882.09 crowns for income in Period 3 includes the 729 crowns from the re-spending effect of the first loan (900 crowns) and 72.90 crowns from the respending effect of the second loan (81 crowns), but it also includes two other components. The first of these is a loan of 72.90 crowns made possible by the redeposit of the 81 crowns saved out of the 810 crowns of income in Period 2 deriving from the respending effect of the first loan; the second is a loan of 7.29 crowns made possible by the deposit of the 8.10 crowns in savings from the income generated in the second period as a result of the second loan. In each successive period more and more terms must be added as new simple income-expansion sequences are begun.

Before proceeding further, however, it must be acknowledged that Vining's presentation is open to certain objections. He explicitly identifies his intermediaries as banks, evidently meant in much the same sense as our useage, but his presentation robs them of two of the characteristics that will interest us most: first, that their obligations serve as money; second, the prompt redeposit of loan proceeds (which is a consequence of the first). For simplicity he assumes the secondary-deposit ratio is zero, which rules out the second characteristic, but he says nothing at all about the first.[3] We have already noted this apparent inconsistency in section 4 of Chapter 1 above, and have offered a partial answer to it. As we will see in section 2 of Chapter 5 below, however, this deficiency can be corrected by a simple modification of his procedure, and it contributes to a clarification of the differences between banks and non-banks in section 2.3 of Chapter 6 below.

---

[3] In fairness to Vining it must be noted that these characteristics were of limited interest for his purposes, and disregarding them does not invalidate his argument, which was addressed to the achievement of long-run equilibrium.

1.3. Algebraic Formulation

Vining's own presentation[4] is heavily algebriac, but in order to make it more compatible with the models we have used in the preceding chapters we will use a different notation. As in Period 1 of column 1 of Table 4.1, let G crowns of previously-hoarded coin be placed with the intermediary, which observes a reserve ratio of r, and let the marginal propensity to save be s — subject to the constraint that $0 \leq r, s, \leq 1$. By hypothesis $(1-r)G$ crowns are borrowed and spent (column 3) and generate new income (column 4) of the same amount in the same income-period. Of this, $(1-s)(1-r)G$ crowns will be spent, to become income in the next period, and $s(1-r)G$ crowns will be saved. In Period 2 the $s(1-r)G$ crowns saved in Period 1 will be redeposited, leading to new loans (column 3) and new income (column 4) of $s(1-r)^2G$ crowns. But by hypothesis the spending of $(1-r)(1-s)G$ crowns in Period 1 will also generate like income in Period 2, so total income in the period becomes $s(1-r)^2G + (1-r)(1-s)G$, or $(1-r)G[(1-s) + s(1-r)]$, which reduces to $(1-r)(1-rs)G$. We thus have a set of converging geometric progressions starting with Period 1 for columns 4 to 6 and Period 2 for columns 1 to 3, each having $(1-rs)$ as a common ratio.

Table 4.2 demonstrates how these complex sequences may be dis-aggregated into the components of a succession of standard-income-multiplier sequences. The spending of the first loan from the intermediary generates the first income-sequence, designated (a), which starts in Period 1 (column 3) and continues in subsequent periods as $(1-r)G + (1-s)$ $(1-r)G + (1-s)^2(1-r)G \ldots \rightarrow (1-r)G/s$. The savings of $s(1-r)G$ generated by the first term of income-sequence (a) (in column 5) are placed with the intermediary in Period 2 (column 1) and give rise to new lending and spending and therefore to a new income-sequence, designated (b), which begins in Period 2 and continues in subsequent periods as $s(1-r)^2G$ $+ (1-s) . s(1-r)^2G + (1-s)^2 . s(1-r)^2G + \ldots \rightarrow (1-r)^2G$. The savings generated by the second term of income-sequence (a) and the first term of income-sequence (b) start further income-sequences, designated (c) and (d) respectively, in Period 3; and so on. Each income-sequence generates a proportionate increase in savings, which are placed with the intermediary in the next period; and placement with the intermediary starts a new sequence of lending, spending, and income-creation in the same period. Among other things this means (a) that the number of income-sequences doubles in each successive income-period, and (b) that the secondary increase of claims against the intermediary (i.e. the total increase in claims after Period 1) is identical to the total savings generated in the entire income-

---

[4] We will be primarily concerned with the elaboration of Vining's basic model as presented in his first eleven pages, to the end of "sequence (5)" in the middle of page 609.

Table 4.2. Algebraic Disaggregation

Period	Sequence	New obligations	New loans[2]
		(1)	(2)
1 ...	—	G	$G.(1-r)$
2 ...		...	...
	$(a-1)$	$s(1-r)G$	$s(1-r)G.(1-r)$
3 ...		...	...
		...	...
	$(a-2)$	$(1-s).s(1-r)G$	$(1-s).s(1-r)G.(1-r)$
	$(b-1)$	$+\ \ s^2(1-r)^2G$	$+\ \ s^2(1-r)^2G.(1-r)$
		$=\ \ (1-rs).s(1-r)G$	$=\ \ (1-rs).s(1-r)G.(1-r)$
4 ...		...	...
		...	...
		...	...
		...	...
	$(a-3)$	$(1-s)^2.s(1-r)G$	$(1-s)^2.s(1-r)G.(1-r)$
	$(b-2)$	$+\ (1-s).s^2(1-r)^2G$	$+\ (1-s).s^2(1-r)^2G.(1-r)$
	$(c-1)$	$+\ s^2(1-r)^2(1-s)G$	$+\ s^2(1-r)^2(1-s)G.(1-r)$
	$(d-1)$	$+\ s^3(1-r)^3G$	$+\ s^3(1-r)^3G.(1-r)$
		$=\ (1-rs)^2.s(1-r)G$	$=\ (1-rs)^2.s(1-r)G.(1-r)$
	.	.	.
	.	.	.
	.	.	.
	(Σa)	$(1-r)G$	$(1-r)G.(1-r)$
	(Σb)	$+\ \ s(1-r)^2G$	$+\ \ s(1-r)^2G.(1-r)$
	(Σc)	$+\ s(1-r)^2(1-s)G$	$+\ s(1-r)^2(1-s)G.(1-r)$
	(Σd)	$+\ \ s^2(1-r)^3G$	$+\ \ s^2(1-r)^3G.(1-r)$
	.	$+$.	$+$.
	.	.	.
	.	.	.
	.	.	.
	.	.	.
		$=\ \ (1-r)G/r$	$=\ \ (1-r)^2G/r$
Σ_1^∞		G/r	$(1-r)G/r$

[1] Assuming an acceptance ratio of 100 per cent. The reserve ratio is r and the marginal propensity to save is s.

[2] These sums are spent and become income in the same period.

of Vining's Expansionary Sequence[1]

New income

Sequence		Total income		Spent[3]		Saved[4]
		(3)		(4)		(5)
$(a-1)$		$(1-r)G$		$(1-r)G.(1-s)$		$(1-r)G.s$
$(a-2)$		$(1-s).(1-r)G$		$(1-s).(1-r)G.(1-s)$		$(1-s).(1-r)G.s$
$(b-1)$	$+$	$s(1-r)^2G$	$+$	$s(1-r)^2G.(1-s)$	$+$	$s(1-r)^2G.s$
	$=$	$(1-rs).(1-r)G$	$=$	$(1-rs).(1-r)G.(1-s)$	$=$	$(1-rs).(1-r)G.s$
$(a-3)$		$(1-s)^2.(1-r)G$		$(1-s)^2.(1-r)G.(1-s)$		$(1-s)^2.(1-r)G.s$
$(b-2)$	$+$	$(1-s).s(1-r)^2G$	$+$	$(1-s).s(1-r)^2G.(1-s)$	$+$	$(1-s).s(1-r)^2G.s$
$(c-1)$	$+$	$s(1-r)^2(1-s)G$	$+$	$s(1-r)^2(1-s)G.(1-s)$	$+$	$s(1-r)^2(1-s)G.s$
$(d-1)$	$+$	$s^2(1-r)^3G$	$+$	$s(1-r)^3G.(1-s)$	$+$	$s^2(1-r)^3G.s$
	$=$	$(1-rs)^2.(1-r)G$	$=$	$(1-rs)^2.(1-r)G.(1-s)$	$=$	$(1-rs)^2.(1-r)G.s$
$(a-4)$		$(1-s)^3.(1-r)G$		$.$		$.$
$(b-3)$	$+$	$(1-s)^2.s(1-r)^2G$		$.$		$.$
$(c-2)$	$+$	$(1-s).s(1-r)^2(1-s)G$		$.$		$.$
$(d-2)$	$+$	$(1-s).s^2(1-r)^3G$		$.$		$.$
$(e-1)$	$+$	$s(1-r)^2(1-s)^2G$		$.$		$.$
$(f-1)$	$+$	$s^2(1-r)^3(1-s)G$		$.$		$.$
$(g-1)$	$+$	$s^2(1-r)^3(1-s)G$		$.$		$.$
$(h-1)$	$+$	$s^3(1-r)^4G$		$.$		$.$
	$=$	$(1-rs)^3.(1-r)G$				
$.$		$.$		$.$		$.$
$.$		$.$		$.$		$.$
$.$		$.$		$.$		$.$
(Σa)		$(1-r)G/s$		$.$		$.$
(Σb)	$+$	$(1-r)^2G$		$.$		$.$
(Σc)	$+$	$(1-r)^2(1-s)G$		$.$		$.$
(Σd)	$+$	$s(1-r)^3G$		$.$		$.$
$.$	$+$	$.$		$.$		$.$
$.$		$.$		$.$		$.$
$.$		$.$		$.$		$.$
$.$		$.$		$.$		$.$
	$=$	$(1-r)G/rs$	$=$	$(1-r)G.(1-s)/rs$	$=$	$(1-r)G/r$
Σ_1^∞		$(1-r)G/rs$		$(1-r)G.(1-s)/rs$		$(1-r)G/r$

[3] These sums become income in the next period.

[4] These sums are placed with the intermediary in the next period.

expansion process. Each expansionary sequence in columns 3 to 5, and in columns 1 and 2 from Period 2 on, constitutes a converging geometric progression with a common ratio of $(1-s)$. Their numbers increase without limit, and the rate at which new sequences appear raises the effective common ratio per period to $(1-rs)$.

Alternatively, we can deduce the equilibrium values for domestic financial assets and its components for any acceptance ratio by considering the proportionate distribution of standard money independently of the detailed sequence analysis, as we did on page 26 above, and derive the equilibrium values of income (Y) and savings (S) therefrom. Setting $d=0$ in equation 1.8, we derive $L=a(1-r)G \big/ [1-a(1-r)]$; by hypothesis $Y=L/s$ and $S=s.Y$, hence $Y=a(1-r)G \big/ s[1-a(1-r)]$ and $S=a(1-r)G \big/ [1-a(1-r)]$ $(=L)$. Setting $a=1$, as Vining assumes, we get the same formulas as before for income, spending, and saving. The corresponding equations from section 3.3 of Chapter 5 are 5.19 to 5.27 on page 126, setting $d=m=z=0$ and $n=1$.

2. Implications for Multiplier Analysis

2.1. Families of Multipliers

As used in economic analysis, a multiplier may be defined as a proportionate relationship between two economic variables such that an exogenous change in one (usually the smaller) will lead to a corresponding change in the other. Multipliers are of considerable use in banking theory and in income-flow analysis, and Vining's analysis brings out some important interrelationships between the two uses.

In many cases we can identify families of multipliers. One example was pointed out on pages 26f above in the open-economy version of the model: by setting $G=1$ in equations 1.1 to 1.8 we can derive a series of related multipliers for total financial assets, domestic financial assets, foreign financial assets, currency in circulation, domestic claims, loans generated, the reserves of the intermediary, and the external drain. The loan multiplier is commonly called the credit multiplier, and if we identify our intermediary as a bank or other depository then the domestic-financial-asset multiplier assumes the more familiar title deposit multiplier;[5] the other

---

[5] A word of warning may be in order about the use of the term "deposit multiplier": it is sometimes carelessly used to mean simply the reciprocal of the reserve ratio. The deposit multiplier derived from equation 1.1 on page 26 is $a/[1-a(1-r)+d]$; in the closed economy case with an acceptance ratio of 100 per cent ($d=0$ and $a=1$) it does indeed reduce to $1/r$, but not otherwise. It is of course true that multiplying the reserves actually retained at the end of an expansionary sequence by $1/r$ will give total deposits, but that amounts merely to saying that if $Gk=r.K$ then $K=Gk/r$, it has

multipliers are not commonly used, but can be clearly identified in the formulation presented here. Similarly, we can identify families of income-related multipliers; the standard income-multiplier itself, and the associated multipliers by means of which we can derive the corresponding totals for domestic consumption, savings, the import leakage, and perhaps other related variables.

Mathematically speaking, in the preceding paragraph we have identified the various multipliers by their *products*; but we can find other families of multipliers classified according to the *multiplicand*. So far we have only looked at multipliers designed to be applied to a new injection of standard money into an economy, but this is not the only possibility. For example, we might wish to derive multipliers that apply to the free reserves available for lending regardless of how they might arise. We can easily derive them by noting that (1) by hypothesis a loan of 1 crown from free reserves will put 1 crown of additional coin in the hands of the public, and (2) from that point on the expansion will proceed exactly as before. Hence, setting $G = 1$ in equations 1.1 and 1.5 to 1.7 on page 26 we find that the same multipliers that apply to a new injection of G crowns into the economy will give us Ad, Gp, K, and G when applied to net free reserves. In the case of L, however, this multiplier will give us the *secondary* expansion (i.e. the sum of all loans except the initial loan from free reserves); in this case therefore the free-reserve multiplier becomes $1 + a(1-r) / [1-a(1-r)] = 1 / [1-a(1-r)]$. We will explore these relationships further in section 3.3 of Chapter 5 below.

There is still another dimension in which we could look for new families of multipliers: those applicable to a marginal increment of standard money injected into the system need not be identical with those that apply on the average to the existing stock of standard money. It may be for example that, as a nation grows, the increase in spending on things that come in large units (cars, appliances, etc.) or that for other reasons tend to be paid for by cheque is proportionately greater than the increase of spending on those things like newspapers, bus fares, food, and other things that tend to be paid for in cash. Or, to put it more generally, many of the parameters in our model that we have tacitly assumed to be constants may actually be variables, and perhaps rather complex variables at that.

2.2. Compound Multipliers
Vining's analysis will serve to introduce what we may call the "total

---

some practical uses on occasion but it does not permit one to derive K from an increase of standard money available to the community, nor from free reserves, nor from other exogenous variables. Moral: all multipliers are ratios, but not all ratios are multipliers.

income multiplier". In this particular model it is the product of the credit multiplier and the standard income-multiplier, and is designed to be used with the initial injection of gold coin (standard money) as the multiplicand. In our numerical example it is 9×10 or 90; more generally, it is $a(1-r) / [1-a(1-r)] \times 1/s$. In this closed-economy model the two components are completely independent of one another, not only in the sense that each can be separately computed, given the values of the necessary parameters, but also in the sense that each is determined by a completely different set of parameters—the acceptance and the reserve ratios in the case of the credit multiplier, the marginal propensity to save in the case of the standard income-multiplier.

The interaction between the credit multiplier and the standard income-multiplier may be called The Compounding Effect. It helps to bring out the fact that the total income-expansion associated with a given credit expansion may be anything within a wide range. The credit multiplier itself may lie anywhere between zero ($a=0$ or $r=1$) and infinity ($a=1$ and $r=0$). However, the standard income-multiplier may also vary widely—from unity ($s=1$) to infinity ($s=0$). It follows that the total-income-multiplier may be little larger than the credit multiplier, since the two become virtually identical as the marginal propensity to save approaches unity. But it also follows that a very small expansion of credit may lead to a virtually unlimited expansion of income if the marginal propensity to save approaches zero. Specifically, with any credit multiplier that is significantly greater than zero we can associate any total-income-multiplier we choose, between the value of the credit multiplier itself and infinity, by postulating whatever standard income-multiplier suits our purpose.

It may also be illuminating to note that a very modest relaxation of our assumptions will permit us to extend the range of possible values of the total-income-multiplier down to zero even if the credit multiplier is substantially greater than zero: we have merely to suppose that money may be borrowed not only to be spent, as we have postulated so far, but also to increase the borrower's liquidity as a protection against real or apprehended future needs (as does happen at times in the real world, e.g. when business firms with uncompleted capital-spending programs anticipate severer credit restraints in the near future). Conceivably the entire expansionary sequence depicted in Table 4.1 may be generated by willing and credit-worthy borrowers who wish only to add to their holdings of gold coins for liquidity purposes and who add not a penny to their spending. With no new spending there will be no generation of new income, no matter what values we assign to the credit multiplier and the standard income-multiplier. More generally, if n ($0 \leq n \leq 1$) is the proportion of new borrowing that is spent and becomes income, the total-income-multiplier becomes $n \times a(-r) / [1-a(1-r)] \times /s$

$= an(1-r)/s[1-a(1-r)]$; if $n = 0$ then the total-income-multiplier becomes zero.

3. An Open-Economy Model

3.1. A Numerical Example

Vining does not extend his model to open-economy conditions, but it is not hard to do so. In section 2.3 of Chapter 1 above we noted that the principal adjustment needed to adapt our model to open-economy conditions is the introduction of the external drain; the main effect on the financial structure is a material reduction in the expansion of credit and of domestic financial assets. As far as the income effects are concerned, the main result is to add the import leakage to the savings leakage, which brings a substantial reduction in the standard income-multiplier. With both components thus reduced, the total-income-multiplier suffers a double contraction.

For purposes of illustration let us retain Vining's assumption that the marginal propensity to save is 10 per cent, and postulate that the marginal propensity to import is 20 per cent. This reduces the standard income-multiplier from 10 (as in Table 4.1) to 3 1/3. We will continue with the constrained-equilibrium interpretation we have used previously, i.e. we will continue to ignore the external repercussions, and with the assumption that all borrowing is spent on domestic goods and services. We will also assume, as before, that the financial system receives 1,000 crowns in standard money (gold coin) in a form that does not constitute income. However, we will now assume that the external drain is composed entirely of the import leakage out of the income generated by the credit expansion, whereas in Chapter 1 we assumed it was entirely composed of the acquisition of external financial claims.[6] We will continue to assume that the reserve ratio is 10 per cent, to simplify the arithmetic; but this time let us suppose the acceptance ratio is 90 per cent instead of 100 per cent, in order to illustrate the effect of the currency drain.

Table 4.3 summarizes the combined credit-and-income sequence based on these assumptions. In Period 1 1,000 crowns of new standard money enter the system, perhaps from dishoarding, and 900 of these crowns are promptly placed with the intermediary. The sequence then proceeds as in Table 4.1, except that we must now introduce new columns for currency in circulation and for income spent abroad, and the new income generated in each period is correspondingly less. Evidently the credit multiplier applicable to an injection of new standard money under these circum-

---

[6] A third possibility is that a portion of loan proceeds may be spent abroad. All three components of the external drain are separately identified in the algebraic formulation presented in section 3.3 of Chapter 5 below.

**Table 4.3. Combined Credit-and-Income Expansion
in an Open Economy** [1]

Period	Public		Intermediary		Income			
	Coin	Claims	Reserve	Loans[2]	Total	Spent at home[3]	Spent abroad	Saved[4]
	(1)	(2)	(3)	(4)	(5)	(6)	(7)	(8)
1	100.00	900.00	90.00	810.00		810.00	567.00	162.00	81.00
		(1000.00)							
2	8.10	72.90	7.29	65.61	65.61				
		(81.00)			567.00	632.61	442.83	126.52	63.26
3	6.33	56.93	5.69	52.24	52.24				
		(63.26)			442.83	494.07	345.85	98.81	49.41
4	4.94	44.47	4.45	40.02	40.02				
		(49.41)			345.85	385.87	270.11	77.17	38.59
	.	.	.	.	.	.	.	.	.
	.	.	.	.	.	.	.	.	.
Σ_2^∞	36.99	332.88	33.29	299.59		(2888.63)	(2022.04)	(577.73)	(288.86)
		(369.86)							
Σ_1^∞	136.99	1232.88	123.29	1109.59		3698.63	2589.04	739.73	369.86
		(1369.86)							

[1] A numerical illustration, assuming an acceptance ratio of 90 percent, a reserve ratio of 10 percent, a marginal propensity to import of 20 percent, and a marginal propensity to save of 10 percent. Figures in parenthesis are relatively unimportant.

[2] Assumed to be spent entirely on domestic goods and to become income in the same period.

[3] Assumed to become income in the next period.

[4] Divided between coin and claims in the next period.

N.B.: Detailed figures may not add exactly to totals because of rounding.

stances is about 1.1, the standard income-multiplier is 3 1/3, and the total-income-multiplier is about 3.7. It may be noted that the common ratio in columns 5 to 8 and from Period 2 on in columns 1 to 4 is 0.781. Also, the equilibrium values may be derived by noting that each crown of domestic financial assets requires 0.1 crowns of gold in circulation and 0.09 crowns in institutional reserves, and is also associated with 0.81 crowns of loans, which The Leakage Principles tell us will generate an external drain of 0.54 crowns (since the marginal propensity to import is 0.2 and the marginal propensity to save is 0.1). Each crown of financial assets will thus deplete the initial gold supply by 0.73 crowns, so 1,000 gold crowns will produce 1,000/0.73 or approximately 1,370 crowns of domestic financial assets.

Note that, as on page 20 above, we can identify the credit expansion (1,109.59 crowns in column 4) with the sum of the secondary increase in domestic financial assets (369.86 crowns in columns 1 and 2) and the external drain (739.73 crowns in column 6). Also, as in Table 4.1, savings out of income equal the secondary or induced expansion of domestic financial assets: the last figure in column 8 is identical to the sum of the second-last figures in columns 1 and 2.

Furthermore the import leakage (which we are now identifying with the external drain) and the *secondary* expansion of domestic financial assets are in the ratio of the marginal propensity to import to the marginal propensity to save. This in turn leads to an instructive comparison with the constrained-equilibrium interpretation of Table 1.2 above, where the expansion of external claims (which is there identified with the external drain) and the *total* expansion of domestic financial assets are equal. The main difference between the two cases is that in Chapter 1 we assume that the new injection of standard money is immediately subdivided between domestic and external assets, whereas now we treat the entire sum as domestic assets and identify the external drain with the import leakage from the income generated by the spending of borrowed money. These are two out of several variants of the asset-substitution version of the combined credit-and-income-expansion sequence, explained in section 3.1 of Chapter 5 below and treated algebraically in section 3.3 thereof.

Table 4.4, supplementing Table 4.3, shows by means of T-square accounts the asset and liability patterns that obtain at each stage of the credit-and-income-expansion sequence. Table 4.3 focuses on the income-generating effects of spending, which, as we have seen, can be translated into a rate of flow. Table 4.4 focuses on the stocks of money-to-hold and money-to-spend at particular points of time.

The numbered columns in Table 4.4 represent the balance sheets at given points in time. The unnumbered intervening columns represent changes in the interval between balance sheets; the symbol # is used to mark what is deemed to be the initiating transaction. In column 1 the public has received 1,000 crowns in new money and has allocated it between holdings of coin and holdings of claims, but this puts the intermediary in disequilibrium, indicated by holdings of 810 crowns of free or excess reserves. The intermediary then lends out its free reserves, and the loan is spent by the borrower and produces domestic income, as in Period 1 of Table 4.3, so that in column 2 of Table 4.4 the public holds 810 crowns of new income it is about to spend (indicated by an asterisk). This is money-to-spend, not money-to-hold; as in Period 1 of Table 4.3, the spending of it generates an exchange drain of 162 crowns and new savings of 81 crowns, the savings being divided into 8.10 crowns in coin in circulation and 72.90 crowns of new deposits with the intermediary, but through the familiar

Table 4.4. T-Square Accounts in an Open-Economy Credit-and-Income Expansion[1]

Item	(1)	(2)	(3)	(4)	(5) (∞)
General Public					
A Coin to spend	+810	810* −243.00	567.00 +65.61	632.61* ..	—
Coin to hold	100	100 + 8.10#	108.10	108.10 ..	136.99
Claims	900	900 + 72.90#	972.90	972.90 ..	1232.88
Domestic assets	1000 +810	1810 −162.00	1648.00 +65.61	1713.61 ..	1369.86
L Debts	+810	810	810.00 +65.61	875.61 ..	1109.59
Net worth	1000	1000 −162.00	838.00	838.00 ..	260.27
Intermediary					
A Req'd reserves	90	90 + 7.29	97.29	97.29 ..	123.29
Free reserves	810 −810	+ 65.61	65.61 −65.61	..	—
Loans	+810#	810	810.00 +65.61#	875.61 ..	1109.59
L Obligations	900	900 + 72.90	972.90	972.90 ..	1232.88
Memorandum:					
External drain		+162.00#	162.00	162.00 ..	739.73

[1] Same assumptions as Table 4.3.

* Received and spent as domestic income. Composed of the respending component of income at the previous stage (odd-numbered columns) plus new loans.

\# Transaction which initiates changes in other items.

N.B.: Detailed figures may not add exactly to totals because of rounding.

respending effect it creates new income and therefore new money-to-spend of 567 crowns, as in column 3 of Table 4.4. At this stage the intermediary again has free reserves, so the expansion continues. Equilibrium is attained in column 5 with the elimination of all money-to-spend either through the external drain or by conversion into money-to-hold—either directly, as willingly-held coin, or indirectly, as required reserves for willingly-held claims.

Like Tables 1.1 and 1.2 but unlike Table 4.3, Table 4.4 permits us to continually identify the whereabouts of the 1,000 crowns of standard money that has been deemed to be injected into the financial system. This in itself is a mechanical matter of limited significance, but it does bring out clearly the fact that it is difficult to interpret our intermediary's function as that of a bank, since all transactions appear to be effected with standard money withdrawn from the intermediary, and redeposits appear to be limited to the money saved out of income. We will return to this problem in section 2 of Chapter 5.

3.2. Algebraic Formulation

In section 1.3 above we employed the commonly-used symbols for income (Y), savings (S), and the marginal propensity to save (s), as well as the symbols first introduced in section 2.5 of Chapter 1 above. For the open-economy case we may add M for imports and m for the marginal propensity to import. Also, we are presently setting $Gd=M$. This done, the various sequences of Table 4.3 may be generalized and additional components identified as follows:

$$Ad = \quad G \quad + \quad as(1-r)G \;+\ldots= \quad \frac{(m+s)G}{(m+s)-as(1-r)} \quad (4.1)$$

$$Gp = \quad (1-a)G \quad + \quad (1-a).as(1-r)G \;+\ldots= \quad \frac{(1-a)(m+s)G}{(m+s)-as(1-r)} \quad (4.2)$$

$$K = \quad a.G \quad + \quad a.as(1-r)G \;+\ldots= \quad \frac{a(m+s)G}{(m+s)-as(1-r)} \quad (4.3)$$

$$Gk = \quad ar.G \quad + \quad ar.as(1-r)G \;+\ldots= \quad \frac{ar(m+s)G}{(m+s)-as(1-r)} \quad (4.4)$$

$$L = \quad a(1-r)G \quad + \quad a(1-r).as(1-r)G \;+\ldots= \quad \frac{a(1-r)(m+s)G}{(m+s)-as(1-r)} \quad (4.5)$$

$$Y = \quad a(1-r)G \quad \left\{ \begin{array}{l} + \quad a(1-r).as(1-r)G \\ + \quad (1-m-s).a(1-r)G \end{array} \right\} +\ldots= \quad \frac{a(1-r)G}{(m+s)-as(1-r)} \quad (4.6)$$

$$M = \quad m.a(1-r)G \quad \left\{ \begin{array}{l} + \quad m.as^2(1-r)^2G \\ + \quad m.a(1-m-s)(1-r)G \end{array} \right\} +\ldots= \quad \frac{am(1-r)G}{(m+s)-as(1-r)} \quad (4.7)$$

$$S = \quad s.a(1-r)G \quad \left\{ \begin{array}{l} + \quad s.as^2(1-r)^2G \\ + \quad s.a(1-m-s)(1-r)G \end{array} \right\} +\ldots= \quad \frac{as(1-r)G}{(m+s)-as(1-r)} \quad (4.8).$$

The sums of these series may be found by noting that the income-related sequences, and also the credit-related sequences excluding their first terms, are converging geometric progressions with a common ratio of $1+as(1-r)$ $-(m+s)$. Note that $Gp+Gk+Gd=G$, that $Y=L/(m+s)$, that the secondary expansion of Ad (i.e. the sum from the second term on) is identical to S, that the secondary expansion of Ad plus the external drain equals the credit expansion (i.e. $AD-G+M=L$), and that $M{:}S=m{:}s$.

Alternatively, we can derive the equilibrium values without recourse to the sequence analysis as such by considering the proportionate distribution of G. Each crown of Ad requires $1-a(1-r)$ crowns of gold for circulation and for the intermediary's reserves. In addition, however, there is the external drain to consider, resulting from the import leakage out of the income generated by the spending of borrowed money. Each crown of domestic financial assets enables the intermediary to make loans of $(1-r)$ crowns; hence, since $K=a.Ad$, each crown of Ad implies $a(1-r)$ crowns of loans. Also, since the spending of borrowed money is the only income-generating factor, The Leakage Principles tell us that the import leakage is equal to $m/(m+s)$ per crown of loans; loans of $a(1-r)$ crowns will therefore generate an external drain of $am(1-r)/m+s$ crowns. This gives a total of $1-a(1-r) + am(1-r)/(m+s)$ crowns in gold per crown of domestic financial assets. Simplifying this expression and dividing it into G, we find that G crowns of standard money will support $(m+s)G/[(m+s)-as(1-r)]$ crowns of Ad. From this we can deduce the values of Gp, K, Gk, and L from the acceptance and the reserve ratios, and from L we can derive Y, M, and S by the use of the marginal propensities to import and to save. Alternatively, all these variables can be derived from equations 5.19 to 5.27 on page 126 below, by setting $d=z=0$ and $n=1$.

3.3 Compound Multipliers

In the open-economy case, as in the closed-economy case, the total income-multiplier appropriate to the present assumptions can be identified as the product of the credit multiplier and the standard income-multiplier. As before, the two components can be separately computed; we have already made use of this fact on page 103 in discussing Table 4.3. They are no longer completely independent, however, because the marginal propensity to import enters into both of them. The credit multiplier can be derived by setting $G=1$ in equation 4.5 on page 105, and the standard income-multiplier takes the usual value $1/(m+s)$. Furthermore if we again identify n as the portion of new loans that is spent and becomes income we get a total-income-multiplier of $n \times a(1-r)(m+s)/[(m+s)-as(1-r)] \times 1/(m+s)$, which reduces to $an(1-r)/[(m+s)-as(1-r)]$. This formula can be reconciled with the closed-economy formula given on page 100 above by setting $m=0$ and $n=1$.

CHAPTER 5

IMPROVED MODELS

1. Alternative Long-Run Models

1.1. The Use of Loan Proceeds

We have usually assumed that all loan proceeds are spent on domestic goods and services and therefore produce domestic income to the full amount of the loan. On the face of it this is not very plausible. It is possible that some of it may in effect be added to the working balance of business enterprises or may be spent on imported materials, components, or equipment and will therefore generate no domestic income. Any such purchase of imports would of course increase the external drain and further reduce both the domestic credit expansion and the income expansion. Additions to working balances, on the other hand, would be treated similarly to savings generated out of income, i.e. they would in effect be either held in cash or redeposited with the intermediaries.

We will not spare the space to illustrate these possibilities in a new table, as there is a danger the procedure may degenerate into a mere exercise in arithmetic, but the general principles involved are straightforward. The loan totals would be subdivided into three subcategories, "loans spent at home", "loans spent abroad", and "loans saved", just as income is subdivided in the preceeding exposition—but of course the proportions might be quite different, because borrowed money is disposable capital rather than income and its spending is likely to be controlled by different considerations. Only the first subcategory would directly produce income at home. The second would become an additional component of the external drain. The third would be further subdivided between holdings of standard money and holdings of claims on the intermediary, like savings out of income, though not necessarily in the same proportions, and would become part of the lending-and-redepositing sequence.

1.2. New Income in Standard Money
1.2.1. A Closed-Economy Model

In none of the sequences used so far does the first step involve any increase in anyone's income. All that happens initially is that standard money is placed with some intermediary in exchange for claims on that intermediary,[1] be they bank notes, chequeable deposits, cash surrender values

---

[1] The same principles apply to direct contracts between primary lenders and ultimate borrowers, of course, as noted on pp. 16 and 75 above and illustrated in Table 3.1.

of life insurance policies, private claims, government debt, or whatever. Incomes are only affected as the intermediary lends some of the money it receives and that money is spent. However, we can easily think of examples of increases in liquid assets that are linked to equal increases in income. In a gold-coin-using economy one obvious way of linking them would be to suppose that someone sets to work mining gold; the new gold he puts into circulation or deposits with an intermediary clearly represents new income to him and to the economy. In a closed-economy cartalist monetary system, new income might be created by government deficit-spending financed by the credit expansion. In an open economy, whether the monetary system was metallist or cartalist, net export earnings would provide new income to the exporter and to the economy.

The incorporation of this modification in the closed-economy model is quite simple. The expansion of claims against and loans by the intermediary will be unchanged, but the total income generated will be increased. We have already noted (in sections 1.2 and 1.3 of Chapter 4 above) that the sequence initiated by the spending of borrowed money can be disaggregated into a series of standard-income-multiplier sequences, each initiated by a particular loan from the intermediary; to this we now add a new standard-income-multiplier sequence, stemming from the initial receipt of standard-money-as-income. We may view the logical relationship as if the initial standard-income-multiplier sequence "goes to completion" first and the savings thus generated are then deposited with the intermediary. The Leakage Principles tell us that these savings will equal the initial injection of income, since there is no other leakage, so the new standard-income-multiplier sequence is simply added to the credit-induced expansion of income. Suppose the standard money is a riyal. In terms of Vining's sequence analysis, the new expansionary element will be incorporated in a stage-by-stage process: the first entry in Table 4.1 on page 92 will be 1,000 riyals in column 4 instead of column 1 in Period 1, subdivided into 900 riyals in column 5 and 100 riyals in column 6; in Period 2 the deposit becomes 100 riyals, loans 90 riyals, and income $900+90=990$ riyals instead of $810+81=891$ riyals; the redeposit in Period 3 will therefore be 99 riyals instead of 89.10 riyals; and so on. The institutional totals (columns 1 to 3) will of course be the same—the sum of the series $100+99+98.01+\ldots$ is the same as the sum of $1,000+90+89.10+\ldots$ — but the equilibrium value of total income (column 4) will now be 100,000 riyals instead of 90,000.

One difference that may be observed between this version of the model (which may be called the injection-of-income version or simply the "income" version) and the one used in Chapter 4 is that we can now identify the new savings generated out of income with the total increase in domestic financial assets, whereas in the earlier version we identified it with the secondary expansion only. The explanation lies in the obvious fact that any version of the model can explain only those values of the variables that accrue after and consequent to whatever exogenous event is deemed to start the expansion going. In the income version that event is the initial receipt of 1,000 riyals as income; the sequence does not "explain" it in any sense, it merely explains how additional income is generated by the respending effect and by the spending of borrowed money, and how the savings generated by the initial income plus the subsequent additions to it become embodied in new financial assets. In Chapter 4 the exogenous injection of new money occurred as an addition to the public's holdings of standard money, and the sequence merely explained the subsequent generation of income, savings, and financial assets; the operative force was the effort of the public to substitute other assets for its surplus holdings of standard money, so we may call it an asset-substitution version (or a "substitution" version for short).

1.2.2. An Open-Economy Model

The open-economy case of the receipt of new income in the form of standard money is a little more complex than the closed-economy case. The new income might come, say, from an increase in exports paid for in gold or the equivalent. Here again the situation is most easily visualized if we think of the initial standard-income-multiplier sequence "going to completion" before any credit expansion occurs. The Leakage Principles tell us that the savings generated will be the product of the ratio $s{:}(m+s)$ and the initial injection of income, so the initial and subsequent deposits with the intermediary will be reduced proportionally compared to our previous assumptions. In terms of Table 4.3 on page 102, with a marginal propensity to import of 0.2 and a marginal propensity to save of 0.1, an injection of 1,000 riyals constituting new income will give an external drain of 666.67 riyals and savings of 333.33 riyals; feeding the latter figure into the credit-and-income-expansion sequence generates only one third of the totals previously derived. Thus domestic financial assets will rise by 456.62 riyals (45.66 in coin and 410.96 in claims) and loans by 369.86 riyals; the increase in income attributable to the credit expansion will be only 1,232.88 riyals, but in addition of course there will be the 3,333.33 riyals of income attributable to the initial income-expansion sequence itself, so the total increase in income will be 4,566.21 riyals.[2] In other

---

[2] In algebraic terms, let Y' and L' be total income and total loans respectively according to the new assumptions. From The Leakage Principles we know that the injection of G riyals in standard-money-as-income will produce new savings of $s.\,G/(m+s)$ riyals through the operation of the standard-income-multiplier sequence without a credit

words the total income multiplier will be nearly 4.7, but the credit multiplier will be less than 0.4.[3]

1.3. The Acquisition of External Assets

There are three principal components of the external drain: the acquisition of foreign assets, import spending out of income, and the spending of borrowed money on imports. In Chapter 1 above, where our discussion was directed to domestic credit expansion as such without reference to any associated income-expansion, we identified the entire external drain with the first; in Chapter 4 we focused primarily on the second; and in section 1.1 of this chapter we introduced the third as well. We must now take a further look at the matter and integrate all three components into our combined credit-and-income-expansion model.

As a starting point we may take a situation in which the public's asset-holdings are in equilibrium with respect to one another and with respect to income. We will address ourselves to the increment of various alternative assets, domestic and foreign, and the associated income-expansion resulting from an injection of new standard money (gold coin in our example) into the financial system. We will again assume that the coefficients of substitution are constants. Presumably the public's initial holdings of domestic and foreign assets will have been acquired by a similar process of combined credit-and-income expansion in the past, but we need not specify whether the new injection does or does not in itself constitute income, and we will not be particularly concerned with whether the past values of the various parameters in our model have or have not been the same as those we will now use—i.e. with whether their average and marginal values are or are not identical.

These considerations out of the way, the enlargement of the model is simple enough: it focuses on how the public chooses to allocate the savings accruing out of the income generated by the credit expansion. In Tables 4.3 and 4.4 on pages 102 and 104 above we have already accommodated the division of these savings between standard money in circulation and claims against the intermediary, and in principle (since our single intermediary

---

expansion, compared to savings of G riyals in the closed-economy case. It follows that L' will bear the same relationship to the loans generated in the closed-economy case, i.e. $L'=s.L\big/(m+s)$. Also, by hypothesis, $Y'=(G+L')\big/(m+s)$. Substituting $a(1-r)(m+s)G\big/[(m+s)-as(1-r)]$ for L, as given on page 105, we derive $L'=as(1-r)G\big/[(m+s)-as(1-r)]$ and $Y'=G\big/[(m+s)-as(1-r)]$.

[3] The stage-by-stage sequence can be derived by feeding 1,000 riyals into column 5 of Table 4.3 at Period 1, thus generating savings of 100 riyals, of which 90 riyals will be redeposited with the intermediary in Period 2 and generate loans of 81 riyals. The loan, combined with 700 riyals of respending from Period 1, will generate income of 781 riyals in Period 2. And so on.

may be interpreted as the weighted average of various types of intermediaries) it also accomodates a variety of other domestic financial assets. Each type will absorb some portion of the available standard money as reserves, ranging from 100 per cent of the particular asset (e.g. if the medium of hand-to-hand circulation is a full-bodied gold coin) down to zero (e.g. claims against a pension fund or other intermediary whose reserve needs might be fully met by the pyramiding of transferable claims on other intermediaries), and the credit counterpart or "backing" for each will lead to some external drain as borrowed money is spent and generates income. In order to introduce the additional possibility that the public may chose to allocate some of its new savings out of income to increased holdings of foreign assets as well as or instead of domestic assets, all we have to do is to treat it as if it were a new form of domestic asset subject to a 100 per cent reserve ratio.

2. Bank-Credit Sequences

2.1. A Closed-Economy Model
2.1.1. A Numerical Example
So far we have been content to follow Vining's treatment of the combined credit-and-income-expansion sequence quite closely, including our adaptation of it to open-economy conditions, despite the fact that it is clearly more applicable to near-banking functions than to banking functions. The main justification for this is to emphasize the similarities between credit expansion through banks and through other financial intermediaries, which are strongest in the long-run static-equilibrium position. In spite of important similarities between money-proper and other financial assets, however, there are major differences between them which are of great importance for economic analysis. Let us therefore look specifically at the expansionary process as it applies to an intermediary whose obligations are accepted as money-proper.

It is easy enough to modify Vining's sequence analysis to make it compatible with bank expansion: we have only to postulate that all payments are made by tendering banknotes or by writing cheques, that all money-to-spend as well as money-to-hold is retained in the form of claims on the banking system, and that an efficient clearing system permits interbank settlements by the transfer of reserve assets among them; if there are competing banks of issue, a surplus of notes of any one bank in the hands of others can be cleared to the issuer in the same way as cheques.

Table 5.1 illustrates the modified closed-economy sequence that will result. We have retained the same assumptions as in Table 4.1 on page 92 above in all respects except one: for the sake of variety we have

Table 5.1. A Bank-Credit-and-Income Expansionary Sequence in a Closed Economy[1]

Period	Income expansion			Bank expansion		Cumulative deposit totals		
	Total	Spent[2]	Saved	Deposits	Free reserves[3]	Total	To hold	To spend
	(1)	(2)	(3)	(4)	(5)	(6)	(7)	(8)
1	1,000[4]			1,000	900	1,000	—	1,000
	900 1,900	1,710	190	900	810	1,900	190	1,710
2	1,710							
	810 2,520	2,268	252	810	729	2,710	442	2,268
3	2,268							
	729 2,997	2,697	300	729	656	3,439	742	2,697
4	2,697							
	656 3,353	3,018	335	656	590	4,095	1,077	3,018
5	3,018							
	590 3,609	3,248	361	590	531	4,686	1,438	3,248
6	3,248							
	531 3,779	3,401	378	531	478	5,217	1,816	3,401
7	3,401							
	478 3,880	3,492	388	478	430	5,695	2,204	3,492
8	3,492							
	430 3,922	3,530	392	430	387	6,126	2,596	3,530
9	3,530							
	387 3,917	3,526	392	387	349	6,513	2,988	3,526
10	3,526							
	349 3,874	3,487	387	349	314	6,862	3,375	3,487
.	.	.	.	.	.	.	.	.
.					Loans			
Σ_1^∞	100,000	90,000	10,000	10,000	9,000	10,000	10,000	—

[1] A numerical example, assuming an acceptance ratio of 100 per cent, a reserve ratio of 10 per cent, and a marginal propensity to save of 10 per cent. Due to rounding, detailed figures may not add exactly to totals.

[2] Becomes income in the next period.

[3] Generate loans in the next phase or period, which are then spent and become income in the same period.

[4] An exogenous receipt of new income in standard money which is deposited with a bank and spent by cheques or banknotes.

chosen to illustrate the income version instead of a substitution version, and we have changed the order of the columns accordingly. We will also make use of the usual conventions in the explanation of bank-credit expansion, including the assumption that the initial deposit is made with one of many competing banks (let us call it Bank A). Presumably the flow of receipts by Bank A's customers from customers of other banks was in balance with their flow of payments to customers of other banks before the new deposit was made, but its new loan of 900 riyals will be a net addition to the flow of funds and will be likely to end up immediately in the hands of other banks which will demand settlement in standard money. (If the borrower takes his loan in banknotes issued by Bank A, they too will likely be paid into other banks, which will present them for redemption in standard money and pay out their own notes instead.) Thus we may assume that 900 riyals of the newly-increased money supply is in the hands of people who will deposit it in some other bank or banks than Bank A, which we may identify notionally as Bank B. This bank thus receives net new deposits of 900 riyals, of which it can lend 810 riyals, and the process continues until the entire sum of 1,000 newly-injected riyals is absorbed into bank reserves.[4]

In Period 1 1,000 riyals of new standard money is received as income (perhaps from the production of new gold) and deposited in chequeing accounts or converted into banknotes; this permits the bank to lend 900 riyals, which is spent and becomes income in the same period, so total income received and spent in Period 1 is 1,900 riyals. The lending and spending of 900 riyals generate either new deposits of a like amount or a net increase in banknotes in circulation, so the money supply rises by 1,900 riyals. We can identify 190 riyals of this as having been saved out of income in the period; by hypothesis there is no savings vehicle available except standard money itself, so it is retained as claims against the banking system.[5] The rest of the new money, namely 1,710 riyals, is

---

[4] As a somewhat more realistic alternative we may assume (1) that each bank in the system receives its *pro rata* share of the net additional deposit of 1,000 riyals; (2) that each is unaware that the reserves of the others have been similarly increased, hence believes it can safely lend only its net free reserves, which amount to 90 per cent of its new deposits; and (3) that each receives as new deposits in the same period its *pro rata* share of all new bank loans granted in any given period.

[5] If we waive the (temporary) assumption that all intermediaries are banks in the strict sense defined on page 6 above, it is tempting to identify the 190 riyals with interest-bearing non-chequeable savings deposits; but this would be incorrect. It would be reasonable enough to suppose that the 1,710 riyals in the process of being spent was held as chequeing deposits or banknotes, but in the sense here relevant the amounts "saved out of income" will include the increase in chequeing accounts and banknotes appropriate to the new higher level of income now attained.

evidently in the hands of people who find their cash balances undesirably high in relation to income and other factors; it constitutes "undigested" cash balances, or money-to-spend instead of money-to-hold.

The various sequences in this table differ materially from their counterparts in Table 4.1. The deposit-loan-redeposit sequence (columns 4 and 5) follows the traditional version of bank-credit expansion, instead of the sharp step-down from Period 1 to Period 2 and the slower convergence thereafter. The increments of income (column 1) at first increase, peak in Period 8, and thereafter decline, because the initial increments of loan-induced spending are of the same order of magnitude as the respending of the previous increments of income whereas the savings leakages (which rise and fall with income) are still relatively small; but by Period 8 the savings leakage (column 3) exceeds the new loans that will be granted in Period 9 (column 4). Column 6 shows the cumulative totals of bank deposits from column 4, rising ultimately to 10,000 riyals on the assumptions made here. Column 7 shows the gradual accumulation of money-to-hold through savings out of income; equilibrium is not restored (the respending effects do not come to an end) until the total increase in money balances is held by willing holders (i.e. is "saved" out of income) and undigested money-to-spend is reduced to zero; and in this model an increase in income is the only way an increase in the money supply can be digested. Column 8 shows the course of undigested money-to-spend; it rises to a peak in Period 8, since on the assumptions here made the initial increments of deposits (column 4) greatly exceed the increments of savings (column 3), but declines thereafter as the increments of savings exceed the increments of deposits, and is eventually extinguished when the newly-expanded money supply is in equilibrium with the new level of money income.

In the last line of Table 5.1 (at the end of the sequence) there is of course no change from Table 4.1 as far as the total of deposits, reserves, and loans is concerned—given the assumptions of a closed economy, an acceptance ratio of 100 per cent, and a reserve ratio of 10 per cent, the equilibrium position is set. There is a 10,000-riyal increase in total income, it is true, but that is solely the result of shifting from a substitution version to the income version. The one analytically significant change stemming from the redeposit of money-to-spend as well as money-to-hold is that the series converges much more rapidly: further credit expansion need not wait on the completion of each step of the income-expansion and the redeposit of the savings thus generated, it can proceed immediately. Thus the implications for short-run and dynamic analyses are very different.

You may notice that the public sector is tacitly assumed to be passive in the process set out in Table 5.1; its spending decisions depend on income only, and therefore the lending decisions of bankers are the main operative factor. It would be more realistic to assume that the public's spending decisions are also affected by wealth, portfolio choices, and perhaps other considerations. For example, even on our presently-restricted assumptions we might suppose that spending in each period would be greater than the table indicates because the public would try to equate its actual cash holdings with its desired cash holdings by spending more than the normal portion of its income. However, we can easily incorporate this consideration in our discussion without further complicating the arithmetic: we can postulate that the figures shown are simply a first approximation subject to the usual *ceteris paribus* qualification, and that spending is also stimulated in some direct but unstated proportion to the stock of undigested money-to-spend. Any additions to spending in this or other ways will accelerate the expansion without altering the final equilibrium position.

2.1.2. Algebraic Formulation

Generalizing this adaptation of Vining's sequence analysis in terms of the notation used in section 1.3 of Chapter 4 above, we are now postulating that the initial injection of G riyals in gold coin constitutes new income in Period 1. By hypothesis the public's financial assets consist solely of claims on the banking system, so the G riyals of new standard money are deposited with (or given in exchange for the banknotes of) some bank or banks, which can thus lend $(1-r)G$ riyals. Loans are spent and become income in the same period, hence the total amount of income in Period 1 is $G+(1-r)G$ *or* $(2-r)G$ riyals. Of this, $s.(2-r)G$ riyals are saved and immediately redeposited with one or more banks as money-to-hold. But, since we are postulating an acceptance ratio of 100 per cent, the remainder of the loans, i.e. $(1-r)G-s(2-r)G$ riyals, is also redeposited (as money-to-spend); the redeposits in each phase or period are equal to the total loans granted in the same phase or period and are entirely independent of the increments of income and savings those loans give rise to. The banks as a group can thus lend $(1-r)^2$ riyals in Period 2, generating a like increment of income. The respending effect from the income of Period 1 will simultaneously give rise to new income of $(1-s).(2-r)G$ riyals, however, so the total increment of income in Period 2 becomes $[(1-r)^2+(2-r)(1-s)]G$ riyals.

Table 5.2 summarizes the various sequences that result, though in order to save space only the columns for income, savings, deposits, and free reserves have been shown. The redeposit sequence (column 3) takes the traditional form of a converging geometric progression with a common ratio of $(1-r)$. Loans are not shown as such but appear as free reserves at the end of each phase or period and as the first terms of new income-sequences in column 1. As before, the total income-sequence can be disaggregated into a series of simple-income-multiplier sequences (column 1). In fact this is the only feasible way of showing it in this case, because

Table 5.2. An Algebraic Bank-Credit-and-Income Sequence in a Closed Economy[1]

Period	Sequence	Income[2] (1)	Savings[3] (2)	Deposits (3)	Free Reserves[4] (4)
1	(a-1)	G[5]	$s.G$	G	$(1-r).G$
	(b-1)	$(1-r).G$	$s.(1-r)G$	$(1-r)G$	$(1-r)^2G$
2	(a-2)	$(1-s).G$	$s.(1-s)G$	—	—
	(b-2)	$(1-s).(1-r)G$	$s.(1-s)(1-r)G$	—	—
	(c-1)	$(1-r)^2G$	$s.(1-r)^2G$	$(1-r)^2G$	$(1-r)^3G$
3	(a-3)	$(1-s)^2.G$	$s.(1-s)^2G$	—	—
	(b-3)	$(1-s)^2.(1-r)G$	$s.(1-s)^2(1-r)G$	—	—
	(c-2)	$(1-s).(1-r)^2G$	$s.(1-s)(1-r)^2G$	—	—
	(d-1)	$(1-r)^3G$	$s.(1-r)^3G$	$(1-r)^3G$	$(1-r)^4G$
4	(a-4)	$(1-s)^3.G$	$s.(1-s)^3G$	—	—
	(b-4)	$(1-s)^3.(1-r)G$	$s.(1-s)^3(1-r)G$	—	—
	(c-3)	$(1-s)^2.(1-r)^2G$	$s.(1-s)^2(1-r)^2G$	—	—
	(d-2)	$(1-s).(1-r)^3G$	$s.(1-s)(1-r)^3G$	—	—
	(e-1)	$(1-r)^4G$	$s^2.(1-r)^4G$	$(1-r)^4G$	$(1-r)^5G$
		.	.	.	.
		.	.	.	.
				Loans	
Σ_i^∞		$G/s + (1-r)G/s = G/rs$	$s.G/rs = G/r$	G/r	$(1-r)G/r$

[1] Assumes an acceptance ration of 100 per cent. The reserve ratio is r and the marginal propensity to save is s.

[2] Spending in each period is *(1-s)* times income, and becomes income in the next period.

[3] Savings in each period are a part, but only a part, of the deposits in the next period.

[4] Generate loans in the next phase or period, which are then spent and become income in the same period.

[5] An exogenous receipt of income in standard money which is deposited with a bank and spent by cheques or banknotes.

making the redeposit sequence independent of the current increments of savings means that incomes in successive periods do not form a simple geometric progression or other readily summable series. The total income generated at the end of the sequence can of course be found by applying the standard algebraic techniques for the summation of converging series, but a simpler procedure is available. By hypothesis the only income-stimulating elements are (1) the initial receipt of G riyals of income and (2) the spending of the loans granted, which do follow a simple geometric progression and total $(1-r)G/r$ riyals; applying the standard income-multiplier of $1/s$ to both elements, we get total income of G/rs riyals. Current spending out of income is not shown as such, but appears as new income in the next period; the total at the end of the sequence is $(1-s)G/rs$. Total savings at the end of the sequence (G/r, equal to the total increase in deposits) can be derived by multiplying total income by s. Undigested money-to-spend (cf. column 9 of Table 4.3) is not shown but can be derived at the end of any period by deducting the cumulative total of new savings from the cumulative total of new deposits.

The more general case, in which the acceptance ratio is not necessarily 100 per cent, can be derived form equation 1.8 on page 26 above, paralleling the procedure at the end of section 1.3 of Chapter 4. In the final equilibrium $L=a(1-r)G/[1-a(1-r)]$; since the standard income-multiplier is $1/s$, and since we are now assuming that both G and L initiate income-expansion sequences, in equilibrium $Y=G\big/s+a(1-r)G\big/s[1-a(1-r)]$ $=G\big/s\,[1-a(1-r)]$.

This algebraic formulation throws additional light on the factors which lead to increasing increments of income in the first few periods in Table 5.1. The change between one income-period and the next is the net result of an increase due to the start of a new loan-financed income-expansion sequence and a decrease due to the savings leakage from the previous period's income. The positive element in the nth period is $(1-r)^n G$, which steadily declines in successive periods, but in the early stages it is a substantial portion of G unless r is relatively high. The negative element is the product of s and the previous period's income, which rises and falls with the increments of income but in the early stages is a relatively small portion of G unless s is relatively large. Ultimately, however, the negative element must prevail, because the positive element declines geometrically whereas the negative element changes in direct proportion to income.

The Compounding Effect noted in section 2.3 of Chapter 4 above is also relevant here. As far as the pure algebra of the matter is concerned, we can produce an unlimited expansion of money-income by letting s approach zero even if we arbitrarily choose a credit multiplier so low that only one riyal of credit-expansion can occur, but this is strictly a limiting case having

117

little practical significance. Reserve ratios approximating 100 per cent of total financial claims have actually occured in the real world, as when full-bodied coins have been virtually the only available financial asset; and marginal propensities to save (referring to savings in the form of financial claims) approximating zero have also been observed, as in the advanced stages of hyperinflation when confidence in the currency has been completely destroyed; but it is hard to imagine plausible circumstances in which the two could occur simultaneously. Nevertheless it is worth remembering that the effects of a change in either one on money income may be either offset or reinforced by a simultaneous change in the other.

2. 2. An Open-Economy Model

2. 2. 1. A Numerical Example

On page 32 above it was suggested that there might be an initial over-expansion of credit which had to be reversed later. One such possibility is that there may be some lag before the external drain is fully felt. So far we have tacitly assumed that it asserts itself instantly, but in practice it would seem likely that there would be some delay before the public's increased purchases of imported goods and of goods in which imported materials and components are important showed up in the depletion of import inventories and led to an actual increase in import orders. Further delays might well occur before these orders had to be paid for. In that case something like closed-economy conditions would obtain for a time, and both the credit expansion and the income expansion might come to temporarily exceed their equilibrium levels.

Even if we ignore this lag effect and follow Vining's combined sequence strictly, assuming that the banks respond promptly to free or deficient reserves in the traditional way, there is likely to be an initial overexpansion of loan-financed expenditure which reinforces the initially-high responding effect of the standard income-multiplier This is set out schematically in Table 5.3. The assumptions are the same as in Table 5.1 except for the introduction of the marginal propensity to import of 0.2. In Period 1 1,000 riyals of new standard money (gold or foreign exchange) is received as income, deposited in a bank, and spent; but, as in the closed-economy case, the banking system is simultaneously able to lend 900 riyals, which are also spent and become income. Hence 380 riyals is withdrawn to buy foreign exchange in order to pay for imports, leaving a net increase in exchange reserves and a net redeposit of 520 riyals. Total deposits rise to 1,520 riyals, of which 190 riyals is willingly held as new savings out of income and the balance is money in the process of being spent. Required reserves absorb 52 riyals of these funds, leaving free reserves of 468 riyals which are re-lent in Period 2; the spending of this sum plus the respending of 1,330 riyals from Period 1 gives new income of 1,798 riyals, of which 180

118

riyals is saved and added to willingly-held balances. However, a further 360 riyals must now be withdrawn to cover the external drain, so the net increase in deposits is 1,628 riyals and in exchange reserves 260 riyals; required reserves thus rise to 163 riyals, so free reserves of gold or foreign exchange are now reduced to 98 riyals. By the end of Period 3 there is a deficiency of 156 riyals in the banks' reserves of gold or foreign exchange, so they must call loans of a like amount and start a credit contraction. Nevertheless the momentum of the respending effect means that income continues to expand until the end of Period 5, by which time the deficiency of external reserves has risen to 304 riyals. There follows a series of damped oscillations which converge on the equilibrium position: the net increase in deposits is 476.19 riyals, and the net gain in income is 4,761.90 riyals.

The equilibrium position can of course be found directly, by noting that the 1,000 riyals of foreign exchange initially acquired must be divided between the external drain and reserves against the increase in deposits: given the parameters assumed, each riyal of income implies 0.2 riyals of external purchases and 0.1 riyals of savings, requiring 0.2+0.01 riyals of gold or foreign exchange, so the equilibrium level of income is 1,000/0.21 = c.4,761.90 riyals. In this or any other particular model, however, even with given values for the acceptance and reserve ratios and for the marginal propensities to import and to save, the path to equilibrium will be strongly affected by the assumed behaviour of both the public and its bankers. If we suppose the public increases its spending when it has undigested money-to-spend and reduces its spending when it holds less cash than it wishes, then the oscillations will be accelerated. If we suppose that bankers are alert to the likelihood of an external drain and to the possibility of overexpansion, then the oscillations will be damped or even eliminated. Allowing each individual standard-income-multiplier sequence to go nearly to completion before a new loan is granted may bring a fairly smooth expansion without oscillations.

No one version of the equilibrating sequence has any particular claim to being more "right" than another, and each has at least some didactic value. Nevertheless it may be worth noting that the oscillating version, crude though it is, may have some application in the real world. It is a matter of empirical observation that central banks in very small open economies seem to be able to achieve a degree of success in money-management that is surprising in view of their limited scope for the use of open-market operations and other sophisticated tools of monetary policy. If domestic credit expansion is causing an exchange drain, merely stopping the expansion seems to end the drain quickly and may even bring a return flow of reserves. The overshooting effect demonstrated in the oscillating approach to equilibrium may offer a clue to the reasons for the success of such policies.

Table 5.3. A Bank-Credit-and-Income Expansionary Sequence In An Open Economy[1]

Period	Income expansion				Bank expansion						
	Total	Domestic Spending[2]	Imports	Savings		Deposits			Reserves[3]		Loans
					Total	To hold	To spend	Total	Required	Free[4]	
	(1)	(2)	(3)	(4)	(5)	(6)	(7)	(8)	(9)	(10)	(11)
1	1,000[5]				(1,000)	(—)	(1,000)	(1,000)	(100)	(900)	
	900	1,330	380	190	− 380			− 380	+52	− 380	900
					+ 900					− 52	
	1,900				+ 520						
					(1,520)	(190)	(1,330)	(620)	(152)	(468)	
2	1,330										
	468	1,259	360	180	− 360			− 360	+11	− 360	468
		(2,589)	(740)		+ 468					− 11	
	(3,698)			(370)	+ 108						
					(1,628)	(370)	(1,259)	(260)	(163)	(98)	
3	1,259										
	98	949	271	136	− 271			− 271	−17	− 271	98
		(3,538)	(1,011)		+ 98					+ 17	
	(5,054)			(505)	− 174						
					(1,455)	(505)	(949)	(−11)	(145)	(−156)	
4	949										
	−156	555	159	79	− 159			− 159	−31	− 159	− 156
		(4,093)	(1,169)		− 156					+ 31	
	(5,847)			(585)	− 315						
					(1,140)	(585)	(555)	(−169)	(114)	(−283)	
5	555										
	−283	190	54	27	− 54			− 54	−34	− 54	− 283
		(4,283)	(1,224)		− 283					+ 34	
	(6,119)			(612)	− 338						
					(802)	(612)	(190)	(−224)	(80)	(−304)	

6	190 −304 (6,005)	−114 (4,204)	−80 (1,201)	−23 (601)	+23 −11 −303 −281 (521)	+23 (601)	+23 −201 (−201)	−28 (52)	+23 +28 −304 (−253)
13	−25 +62 (4,515)	37 (3,160)	26 (903)	7 (451)	−7 4 +62 +55 (477)	−7 (451)	−7 (97)	+5 (48)	−7 −5 62 (49)
20	+4 −18 (4,842)	−14 (3,389)	−10 (968)	−3 (484)	+3 −1 −18 −15 (453)	+3 (484)	+3 (32)	−2 (45)	+3 +2 −18 (−13)
Σ_1^∞	4,761.90	3,333.33	952.38	476.19	476.19	476.19	47.62	47.62	428.57

[1] A numerical example, assuming an acceptance ratio of 100 per cent, a reserve ratio of 10 per cent, a marginal propensity to import of 20 per cent, and a marginal propensity to save of 10 per cent. Figures in parenthesis are cumulative totals. Due to rounding, detailed figures may not add exactly to totals.

[2] Becomes income in the next period.

[3] Increments of reserve holdings of standard money (gold coin or the equivalent). A negative figure for the cumulative total represents an impairment of previously-held reserves.

[4] A positive figure for the cumulative total permits loans in the next phase or period, which are then spent and become income in the same period; a negative figure causes loans to be called and incomes reduced.

[5] An exogenous receipt of new income in standard money, which is deposited with a bank and spent by cheques or banknotes.

121

2. 2. 2. Algebraic Formulation

The format of Table 5.2 on page 116 can be adapted to the open-economy model by incorporating the effects of the import leakage in the income-sequence and the redeposit-sequence. For incomes the adjustment is simple: each individual income-sequence (sequences a, b, c, ... in column 1) will now have a common ratio of $(1-m-s)$ instead of $(1-s)$; the various increments of savings (coumn 2) will continue to be s times the corresponding increments of income; and a new column may be added for the import leakage, each increment of which will be m times the corresponding increment of income. For redeposits the adjustment is much more complex. If D_n and Y_n are respectively the totals of the redeposit (secondary expansion) and the income entries in the nth period then $D_n = (1-r)D_{n-1} - m . Y_n$. There will be no simple relationship between the total entries for successive periods in any column, though of course their sums can be determined by the use of standard algebraic techniques.

Since the final equilibrium position is independent of the path by which it is reached, the various totals appropriate to our present assumptions can be derived from equations 4.1 to 4.8 on page 105 above. First, suppose the standard-income-multiplier expansion resulting from the initial injection of G riyals of income in standard money is allowed to go to completion before any credit expansion is allowed to occur; call the resulting total Y'. The standard income-multiplier is $1/(m+s)$, hence we know that $Y' = G/(m+s)$, $M' = m . G/(m+s)$, and $S' = s . G/(m+s)$. This leaves the banking system with $sG/(m+s)$ riyals in deposits and a like sum in reserves of standard money (gold or the equivalent). Now feed this into equations 4.1 to 4.8 in place of G; the results will be $s/(m+s)$ times those there shown. Call the reduced level of loans L'' and the associated level of income Y'': then $L'' = s / (m+s) \times a(1-r)(m+s)G / [(m+s)-as(1-r)]$ and $Y'' = s / (m+s) \times a(1-r)G / [(m+s)-as(1-r)] = L'' / (m+s)$. Total loans appropriate to our present assumptions are $L'' = as(1-r)G/[(m+s)-as(1-r)]$, and total income is $Y = Y' + Y'' = Y' + L'' / (m+s) = G/(m+s) + as(1-r)G / [(m+s)-as(1-r)] = G / [(m+s)-as(1-r)]$. The same result can be derived from equation 5.1 on page 125 below, by setting $d=z=0$ and $n=1$.

3. A Generalized Presentation

3.1. The Consolidated Model

On page 31 above we noted that the simple one-intermediary model used in Chapter 1 may be interpreted as an accounting consolidation of all the various intermediaries operating in the economy. Let us revert to that interpretation as the basis for a generalized presentation through which we may summarize the pure theory of financial intermediation.

On pages 108f above we identified the "income" version of the model, and distinguished it from the "substitution" version used in Chapter 4. (The models used in Chapters 1 to 3 inclusive may also be interpreted as substitution versions, though we were then abstracting from both prior and subsequent changes in income.) However, the substitution version may be subdivided into at least four variants, according to where the injection of new money occurs (or where it is first identified). First, it may occur as an increment of total financial assets, and be divided among external and domestic claims according to the general public's coefficients of substitution. Second, it may first be identified at the domestic-asset level, net of any initial allocation to external assets. Third, it may first be observed as new claims against domestic financial intermediaries, after any initial allocation to external assets or to hand-to-hand currency. Fourth, it may first appear as free reserves in the hands of financial intermediaries. These variants are explained algebraically in section 3.3 below. There is no need to give detailed illustrations of them here, but a few points merit mention.

All four variants of the substitution version may be seen as a succession of stages in a single overall sequence, even though the earlier stages may sometimes be ignored. It may be, for example, that we are interested in the income generated (or the financial assets accumulated, or both) as a result of the receipt of 1,000 riyals as income. For other purposes, however, we may be interested only in what happens after 1,000 riyals are identified as new savings, or as new savings in the specific form of domestic assets, or as new savings placed with domestic financial intermediaries, or as free reserves in the hands of intermediaries. Thus the version used in Chapter 4 may represent merely the notional separation of Vining's credit-and-income-expansion sequence from the standard-income-multiplier sequence, even though both are proceeding simultaneously. Alternatively, the two components may be distinctly separated in time: the public's stock of standard money may have been saved out of income and brought into equilibrium with its flow of income at some time in the past, then the opening of new intermediaries (as postulated in Chapter 1 above) or a change in the public's coefficients of substitution may set off a new credit-and-income-expansion sequence.

However, it does not follow that all the stages will be present or must already have occurred at some earlier date. For example, central-bank open-market purchases from the general public may create a temporary surplus of standard money in circulation without any previous expansion of income. Or central-bank rediscounts for financial intermediaries may produce free reserves without any previous increase in their obligations to the public.

3.2. The Activation of Idle Balances

The money-and-banking literature recognizes the "activation of idle balances" as an alternative way of stimulating income-expansion sequences, distinct from the essentialy-quantitative effects of traditional monetary policy. This possibility is included in our consolidated model in that it would constitute a change in the public's coefficients of substitution and is therefore subsumed in the substitution version.

In a very loose sense the withdrawal of funds from some form of near-money or from still-less-liquid financial assets in order to spend them may be described as the "activation" of the balances previously so held, but it is rather poor usage. What is actually involved is the conversion of some other financial asset into money-proper and the activation of the money-proper so obtained; the previously-held asset must either be extinguished or sold to a third party for what it will bring. It therefore seems preferable to restrict the term "activation of idle balances" to decisions to spend sums of money-proper previously held unspent (perhaps for precautionary or speculative reasons). In addition, however, we must include cases in which a holder of money-proper buys some other financial claim (or for that matter an existing physical asset) from a third party, provided the third party in his turn spends the money so obtained.

The importance of the activation of idle balances is that it sets off a new chain of spending, generates new income and new savings, and causes a secondary expansion of domestic assets as well as an external drain.

3.3. Algebraic Formulation

Some changes in the notation previously used will be required in order to adapt the simplified model of the expansion of credit and financial assets we used in Chapter 1, in which domestic assets are confined to standard money and an accounting consolidation of all financial intermediaries, to a generalized presentation of the simultaneous expansion of income and credit. Some new symbols have already been introduced in Chapter 4 and in the preceding sections of this chapter, but they bear repeating for the sake of ready reference. The notation used in section 2.5 of Chapter 1 above may be given the following additions and modifications:

(1) The usual symbols Y, C, M, and S for money income, consumption (in this case meaning domestic spending, including spending out of income on physical capital), imports, and financial savings respectively, and m and s for the marginal propensities to import and to save.

(2) The portion of loans (L) spent domestically will be n, the portion saved z, and the portion spent on imports ($1-n-z$); and the cumulative savings out of loans will be Z. Note that S and Z need not be subdivided between Gp and K in the same proportions; a must be interpreted as the weighted average acceptance ratio for borrowing and non-borrowing members of the public.

(3) *Af* will mean only those foreign claims intended to be held more or less indefinitely as assets.

(4) The external drain (Gp) becomes $Af+mY+(1-n-z)L$.

(5) A symbol having the Greek letter Δ prefixed to it represents the increment of value subsequent to the initial injection of money, when that injection consists of or includes an allocation of the variable in question; for example, in the income version of the model $\Delta Y = Y-G$, $\Delta M = m(Y-G)$, etc. This prefix will also be applied to those values of *At* and its components that are wholly derived within a sequence.

(6) A symbol with an asterisk appended to it represents the secondary expansion of that variable, when the initial injection of money has been addressed to that variable or may reasonably be deemed to have been so addressed; for example, $At^* = At-G$. Note that by hypothesis $At = Af+Ad = Af+Gp+K = Af+Gp+Gk+L$, hence $At^* - Af+Ad^* = Af+Gp+K^* = Af+Gp+Gk+L^*$.

(7) $Q = (m+s)[1+d-az(1-r)] -ans(1-r)$. The derivation of this expression is explained below; Q is used for the sake of brevity in the many equations that will be derived.

In the income version of the model G or its equivalent value is received directly by the public and is reallocated among alternative assets in the process of being spent. The equilibrium distribution of G is $G = Gp+Gk+Gd = (1-a)Ad+rK+[Af+mY+(1-n-z)L]$. Substituting $(G+nL)/(m+s)$ for Y and the equivalent multiple of Ad for Af, K, and L, then solving for the equilibrium value of Ad, we get $sG/[(m+s)(1+d-az(1-r))-ans(1-r)] = sG/Q$. Other asset-related variables are derived from their postulated relationship to Ad. Income-related variables are derived from G and L, since by hypothesis $Y = (G+nL)/(m+s)$ Thus we get:

$$Y_y = [1+d-az(1-r)]G/Q \dotfill (5.1)$$

$$M_y = m[1+d-az(1-r)]G/Q \dotfill (5.2)$$

$$S_y = s[1+d-az(1-r)]G/Q \dotfill (5.3)$$

$$At_y = s(1+d)G/Q \dotfill (5.4)$$

$$Af_y = dsG/Q \dotfill (5.5)$$

$$Ad_y = sG/Q \dotfill (5.6)$$

$$Gp_y = s(1-a)G/Q \dotfill (5.7)$$

$$K_y = asG/Q \dotfill (5.8)$$

$$Gk_y = arsG/Q \dotfill (5.9)$$

$$L_y = as(1-r)G/Q \dotfill (5.10)$$

$$Z_y = asz(1-r)G/Q \dotfill (5.11)$$

$$Gd_y = [d(m+s)+m(1-az(1-r))+as(1-r)(1-n-z)]G/Q \ \dots \ (5.12)$$

$$At^*_y = \Delta At_y = [a(1-r)(ns+z(m+s))-m(1+d)]G/Q \ \dots\dots \ (5.13)$$

$$Ad^*_y = [a(1-r)(ns+z(m+s))-m(1+d)-ds]G/Q \dots\dots\dots \ (5.14)$$

$$\Delta Ad_y = [a(1-r)(ns+z(m+s))-m(1+d)]G/Q(1+d) \dots\dots \ (5.15)$$

$$\Delta Y^*_y = [ans(1-r)+(1+d-az(1-r))(1-m-s)]G/Q \dots\dots \ (5.16).$$

The substitution version of the model has several variants, according to the level at which G makes its appearance: e.g., as an addition to At, to Ad, to K, or to free reserves (which will become L). If the public receives G or its equivalent value as an addition to At, and allocates it to Af and Ad in the ratio of $d:1$, then the only change from the income version is that $Y=nL/(m+s)$ instead of $(G+nL)/(m+s)$. Proceeding as before, we derive a second set of equations. The equilibrium values of asset-related variables, but not their increments or their secondary expansions, are $(m+s)/s$ times their respective values in equations 5.1 to 5.16:

$$At_{st} = (1+d)(m+s)G/Q \ \dots\dots\dots\dots\dots\dots\dots\dots\dots\dots \ (5.17)$$

$$Af_{st} = d(m+s)G/Q \dots\dots\dots\dots\dots\dots\dots\dots\dots\dots\dots\dots \ (5.18)$$

$$Ad_{st} = (m+s)G/Q \ \dots\dots\dots\dots\dots\dots\dots\dots\dots\dots\dots\dots \ (5.19)$$

$$Gp_{st} = (1-a)(m+s) \ \dots\dots\dots\dots\dots\dots\dots\dots\dots\dots\dots \ (5.20)$$

$$K_{st} = a(m+s)G/Q \ \dots\dots\dots\dots\dots\dots\dots\dots\dots\dots\dots\dots \ (5.21)$$

$$Gk_{st} = ar(m+s)G/Q \ \dots\dots\dots\dots\dots\dots\dots\dots\dots\dots\dots \ (5.22)$$

$$L_{st} = a(m+s)(1-r)G/Q \ \dots\dots\dots\dots\dots\dots\dots\dots\dots\dots \ (5.23)$$

$$Z_{st} = az(m+s)(1-r)G/Q \ \dots\dots\dots\dots\dots\dots\dots\dots\dots \ (5.24)$$

$$Y_{st} = an(1-r)G/Q \dots\dots\dots\dots\dots\dots\dots\dots\dots\dots\dots \ (5.25)$$

$$M_{st} = amn(1-r)G/Q \dots\dots\dots\dots\dots\dots\dots\dots\dots\dots\dots \ (5.26)$$

$$S_{st} = ans(1-r)G/Q \ \dots\dots\dots\dots\dots\dots\dots\dots\dots\dots\dots \ (5.27)$$

$$Gd_{st} = [d(m+s)+a(1-r)(mn+(m+s)(1-n-z))]G/Q \ \dots\dots \ (5.28)$$

$$At^*_{st} = \Delta At_{st} = a(1-r)[ns+z(m+s)]G/Q \dots\dots\dots\dots\dots \ (5.29)$$

$$Ad^*_{st} = [a(1-r)(ns+z(m+s))-d(m+s)]G/Q \dots\dots\dots\dots \ (5.30)$$

$$\Delta Ad_{st} = a(1-r)[ns+z(m+s)]G/Q(1+d) \ \dots\dots\dots\dots\dots \ (5.31).$$

The relationship between the income version and the At variant of the substitution version can be simply illustrated by subdividing the former into three steps. First, let the standard income-multiplier go to completion from the injection of G, yielding a first income-tranche of $G/(m+s)$.

Second, from The Leakage Principles we know that this will yield savings of $sG/(m+s)$. Substituting $sG/(m+s)$ for G in equation 5.25 we get a second income-tranche, $sG/(m+s)\times an(1-r)/Q$. Third, summing these two tranches, we get equation 5.1.

Other variants of the substitution version may be derived in the same way, noting that the analysis is concerned only with changes in the variables that occur after and consequent to the injection of money that is deemed to initiate the expansion. Thus if G is received or first identified at the Ad level the subsequent values are the same as if $(1+d)G$ had been received at the At level, hence the equilibrium values of all variables (except Gd and secondary expansions) are $(1+d)$ times the corresponding values given in or derived from equations 5.17 to 5.31. The equilibrium values are:

$$Ad_{sd} = (1+d)(m+s)G/Q \dots \dots \dots \dots \quad (5.32)$$

$$Gp_{sd} = (1-a)(1+d)(m+s)G/Q \dots \dots \dots \quad (5.33)$$

$$K_{sd} = a(1+d)(m+s)G/Q \dots \dots \dots \dots \quad (5.34)$$

$$Gk_{sd} = ar(1+d)(m+s)G/Q \dots \dots \dots \dots \quad (5.35)$$

$$L_{sd} = a(1+d)(m+s)(1-r)G/Q \dots \dots \dots \quad (5.36)$$

$$Z_{sd} = az(1+d)(m+s)(1-r)G/Q \dots \dots \dots \quad (5.37)$$

$$Y_{sd} = an(1+d)(1-r)G/Q \dots \dots \dots \dots \quad (5.38)$$

$$M_{sd} = amn(1+d)(1-r)G/Q \dots \dots \dots \dots \quad (5.39)$$

$$S_{sd} = ans(1+d)(1-r)G/Q \dots \dots \dots \dots \quad (5.40)$$

$$Gd_{sd} = [ad(1-r)(ns+z(m+s))+a(1+d)(1-r)(mn \mid (m \mid s)$$
$$(1-n-z))]G/Q \dots \dots \dots \dots \quad (5.41)$$

$$\Delta At_{sd} = a(1+d)(1-r)[ns+z(m+s)]G/Q \dots \dots \dots \quad (5.42)$$

$$\Delta Af_{sd} = ad(1-r)[ns+z(m+s)]G/Q \dots \dots \dots \quad (5.43)$$

$$Ad^*_{sd} = \Delta At_{sd} = a(1-r)[ns+z(m+s)]G/Q \dots \dots \dots \quad (5.44).$$

Similarly, if G is first identified as new claims on the intermediaries (K) the subsequent values are the same as if G/a had been received at the Ad level or $(1+d)G/a$ at the At level: the equilibrium values of all variables (excluding their secondary expansions but including Gd) are $1/a$ times the corresponding values given in or derived from equations 5.32 to 5.44:

$$K_{sk} = (1+d)(m+s)G/Q \dots \dots \dots \dots \quad (5.45)$$

$$Gk_{sk} = r(1+d)(m+s)G/Q \dots \dots \dots \dots \quad (5.46)$$

$$L_{sk} = (1+d)(m+s)(1-r)G/Q \dots \dots \dots \quad (5.47)$$

$$Z_{sk} = z(1+d)(m+s)(1-r)G/Q. \dots\dots\dots\dots\dots\dots\dots \quad (5.48)$$

$$Y_{sk} = n(1+d)(1-r)G/Q \dots\dots\dots\dots\dots\dots\dots\dots \quad (5.49)$$

$$M_{sk} = mn(1+d)(1-r)G/Q. \dots\dots\dots\dots\dots\dots\dots \quad (5.50)$$

$$S_{sk} = ns(1+d)(1-r)G/Q. \dots\dots\dots\dots\dots\dots\dots \quad (5.51)$$

$$Gd_{sk} = [d(1-r)(ns+z(m+s))+(1+d)(1-r)(mn+(m+s)$$
$$(1-n-z))]G/Q. \dots\dots\dots\dots\dots\dots\dots \quad (5.52)$$

$$\Delta At_{sk} = (1+d)(1-r)[ns+z(m+s)]G/Q. \dots\dots\dots\dots \quad (5.53)$$

$$\Delta Af_{sk} = d(1-r)[ns+z(m+s)]G/Q \dots\dots\dots\dots\dots\dots \quad (5.54)$$

$$\Delta Ad_{sk} = (1-r)[ns+z(m+s)]G/Q. \dots\dots\dots\dots\dots \quad (5.55)$$

$$\Delta Gp_{sk} = (1-a)(1-r)[ns+z(m+s)]G/Q \dots\dots\dots\dots \quad (5.56)$$

$$K^*_{sk} = \Delta K_{sk} = a(1-r)[ns+z(m+s)]G/Q \dots\dots\dots\dots \quad (5.57).$$

If **G** is first identified as free reserves in the intermediaries then the equilibrium values of all variables (but not their secondary expansions) are $1/(1-r)$ times the corresponding values given in or derived from equations 5.45 to 5.57:

$$L_{sf} = (1+d)(m+s)G/Q \dots\dots\dots\dots\dots\dots\dots\dots \quad (5.58)$$

$$Z_{sf} = z(1+d)(m+s)G/Q \dots\dots\dots\dots\dots\dots\dots\dots \quad (5.59)$$

$$Y_{sf} = n(1+d)G/Q. \dots\dots\dots\dots\dots\dots\dots\dots\dots \quad (5.60)$$

$$M_{sf} = mn(1+d)G/Q \dots\dots\dots\dots\dots\dots\dots\dots\dots \quad (5.61)$$

$$S_{sf} = ns(1+d)G/Q. \dots\dots\dots\dots\dots\dots\dots\dots\dots \quad (5.62)$$

$$Gd_{sf} = [d(ns+z(m+s))+(1+d)(mn+(m+s)(1-n-z))]G/Q \dots \quad (5.63)$$

$$\Delta At_{sf} = (1+d)[ns+z(m+s)]G/Q \dots\dots\dots\dots\dots\dots \quad (5.64)$$

$$\Delta Af_{sf} = d[ns+z(m+s)]G/Q \dots\dots\dots\dots\dots\dots\dots \quad (5.65)$$

$$\Delta Ad_{sf} = [ns+z(m+s)]G/Q \dots\dots\dots\dots\dots\dots\dots \quad (5.66)$$

$$\Delta Gp_{sf} = (1-a)[ns+z(m+s)]G/Q. \dots\dots\dots\dots\dots \quad (5.67)$$

$$\Delta K_{sf} = a[ns+z(m+s)]G/Q. \dots\dots\dots\dots\dots\dots\dots \quad (5.68)$$

$$\Delta Gk_{sf} = ar[ns+z(m+s)]G/Q \dots\dots\dots\dots\dots\dots\dots \quad (5.69)$$

$$L^*_{sf} = \Delta L_{sf} = a(1-r)[ns+z(m+s)]G/Q \dots\dots\dots\dots \quad (5.70).$$

The following points may be noted:
(1) Increments and secondary expansions in open-economy applications

may be negative if d, m, and r are relatively large and a, n, s, and z are relatively small. This is especially true of the income version, since M will provide a negative component amounting to $mG/(m+s)$ even if there is no credit expansion at all, and only $sG/(m+s)$ will be available to provide a positive component.

(2) In all cases the total savings generated "explains" or is equal to the accrual of total assets that is derived in the course of the expansion. Thus in the income version $S+Z=At$, but in all variants of the substitution version $S+Z=\Delta At$.

(3) In all cases the loans granted are equal to the sum of the external drain and the subsequent increase in domestic assets, as The Leakage Principles dictate. Thus in the income version and in the At and the Ad variants of the substitution version $L=Gp+Ad^*$, but in the K and the L variants of the substitution version $L=Gp+\Delta Ad$.

(4) In all variants of the substitution version the same multiplier, $(1+d)$ $(m+s)/Q$, applies to the variable that is first deemed to receive the injection of G; At in equation 5.17, Ad in equation 5.32, K in equation 5.45, and L in equation 5.58.

(5) In the substitution version the income generated increases progressively as the injection of G is deemed to occur at later points in the overall sequence, unless $a=1$ and $r=0$. The loans granted also increase progressively, unless $a=1$ and $d=r=0$. The changes in Gd are more complex, since they reflect variations in the portions of G that are absorbed by Gp and Gk; in general Gp and Gk both increase progressively (Gd tends to decrease) unless $a=1$ and $r=0$, but there is a significant drop in Gp at the K level (unless $a=1$) and in Gk at the L level (unless $r=0$), with corresponding increases in Gd.

(6) Under closed-economy conditions Ad becomes identical with At. Also, the values of Ad, Gp, and Gk are identical in the income version and in the Ad and the L variants of the substitution version, since $Gd=0$ and Gp and Gk are in the same proportions; in the K version, however, Gk is proportionately greater and Ad is therefore reduced.

CHAPTER 6

THE EQUILIBRATING PROCESS

1. Long-Run Equilibrium in a Complex Financial Structure

1.1. A Closed-Economy Model

Although the long-run-equilibrium relationships among various financial assets and liabilities may be determined without considering the implications for income, the combined credit-and-income-expansion sequence offers a fuller explanation of the equilibrating mechanism. Let us start with a closed-economy injection-of-income model of a society in which the standard money is a dollar and banks in the strict sense are the only financial intermediaries—in other words with essentially the same model as in Table 5.1. Taking some liberties with the time-sequence presentation for the sake of brevity, and using a cash-reserve ratio of 0.2 and a marginal propensity to save of 0.1 in order to avoid posssible confusion of the two expansions, the full credit-and-income-multiplier effect of an injection of $1,000 of income in ultimate standard money may be summarized as follows:

$$Y_1 = 1,000.00 + \quad 900.00 + \quad 810.00 + \ldots \rightarrow \quad 10,000$$
$$Y_2 = \quad 800.00 + \quad 720.00 + \quad 648.00 + \ldots \rightarrow \quad 8,000$$
$$Y_3 = \quad 640.00 + \quad 576.00 + \quad 518.40 + \ldots \rightarrow \quad 6,400$$

$$\cdots$$

$$\Sigma_1^\infty Y = 5,000.00 + 4,500.00 + 4,050.00 + \ldots \rightarrow \quad 50,000.$$

Similarly, the consumption series (each term of which becomes income in the succeeding period) may be set out thus:

$$C_1 = \quad 900.00 + \quad 810.00 + \quad 729.00 + \ldots \rightarrow \quad 9,000$$
$$C_2 = \quad 720.00 + \quad 648.00 + \quad 583.20 + \ldots \rightarrow \quad 7,200$$
$$C_3 = \quad 576.00 + \quad 518.40 + \quad 466.56 + \ldots \rightarrow \quad 5,760$$

$$\cdots$$

$$\Sigma_1^\infty C = 4,500.00 + 4,050.00 + 3,645.00 + \ldots \rightarrow \quad 45,000.$$

Finally, the savings series:

$$S_1 = \quad 100.00 + \quad 90.00 + \quad 81.00 + \ldots \rightarrow \quad 1,000$$
$$S_2 = \quad 80.00 + \quad 72.00 + \quad 64.80 + \ldots \rightarrow \quad 800$$
$$S_3 = \quad 64.00 + \quad 57.60 + \quad 51.84 + \ldots \rightarrow \quad 640$$

$$\cdots$$

$$\Sigma_1^\infty S = \quad 500.00 + \quad 450.00 + \quad 405.00 + \ldots \rightarrow \quad 5,000.$$

Note that the strict time-sequence can be derived by identifying the first term of the Y_1 series with Period 1, the second term of the Y_1 and the first term of the Y_2 series with Period 2, etc. in a diagonal pattern; and similarly with the consumption and the savings series. The credit-expansion resulting from a given injection of money is set out vertically, the income-expansion horizontally; one may treat the sequence as if the income-expansion occurred first and the credit-expansion second, as if the credit-expansion occurred first, or—by combining terms in a diagonal pattern as already explained—as if they proceeded in step. For each tranche and in total, $C+S=Y$; also, the sum of the S's in any line is equal to the corresponding initial value of Y. However, in deriving the savings series we have in effect limited our attention to the accrual of money-to-hold in the banking system and have ignored the temporary build-up of money-to-spend, which is irrelevant in deriving the long-run equilibrium position.

Now let us revoke the assumption that banks are the only intermediaries and the consequential postulate that all financial savings are held in the form of money-proper. Instead, as a first approximation let us suppose that there is also a composite group of other financial intermediaries (non-banks), and that the public allocates marginal increments of savings equally between the two groups. Let us also suppose that the non-banks are able to get along on zero cash reserves (or zero additions to cash reserves for a considerable increase in their obligations); initially, however, they make no loans and are content to hold whatever funds are placed with them in the form of claims against the banking system.

First, the Y_1 sequence may be deemed to go to completion, as before, so that $Y_1 \rightarrow \$10,000$, $C_1 \rightarrow \$9,000$ and $S_1 \rightarrow \$1,000$. Of the total savings generated in this tranche, $500 is held by the public on deposit with the non-banks and $500 with the banking system, all being money-to-hold. The non-banks in turn hold all their $500 of assets on deposit with the banking system, also as money-to-hold (temporarily at least); the banks therefore have total obligations of $1,000. So far as their ability to lend is concerned it makes no difference to the banks who holds their obligations as long as someone does, and in this model there is no leakage of reserves and hence no reduction in the bank expansion. As before, therefore, we may suppose that the $1,000 in new bank claims generates $800 in new bank loans and produces a second tranche of the credit-and-income-multiplier expansion; and similarly for further tranches. Clearly, each savings sequence still represents the addition of money-to-hold at the banks, and the grand total rises to $5,000 as before; but now $2,500 of it is held by the non-banks. We may re-designate the entire initial income-expansion of $50,000 as Y_1, and the associated savings series may be summarized as follows, using S' for the public's holdings of digested bank balances (money-to-hold), S'' for the public's holdings of claims on the non-banks, and S^* for bank balances held temporarily by the non-banks:[1]

$$
\begin{array}{llllll}
S_1 & = & 500.00 + & 450.00 + & 405.00 + \dots & \rightarrow & 5{,}000 \\
S'_1 & = & 250.00 + & 225.00 + & 202.50 + \dots & \rightarrow & 2{,}500 \\
S''_1 & = & 250.00 + & 225.00 + & 202.50 + \dots & \rightarrow & 2{,}500 \\
S^*_1 & = & 250.00 + & 225.00 + & 202.50 + \dots & \rightarrow & 2{,}500.
\end{array}
$$

Now let the non-banks begin to lend their \$2,500 to people who wish to spend their borrowings. By hypothesis the S^* balances are free reserves to the non-banks, and therefore the full amount is lent and sets off a new income-expansion sequence (omitting the consumption component) of:

$$
\begin{array}{llllll}
Y_2 & = & 2{,}500.00 + & 2{,}250.00 + & 2{,}025.00 + \dots & \rightarrow & 25{,}000 \\
S_2 & = & 250.00 + & 225.00 + & 202.50 + \dots & \rightarrow & 2{,}500 \\
S'_2 & = & 125.00 + & 112.50 + & 101.25 + \dots & \rightarrow & 1{,}250 \\
S''_2 & = & 125.00 + & 112.50 + & 101.25 + \dots & \rightarrow & 1{,}250 \\
S^*_2 & = & 125.00 + & 112.50 + & 101.25 + \dots & \rightarrow & 1{,}250.
\end{array}
$$

Thus half the new savings take the form of an increase in the public's holding of money-proper (the conversion of money-to-spend into money-to-hold) and half is redeposited with the non-banks. The latter can now lend a further \$1,250, which sets off another round of income-expansion:

$$
\begin{array}{llllll}
Y_3 & = & 1{,}250.00 + & 1{,}125.00 + & 1{,}012.50 + \dots & \rightarrow & 12{,}500 \\
S_3 & = & 125.00 + & 112.50 + & 101.25 + \dots & \rightarrow & 1{,}250 \\
S'_3 & = & 62.50 + & 56.25 + & 50.63 + \dots & \rightarrow & 625 \\
S''_3 & = & 62.50 + & 56.25 + & 50.63 + \dots & \rightarrow & 625 \\
S^*_3 & = & 62.50 + & 56.25 + & 50.63 + \dots & \rightarrow & 625.
\end{array}
$$

Further sequences will be generated in the same way, giving a series of income-expansions each half as great as the preceding one. By the standard formula for the summation of geometric progressions we therefore get:

$$
\begin{array}{llllll}
\Sigma_2^\infty Y & = & 5{,}000.00 + & 4{,}500.00 + & 4{,}050.00 + \dots & \rightarrow & 50{,}000 \\
\Sigma_2^\infty S & = & 500.00 + & 450.00 + & 405.00 + \dots & \rightarrow & 5{,}000 \\
\Sigma_2^\infty S' & = & 250.00 + & 225.00 + & 202.50 + \dots & \rightarrow & 2{,}500 \\
\Sigma_2^\infty S'' & = & 250.00 + & 225.00 + & 202.50 + \dots & \rightarrow & 2{,}500 \\
S^*_\infty & = & 0 + & 0 + & 0 + \dots & \rightarrow & 0.
\end{array}
$$

[1] Note that total bank deposits are $S' + S^*$.

133

The income-expansion generated by non-bank lending comes to an end when all bank balances have been converted into money-to-hold in the hands of the public. Since by hypothesis the public adds a dollar to its claims on non-banks for every dollar it adds to its equilibrium holdings of money-proper, the end result is an expansion of income and saving by double the amount of the bank-expansion sequence.[2] This may be summarized thus:

$$
\begin{array}{llllllll}
\Sigma_1^\infty\, Y & = & 10,000 + & 9,000 + & 8,100 + & \ldots & \rightarrow & 100,000 \\
\Sigma_1^\infty\, S & = & 1,000 + & 900 + & 810 + & \ldots & \rightarrow & 10,000 \\
\Sigma_1^\infty\, S' & = & 500 + & 450 + & 405 + & \ldots & \rightarrow & 5,000 \\
\Sigma_1^\infty\, S'' & = & 500 + & 450 + & 405 + & \ldots & \rightarrow & 5,000.
\end{array}
$$

The credit expansion is not shown explicitly in this summary presentation, but by hypothesis the equilibrium volume of loans is 80 per cent of bank deposits plus 100 per cent of non-bank claims or $9,000. Since the initial injection of new money is deemed to constitute new income, the standard income-multiplier of $1/s$ or 10 applies to both the initial injection of $1,000 and the loans generated; i.e. the increase in income amounts to ($1,000 + $9,000) / 0.1 = $100,000, as already derived.

By extending the same technique we can incorporate any given number of types of financial claims in the public's portfolio and in the associated income-expansion sequences.[3] If we identify the public's savings held in the form of claims on the banking system (money-proper) as S', claims on the non-banks as S'', government securities as S''' *and private claims as* S'''', we have a summary representation of the financial structure illustrated in Table 3.1 on page 79 above. On the assumptions there made the increase in the public's portfolio of financial claims is four times the increase in its holdings of money-proper, and total loans to ultimate borrowers (including the government) are more than four times as great as loans through the banking system. If the initial injection of new ultimate standard money constitutes new income, and if the marginal propensity to save is 0.1, as we have been here assuming, then the total income generated will be $471,976.40; had there been no non-banks and no lending except through banks the banking system's obligations would have been somewhat smaller (no notes would have been required for non-bank reserves, but by hypothesis note-holdings would have been a larger portion of the public's financial assets)

[2] Cf. A.N. McLeod, "Credit Creation in an Open Economy", *The Economic Journal*, Vol. LXXII, September 1962, paras. 11–19 and paras. 1–9 of the technical notes, pp. 615–618 and 636–638.

[3] A more realistic representation of the approach to long-run equilibrium may be achieved by letting all expansionary sequences proceed simultaneously.

and the income-expansion would have been only \$123,076.92.

Reinterpreting the coefficients of substitution as variables instead of constants even in the short run, we get much more fluid relationships among income and the various assets in the public's portfolio, but the same basic principles are discernible. Any injection of new real income, exemplified in our closed-economy model by new gold production, will of course generate a multiple expansion of money-income both directly and through whatever changes it involves in the community's ultimate reserves (in our model, gold), and therefore in the credit structure; any decreases in real income will have contrary effects. A change in any of the parameters that influence the coefficients of substitution or the constraints on the financial system may act to increase credit expansion, or on the contrary to decrease it, with corresponding multiple effects on money-income. Of course we are unable to say whether these expansions of money-income add equivalently, less, or nothing to real income; that depends on factors we have only briefly and infrequently alluded to and have been unable to integrate systematically into our models.

Specifically, any injection of new spending however accomplished will initiate an expansion of money-income until the volume of new *savings in the form of willingly held money balances* has risen by exactly the same amount. This implies that *savings in all other forms* must have changed in a corresponding way, under the influence of the (possibly changing) co-efficients of substitution. It further implies that in the end the various parameters by and through which these coefficients are influenced must also be in equilibrium with one another and with the other variables in the structure, perhaps themselves being changed as part of the process of mutual adjustment. Similarly, any exogenous change in any coefficient of substitution or in any parameter which induces an increase in the credit structure will induce changes in some or all other coefficients, money-income, savings, liquid assets, and the various parameters that link them, until a new equilibrium is reached. We may perhaps subsume the effects of these exogenous changes in the structure under the concept of "activitation of idle money", in contradistinction from the exogenous injection of new money. In sum, then, we may say that any injection of new money or any activation of previously-idle money means new spending, new income, new savings, and new changes in various liquid assets which will not end until every newly-created or newly-activated dollar is in the hands of someone who wishes to hold it as an addition to his previous stock of money-to-hold.[4]

---

[4] This remains true if the borrowed money is *not* spent—e.g. if it is borrowed for liquidity purposes, as noted on page 100 above. In that case the entire sum borrowed immediately "leaks away" as an increase in idle balances, or in other words is borrowed only to be saved, and the increase in income is zero.

1.2. An Open-Economy Model
1.2.1. Domestic Equilibrium
Let us retain the assumptions of section 1.1 immediately above, except for the addition of a marginal propensity to import of 0.15, and let us continue to disregard the external repercussions. In an open-economy model it is no longer a matter of indifference whether we compute the income-sequence or the credit sequence first, nor can the non-bank-credit expansion be simply added to the bank-credit expansion, as in a closed-economy model. The credit-multiplier and the standard income-multiplier are no longer determined by completely different sets of parameters,[5] and non-bank-credit expansion as well as bank-credit expansion brings a drain of external reserves and thereby reduces the credit base. Recalling the oscillating path to equilibrium depicted in section 2.2.1 of Chapter 5 above, and the technique by which it was avoided, let us suppose that the standard-income-multiplier expansion associated with the injection of $1,000 of ultimate standard money as income is allowed to go to completion before any credit expansion occurs. Again omitting the consumption series, we get:

Y_1	=	1,000 +	750.00 +	562.50 +	... →	4,000
M_1	=	150 +	112.50 +	84.38 +	... →	600
S_1	=	100 +	75.00 +	56.25 +	... →	400
S'_1	=	50 +	37.50 +	28.13 +	... →	200
S''_1	=	50 +	37.50 +	28.13 +	... →	200
$S*_1$	=	50 +	37.50 +	28.13 +	... →	200.

At this point the banking system has $400 in deposit obligations $(S'+S*)$ against which it holds $400 in external reserves (the original receipt of $1,000 less the import drain of $600), so it has free reserves of $320. For their part the non-banks have free reserves of $200, so if we follow the customary practice in illustrations like this and allow both types of intermediary to lend the full amount of their free reserves we will have initial loans of $520, which will produce an initial over-expansion and another oscillating path to equilibrium. While in principle one path to long-run equilibrium is as good as another, in practice it is easier to deal with a smoothly-expanding sequence. Let us therefore suppose that experience has taught all bankers that non-bank-credit expansion will result in a drain on their external reserves even if they themselves grant no loans, and has led them to act as if all their non-bank deposits will be promptly withdrawn in cash; that is, the banking system lends the difference between its free

---

[5] See sections 2.3 and 3.3 of Chapter 4 above.

reserves and its obligations to non-banks ($S*$). This gives combined first-round loans of $320, $200 by the non-banks and $120 by the banking system; we may assume that the spending of them is allowed to have its full income-expanding effect before any more loans are granted:

$$
\begin{aligned}
Y_2 &= 320 + 240 + 180 + \ldots \rightarrow 1{,}280 \\
M_2 &= 48 + 36 + 27 + \ldots \rightarrow 192 \\
S_2 &= 32 + 24 + 18 + \ldots \rightarrow 128 \\
S'_2 &= 16 + 12 + 9 + \ldots \rightarrow 64 \\
S''_2 &= 16 + 12 + 9 + \ldots \rightarrow 64 \\
S*_2 &= 16 + 12 + 9 + \ldots \rightarrow 64.
\end{aligned}
$$

The number of variables to be kept track of in following the subsequent rounds of income-expansion is great enough to make it expedient to supplement these sequences with Table 6.1, which shows the T-square accounts of the various sectors of the economy, just as Table 4.4 supplements Table 4.3. Column 1 represents the position at the end of the Y_1 expansion. The left-hand portion of column 2 shows the granting of the first round of loans by the intermediaries, and the right-hand portion shows the disposition of the funds as the public spends the borrowed money. On the assumptions here made $s \, / \, (m+s)$ of the total loans or $128 is added to domestic financial assets and $m \, / \, (m+s) \times 320$ or $192 is added to the initial external drain of $600. Column 3 shows the next balance-sheet position; the non-banks now have $64 in free reserves and the banking system retains $208 in external reserves ($400-192$), of which $65.60 is required reserves—$0.2 \times (200+64+64)$—and $142.40 is free reserves. Column 4 represents the second round of loans and their disposition, and column 5 the subsequent balance-sheet position; the third round of loans will be $58.37. The various sequences do not constitute simple geometric progressions or other easily-summable series, but the equilibrium position (column 6) is easily found in the usual way by noting the final distribution of the $1,000 of ultimate standard money. Bank reserves will amount to $0.2 \times 0.5 (=0.1)$ times domestic financial assets, and the external drain $m/(m+s)$ or 1.5 times, so $1,000 of ultimate standard money will accommodate $1,000 / 1.6 = \$625$ in domestic financial assets; the other balance-sheet items can be found by applying the appropriate parameters to total domestic financial assets.

Returning to the income-expansion sequences, the second round of loans will be $142.40, $78.40 by the banks and $64 by the non-banks, hence we get:

137

Table 6.1. T-Square Accounts in a Multi-Intermediary Credit-and-Income Expansion in an Open Economy[1]

Item	(1)	(2)	(3)	(4)	(5)	(6) (∞)
General Public						
A Money-proper	200	+ 64	264.00	+28.48	292.48	... 312.50
Non-monies	200	+ 64	264.00	+28.48	292.48	... 312.50
Total	400	+128	528.00	+56.96	584.96	... 625.00
L Debt	—	+320	320.00	+142.40	462.40	... 562.50
Net worth	400	−192	208.00	−85.44	122.56	... 62.50
Non-Banks						
A Money-proper	200	−136	64.00	−35.52	28.48	... —
Loans	—	+200	200.00	+ 64.00	264.00	... 312.50
L Non-monies	200	+ 64	264.00	+28.48	292.48	... 312.50
Banking System						
A Gold	400	−192	208.00	−85.44	122.56	... 62.50
Loans	—	+120	120.00	+ 78.40	198.40	... 250.00
Money-proper	400	− 72	328.00	− 7.04	320.96	... 312.50
L General Public	200	+ 64	264.00	+28.48	292.48	... 312.50
Non-banks	200	−136	264.00	−35.52	28.48	... —
Memoranda:						
Required reserves	80		65.60		64.192	... 62.50
Free reserves	320		142.40		58.368	... —
External Sector						
External drain	600	+192	792.00	+85.44	877.44	... 937.50

[1] Assuming a marginal propensity to import of 15 per cent, a marginal propensity to save of 10 per cent, an acceptance ratio of 100 per cent for money-proper in terms of gold, a reserve ratio of 10 percent for the banking system and zero for the non-banks, and public coefficients of substitution of 1 : 1 for money-proper and non-monies. An initial injection of $1,000 of new income in gold has been allowed to expand income by $4,000, thus generating domestic financial assets of $400 and an external drain of $600.

$$Y_3 = 142.40 + 106.80 - 80.10 + \ldots \rightarrow 569.60$$
$$M_3 = 21.36 + 16.02 - 12.02 + \ldots \rightarrow 85.44$$
$$S_3 = 14.24 + 10.68 - 8.01 + \ldots \rightarrow 56.96$$
$$S'_3 = 7.12 + 5.34 - 4.01 + \ldots \rightarrow 28.48$$
$$S''_3 = 7.12 + 5.34 - 4.01 + \ldots \rightarrow 28.48$$
$$S^*_3 = 7.12 + 5.34 - 4.01 + \ldots \rightarrow 28.48.$$

Subsequent income-sequences may be derived in the same way. Again these series do not constitute easily-summable progressions, but we can derive the equilibrium value of income from the standard income-multiplier $1 / (m+s)$, the initial injection of ultimate standard money ($1,000.00), and the total loans derived as in Table 6.1 ($562.50):

$$\Sigma_1^\infty Y = 1,562.50 + 1,171.88 + 878.91 + \ldots \rightarrow 6,250.00$$
$$\Sigma_1^\infty M = 234.38 + 175.78 + 131.84 + \ldots \rightarrow 937.50$$
$$\Sigma_1^\infty S = 156.25 + 117.19 + 87.89 + \ldots \rightarrow 625.00$$
$$\Sigma_1^\infty S' = 78.13 + 58.59 + 43.95 + \ldots \rightarrow 312.50$$
$$\Sigma_1^\infty S'' = 78.13 + 58.59 + 43.95 + \ldots \rightarrow 312.50$$
$$S^*_\infty = 0 + 0 + 0 + \ldots \rightarrow 0.$$

1.2.2. International Equilibrium

Chapter 8 below treats the external repercussions of the import leakage in the context of a two-country world; in general the result is to offset the exchange drain in part at least, but whether the offset is small or large depends on circumstantial and policy factors that lie largely outside the scope of this book. However, we may easily envisage the asset structure of the final international equilibrium position. First, as in section 1.3 of Chapter 1 above, we may accommodate foreign claims as well as domestic claims in the portfolios of the general public and (we may now add) of domestic financial intermediaries. Second, we must interpret "foreign claims" in the strict sense of claims which the holder wishes to retain more or less permanently in that form and not as including claims which the holder has already converted or is about to convert into foreign-produced goods to be imported into the home country for consumption or for incorporation in physical capital.

As a concrete example of what is involved, Table 6.2 presents a model of a two-country world in which we may postulate that the requirements of a general equilibrium are satisfied. Country B is approximately double Country A in size, and residents of each country hold some financial claims issued in the other. We can confidently say that the final equilibrium must entail the marginal equivalence of the attractions of holding various domestic and foreign claims in each country. And, of course, besides the

Table 6.2. Schematic Illustration of a Two-Country World
in General Equilibrium

Assets	A	B	World	Liabilities	A	B	World
Gold	10	20	30	Foreign debt	200	100	300
Money	400	800	1200	Intermediary debt	800	1600	2400
Near-money	400	800	1200				
Gov't securities	300	600	900	Government debt	300	600	900
Other domestic debt	900	1800	2700	Other domestic debt	900	1800	2700
Shares	100	200	300	Shares	100	200	300
Foreign claims	100	200	300	Net worth	-90	120	30
	2210	4420	6630		2210	4420	6630

factors that operate on domestic coefficients of substitution, it is clear that the international coefficients are affected by such things as the international distribution of resources and technical skills, comparative investment opportunities, development programs in particular countries, exchange rates, exchange controls, wars and rumours of wars (trade as well as military), and in short all the factors that directly or indirectly influence international economic relationships.

In this model the world economy becomes in fact a closed economy. If we choose to ignore the complications of international economic interactions, exchange rates, capital transfers, the balance of payments, and the rest, therefore, we can apply the analysis of our closed-economy models to this new situation. Realistically, of course, we would have to abandon the high combined credit-and-income multipliers we there derived, unless we think of the process as occurring over a very long period of time in which real income could rise more or less in proportion to the increase in money-income, or in which a largely-subsistence economy transferred itself into a largely-money-and-market economy; otherwise multipliers of this magnitude imply severely inflationary pressures. If we want to use our model to help us understand events in a relatively short period of time, especially in the world of the late 20th century, we must suppose that the expansion of credit and of money-income in each country, and therefore in the world as a whole, is kept reasonably well in step with the current full-employment level of real income.

1.3. Algebraic Formulation

In addition to or as modifications of the notation previously used,[6] we may

[6] See especially section 2.5 of Chapter 1, section 3.5 of Chapter 3, and section 3.3 of

identify $A_1d, A_2d, A_3d, \ldots$ as the various categories into which Ad may be subdivided; $r_1, r_2, r_3, \ldots$ as their respective reserve ratios: and $p_1, p_2, p_3, \ldots$ as the respective portions thereof held in the form of claims on the deposit banks rather than the central bank or other issuer of standard money. In the injection-of-income case $Ad=S$, $A_1d=S'$, $A_2d=S''$, $A_3d=S'''$, ... In section 1.1 of this chapter A_1d may be identified as money-proper, A_2d as non-monies, and there are no other categories of domestic financial assets; $a=0.5$, $r_1=0.2$, and $r_2=d=0$. In the illustrations used in section 1.2, $m=0.15$ and $s=0.1$ (or $d=1.5$). For a more elaborate illustration we may use the model set out in section 3.5 of Chapter 3 above, in which $A_1d=Np=$ $(1-a-b-i-j).Ad$, $A_2d=Dp=a.Ad$, $A_3d(=b.Ad)$ means claims on non-banks, $A_4d(=i.Ad)$ means the public's holdings of government securities, $A_5d(=j.Ad)$ means the public's holdings of private debt issues, $r_1=R$, $r_2=r$, $r_3=cr$, and $r_4=r_5=p_1=p_2=0$.

The procedure is the same as before, but because of the number of terms to be accommodated it is expedient to use temporary abbreviations in the equations. Setting $p_1=p_2=0$, we get:

$$Dt = (a+br_3p_3+ir_4p_4+jr_5p_5+ \ldots)Ad=V.Ad \dots \dots \dots \dots \tag{6.1}$$

$$N = [(1-a-b-j-\ldots)+r_2V+r_3b(1-p_3)+r_4i(1-p_4)+r_5j(1-p_5)+ \ldots]Ad$$

$$= [1-a(1-r_2)-b(1-r_3+r_3p_3-r_2r_3p_3)-i(1-r_4+r_4p_4-r_2r_4p_4)- \ldots]Ad=K.Ad \dots \tag{6.2}$$

$$Ad = G/(r_1K+d) \dots \dots \dots \dots \dots \dots \dots \tag{6.3}$$

$$L = (1-r_1)N+(1-r_2)Dt+(1-r_3)A_3d+(1-r_4)A_4d+ \ldots \dots \dots \dots \tag{6.4}$$

$$Y = (G+L)/(m+s) \dots \dots \dots \dots \dots \dots \dots \tag{6.5}.$$

2. Short-Run Dynamics: Banks and Non-Banks

2.1. The Indestructibility Principle

Long-run-equilibrium monetary analysis, to which the bulk of the discussion so far in this book has been addressed, emphasizes the similarities between money and other financial claims and between banks and non-bank financial intermediaries that were first popularized in economic literature in the 1950's, notably but not exclusively by Gurley and Shaw.[7] Short-run monetary analysis, on the other hand, brings out certain crucial differences between money-proper and all other financial claims, even its closest near-money substitutes. These differences centre on the key role of money-proper in the equilibrating process.

The short-run dynamics of money-proper are epitomized in an *obiter dictum* by J.B. Say in explaining his Law of Markets: ". . . the only way of

---

Chapter 5, above.

[7] See footnote 4 on pp. 1f above.

getting rid of money is in the purchase of some product or other."[8] He was undoubtedly thinking in terms of commodity monies, such as full-bodied gold and silver coins, which might be lost or melted down or worn away by much handling but were otherwise indestructible, so we may identify the basic concept as The Indestructibility Principle. Even modern credit-based money is virtually indestructible once issued, despite the fact that it can be cancelled by or with the acquiescence of its issuer; even the extinction of domestic standard money in exchange for foreign monies to make payments abroad merely transfers the equivalent purchasing power to foreign residents.

An individual whose actual holdings of an accepted form of money exceed his desired holdings can easily restore his financial equilibrium by spending the surplus on consumption or buying some other asset, but that merely transfers its possession to someone else, who may very well want money-to-spend rather than money-to-hold. For the community as a whole there are only three ways to eliminate a surplus of domestic money-proper: by the extinction of a credit-based domestic money in exchange for or in extinction of domestic claims held by the issuer (which nowadays usually means a central-bank decision to contract credit); by a similar extinction in exchange for foreign currencies, i.e. a depletion of the external reserves; or by the expansion of domestic money-income until the surplus supply of money is absorbed by rising demand for money-to-hold.

The virtual indestructibility of money-proper in a sophisticated modern economy reflects the fact that, by and large, the public's control over the volume of credit-based money through the acceptance ratio has been abrogated by the rise of efficient central banks.[9] Under the full gold-coin standard the domestic money supply was all too destructible in the face of a "loss of confidence", which might lead to an internal as well as or instead of

---

[8] *A Treatise on Political Economy*, trans. from the 4th ed. of the French by C.R. Prinsep, New American Ed., Philadelphia, Claxton Remsen and Haffelfinger, 1880, pp. 134f.

[9] This does not mean that a modern central bank has precise control over the volume of domestic money-proper, nor that it should. A change in the public's demand for banknotes affects bank reserves; the cash reserves available to commercial banks support their money-proper and near-money obligations in variable proportions; non-bank financial intermediaries may offer good substitutes for the chequeable-deposit obligations of the recognized banks; hence the public still has considerable power to vary its holdings of money-proper even in the short run. With respect to the precise volume of money-proper at any given moment, therefore, it may still be said that the central bank proposes but the public disposes. Furthermore, while this does undoubtedly reduce the control of the central bank over the financial system in the short run, it can be argued that it also produces a useful cushioning of the effects of monetary policy on the general economy.

an external gold drain and cause a monetary contraction that could freeze up the entire financial system. Officially-sanctioned Banks of Issue were able to solve this problem through the lender-of-last-resort function, provided their reserve requirements were sufficiently flexible or could be made so in an emergency; their evolution into true central banks and the centralization of external reserves in official hands have all but eliminated "runs" on banking systems, and have made the money supply a policy variable. Orderly conversion of the domestic currency into foreign currency may be freely possible in settled times, but in most jurisdictions it is no longer a matter of right.

2.2. A Closed-Economy Model

Tables 4.1 on page 92 and 5.1 on page 112 above clearly show the difference that the acceptance of a given type of financial claim as a form of money-proper makes in the rate at which the associated income-expansion sequence operates. However, the contrast can be brought out more effectively in a model that combines both bank and non-bank credit expansion. We may use the same closed-economy model that we used in section 1.1 above to determine the long-run equilibrium position; it assumes that $1,000 of new ultimate standard money is received as income, that the marginal propensity to save is 0.1, that the public assigns half its money-to-hold to the banking system and half to other financial claims, and that the cash reserve ratio is 0.2 for banks and zero for other intermediaries. We may also suppose that the public holds as (undigested) money-proper any receipts it has not yet succeeded in reapportioning according to its equilibrium coefficients of substitution. This last assumption somewhat understates the potential role of financial claims other than money-proper, for the reasons noted on page 146 below, but on the other hand the reserve ratios postulated for the banks and for other intermediaries probably understate the potential of the banks and overstate that of the others.

Since the "periods" of both the income-expansion and the credit-expansion sequences are arbitrary analytical devices in any case, we may as well treat them as identical; probably this, too, understates the rapidity of bank-credit expansion in the real world. Also we may suppose that the free reserves the banking system and the non-banks find themselves with in one period are lent and spent and generate income in the next period. We may confine our attention to the Y_1 sequence of section 1.1 above, the bank lending sequences (which we may now combine as $L'=Y'$), and the non-bank lending sequences ($L''=Y''$), since by hypothesis they are the only generators of income; the accumulation of digested balances of money-proper (S') are subsumed in the growth of the bank obligations. In each period non-bank lending (L'') equals the non-bank allocation of savings

(S'') in the previous period. Thus we may again start with the standard-income-multiplier sequence and its savings derivatives:

$$
\begin{aligned}
Y_1 &= 1{,}000.00 + 900.00 + 810.00 + 729.00 + \ldots \\
S_1 &= \phantom{1{,}00}100.00 + 90.00 + 81.00 + 72.90 + \ldots \\
S'_1 &= \phantom{1{,}00}50.00 + 45.00 + 40.50 + 36.45 + \ldots \\
S''_1 &= \phantom{1{,}00}50.00 + 45.00 + 40.50 + 36.45 + \ldots \\
S*_1 &= \phantom{1{,}00}50.00 + 45.00 + 40.50 + 36.45 + \ldots \; .
\end{aligned}
$$

In Period 1 total income is \$1,000, all from the Y_1 sequence, but in Period 2 it is \$1,750—\$900 from the second term of the Y_1 sequence, \$800 from the first term of the first Y' subsequence, and \$50 from the first Y'' subsequence, which is derived from the figure for $S*$ in the first period. We therefore have the following income and non-bank free-reserve sequences running in Period 2:

$$
\begin{aligned}
Y_1 &= 900.00 + 810.00 + 729.00 + \ldots \\
Y'_1 &= 800.00 + 720.00 + 648.00 + \ldots \\
Y''_1 &= 50.00 + 45.00 + 40.50 + \ldots \text{ (from } Y_1 \text{ in Period 1)} \\
S*_1 &= 45.00 + 40.50 + 36.45 + \ldots \text{ (from } Y_1 \text{ in Period 2)} \\
S*_2 &= 40.00 + 36.00 + 32.40 + \ldots \text{ (from } Y'_1 \text{ in Period 2)} \\
S*_3 &= 2.50 + 2.25 + 2.025 + \ldots \text{ (from } Y''_1 \text{ in Period 2)}
\end{aligned}
$$

For subsequent periods the full derivation becomes increasingly complicated, as the number of new sequences and subsequences doubles each time: there is only one income component in the first period, but there are three in the second, seven in the third, fifteen in the fourth, and so on indefinitely. However, we can reduce this to just two new subsequences per period by combining the many Y'' components into one. By hypothesis the common factor applying to all sequences and subsequences already introduced is 0.9, and the sum of all Y'' components in each period must be 5 per cent of the previous period's total income. Thus in Period 3 the second banking sequence begins (\$640+\$576+\$518.40+...), hence total income is \$1,750×(0.9+0.05)+\$640=\$2,302.50. In the same way we can derive the fourth and subsequent terms as \$2,699.375+\$2,974.00625+.... They increase in size for a time, for the same reason as in Table 5.1: the initial terms of the various banking subsequences are of about the same order of magnitude as the corresponding terms of the Y_1 sequence. After period 9 they decline and approach zero, however, as the characteristics of converging geometric progressions assert themselves. The equilibrium position can be derived as in section 1.1 above.

The significant point in all this is to identify the very different rates of growth of the banking and the non-banking contributions in the early stages of the expansion. In the first three periods $5,052.50 is added to income, of which $2,710.00 or nearly 54 per cent is attributable to the initial injection of income (the Y_1 sequence), $2,160.00 or nearly 43 per cent to the bank-credit sequence, and only $182.50 or 3.6 per cent to non-bank credit. At this point "digested" claims by the public on the banking system are the same as the total obligations of the non-banks (including the new additions that in the case of the non-banks provide free reserves for lending in the next period), i.e. $252.63 or 5.1 per cent of their final equilibrium level, but total claims on the banking system (including not only the claims of the non-banks but also the undigested claims of the public) amount to $2,440.00 or 48.8 per cent of the equilibrium level. By the fourth period bank-credit expansion accounts for 50.3 per cent of the increase in income and bank obligations are 59 per cent of their equilibrium value, compared to 5.4 per cent and 7.8 per cent respectively for the non-banks. That is why acceptance as a form of money-proper makes such a difference in the role of any financial claim.

2.3. Money and Near-Money

Regardless of *why* a particular financial claim, commodity, or object gains acceptance as money-proper and another does not, and regardless of *how* it achieves that status, such acceptance brings a difference in kind and not merely in degree between the two. The very essence of moneyness is general acceptability in exchange for other things. Money-proper is readily acceptable by spenders and savers alike for its own sake, near-money is not—not even the "nearest" of near-monies. Those who want to acquire goods and services can use money-proper at once for their purposes, and those who want to add to their financial or physical assets can immediately use it to acquire any other asset they wish. Near-monies are not normally an acceptable tender in the settlement of transactions, or are acceptable only at their market value (i.e. at the price at which they can be exchanged for money-proper).

No other financial asset is "indestructible" in the sense that money-proper can be said to be—not even its closest substitutes. If an individual has more of a particular non-bank claim (or any other asset) than he now wants he may conceivably be successful in bartering it for something he does want,[10] but even if he merely wishes to exchange one asset for another he will normally sell the first for money-proper and buy the second with the proceeds. He can extinguish the claim in exchange for money-proper on maturity (or in some cases on demand, as with some types of savings deposits) and spend the proceeds, thus unilaterally reducing the total of such assets. Furthermore the actions of the community as a whole in this respect are the sum of

---

[10] If a particular type of financial claim were to become increasingly acceptable in such barter transactions, at some imprecise point it would have to be acknowledged to have become a form of money-proper. Banknotes and chequeable deposits are historical examples.

the actions of its individual members. It may take time, but an oversupply of a given non-bank claim is corrected primarily by its extinction rather than by a stimulus to the expansion of money-income; in the meantime its market value will decline to reflect its altered acceptability.

Without exaggerating the importance of the particular illustrations here used, and without putting too fine a meaning on the successive "periods" they employ, they do graphically illustrate the key role of money-proper in the short-run dynamics of the financial system and in its equilibrating mechanism, as well as the elasticity the acceptance of a credit-backed form of money provides. Given the wide acceptability and the virtual indestructibility that money-proper status entails, the lending-and-redeposit sequence through banks generates a much more rapid rate of expansion of the spending stream than through other intermediaries because their obligations can accommodate not only digested balances of money-to-hold (i.e. balances appropriate to the current level of money-income and wealth) but also undigested balances of money-to-spend. There are indeed feedback effects on income levels from the spending of funds channelled through other intermediaries just as there are through banks, and credit is indeed expanded or "created" in essentially the same way. Nevertheless credit expansion through banks operates much more rapidly and assuredly than through other intermediaries, and the feedback effects on income and savings are much more powerful. If that is merely a difference of degree, it is a degree of difference that will certainly impress the practical policymaker.

This line of argument does not depend on the proposition that all undigested balances are left on deposit with banks, and in fact that proposition is demonstrably false. Some portion of undigested balances may be converted into various forms of near-money and so held for appreciable periods before being reconverted into money-proper and spent. The availability of a suitable choice of liquid (short-dated or readily-marketable) near-monies is an essential condition, and yields thereon must be sufficient to make the exchange worthwhile. The relatively high interest rates of recent years have had a double stimulus here: shifts of smaller sums for shorter periods have become economic, and there is a strong incentive for intermediaries (and markets) to offer new instruments to tempt short-term investors. Clearly, these developments have expanded the roles of near-banks and increased the feedback effects of their lending. The fact remains, however, that it still involves conscious efforts and specific transactions costs to divert short-term balances to a near-bank, then back again when the time comes to spend them, whereas they flow through the holder's bank account with no effort on his part. Furthermore, thanks to The Indestructibility Principle, funds so diverted do not immediately reduce the money supply (and hence the lending capabilities of banks), they merely speed up its rate of turnover, though in due course the central bank may be induced to hold bank expansion below what it would otherwise have been, or the increased external drain may have the same effect.

Thus the analysis of an older generation was largely right in stressing the difference between banks and other financial intermediaries, or between money and other financial assets, but quite wrong in its explanation of the difference. It is substantially but not entirely true in the short run that non-bank lenders may lend only money saved out of income and placed with them, and it is clearly true that under favourable conditions banks can expand or "create" credit much more rapidly. But the difference does not lie in any unique powers in the hands of banks: other intermediaries share those powers in some degree. The superior credit-expansion powers of banks are primarily a dynamic short-term disequilibrium phenomenon, and are due to the ready acceptability of money-proper by those who want money-to-spend as well as those who want money-to-hold.

2.4. Algebraic Formulation

Using the same notation as in section 1.3 above, let us identify S' with the public's digested balances of money-proper and S'', S''', S'''', ... with its non-bank financial assets of various kinds, and let us assume that holdings of those savings vehicles that constitute money-proper include not only digested balances (both customary or required cash reserves of non-banks and the public's money-to-hold) but also undigested balances (the free reserves of the non-banks and the public's money-to-spend). We will treat bank-credit expansion independently, and subsume therein the accrual of digested balances of money-proper. We will also postulate that the free reserves of all financial intermediaries are lent and spent and produce income in the next period. There are thus three income-generating series, each with a common ratio of $(1-s)$: Y_1, with an initial term of G in Period 1; Y', comprising a progression of subsequences starting with $G(1-r_1)$ in Period 2, $G(1-r_1)^2$ in Period 3, and so on; and Y'', which also starts in Period 2 and consists of the non-bank free reserves generated in the previous period (i.e. that period's total income multiplied by $(1-a-b-i-j-$ ... $)$, *less* the cash reserves appropriate to the intermediaries in question).

In the first period the only component of income is G, which is deposited in the banking system in full, including the public's allocations to S' and (temporarily) to S'', S''', ... , amounting to $sG(1-a-b-i-$ ... $)$, asG, bsG, isG, ... respectively. In the second period the income generated includes $G(1-s)$ from the Y_1 sequence, $G(1-r_1)$ from the first Y' subsequence, and $sG[a(1-r_2)+b(1-r_3)+$ ... $]$ from the Y'' sequence. In each succeeding period a new income-sequence will be started for the next term of every sequence already started, and further new terms for the additional accrual of savings to the non-banks. In Period 3, for example, there will be income of $G(1-s)^2$ from the initial income-sequence, $G(1-r_1)(1-s)$ from

147

the first round of bank lending, and $sG[a(1-r_2)+b(1-r_3)+\ldots].(1-s)$ from the first round of non-bank lending, but there will also be four terms from the start of four entirely new series: the spending of the second round of bank loans, $G(1-r_1)^2$; a new round of non-bank lending from the S'', $S''',\ldots$ portions of the savings generated by the spending of $G(1-s)$ in the second period from the initial income-sequence, amounting to $sG(1-s)$ $[a(1-r_2)+b(1-r_3)+\ldots]$; another new round of non-bank lending arising from their share of the savings generated by the spending of the first round of bank loans in Period 2, amounting to $sG(1-r_1)[a(1-r_3)+b(1-r_3)$ $+\ldots]$; and a third new round of non-bank lending generated in the same way from their share of the savings resulting from the spending of their own first round of loans in the second period, amounting to $s^2G[a(1-r_2)+$ $b(1-r_3)+\ldots]^2$. In each period the number of newly-introduced sequences doubles.

3. A Literary Interpretation

Useful as algebraic presentations are for introducing precision into the analysis, their precision must not be pressed beyond the limits of the underlying data. In the real world parameters such as we have used here ($a, b, i, j, r, s,$ etc.) and previously are likely to be complex variables obeying ill-defined laws, instead of constants, so they are more useful for expositional than for operational purposes. A literary interpretation can bring out the essentials more briefly and more effectively.

The substance of the matter is that, although a discrepancy between actual and desired holdings of any asset (financial or physical) will provoke action designed to restore the balance, in the case of a credit-based money-proper such a discrepancy (a) will act rapidly and effectively on the spending stream as well as on the public's asset-holding pattern and (b) can be flexibly managed by the monetary authorities. A credit expansion could indeed occur in a system in which the only money was a full-bodied commodity-money and all financial intermediaries were merely savings institutions, and an easy-credit policy could be employed to stimulate spending when needed, but the credit expansion would be slow and the spending stimulus small. Institutional reserve requirements could be reduced, and loans granted by "writing up" savings deposits on the books of the intermediaries, but the cash drain would immediately wipe out virtually all their free reserves and the resultant redeposits would be slow to materialize.

Any "disturbance" or imbalance in the public's money holdings will quickly set an equilibrating process in motion, which may either expand or contract money-income and the public's holdings of financial assets. Perhaps new external reserves are received from increased net export earnings; perhaps some holder of money balances decides to reduce them, either by spending them or by lending them to someone else who will; perhaps changing circumstances or changing legal provisions permit and encourage some intermediaries to reduce their reserve ratios. Or, more significantly, central-bank monetary-policy initiatives may effect an imbalance in the public's holdings of money relative to other assets. Some of these events will stimulate income-expanding sequences directly, others indirectly, by causing new loans to be granted and (presumably) spent, and some *both* directly *and* indirectly.

The sequences initiated will not end until every newly-received or newly-created or newly-activated sum of money-to-spend *either* leaks away to pay for imports *or* is added to someone's balances of money-to-hold. The associated asset-expansion will spill over into the full panoply of financial intermediaries according to the public's coefficients of substitution among the competing financial claims they offer, leading to a complex set of income-generating, lending, and spending sequences. Each successive holder of the new or newly-activated money will in turn revise his spending and his asset-holding patterns in the light of his new position, and will pass them on to others, except as he may choose to add to his previously-held money balances in view of his increased income and wealth.

Part Three ═══════════════════

INTERNATIONAL FINANCIAL INTERMEDIATION

CHAPTER 7

INTERNATIONAL APPLICATIONS
OF THE FRACTIONAL-RESERVE PRINCIPLE

1. The International Monetary System

The international monetary system still remains, as it has been historically, a federation of national monetary systems. Its evolutionary path seems similar to, but lagging behind, that of domestic financial systems, and has been punctuated by similar aberrations and wanderings in the wilderness. The first domestic monies were inelastic commodity-monies, and the first international systems were simple linkages of national monies using or based on the same commodity-money—typically gold or silver or some combination of the two. Domestic financial systems then developed along automatically-regulated institutional patterns in which the money supply was relatively elastic, because it included a credit-based portion convertible on demand into the basic commodity-money, but which proved vulnerable to convertibility crises. Discretionary procedures gradually replaced automaticity, and further evolution brought the typical modern system illustrated in Chapter 3 above, in which the attributes of an elastic credit-based currency are constrained by money-management techniques. Meanwhile the primitive linkage of domestic currencies through common or similar commodity-money bases was successively replaced by the formalized international gold standard, the gold-exchange standard, and the key-currency-exchange standard (in which other currencies are convertible into a major currency but no currency is convertible as of right into gold or any other commodity). Further rationalization of the international system made some progress after World War II through the International Monetary Fund (the I.M.F. or the Fund), but those arrangements fell into disarray in the 1970's.

It may reasonably be argued that the ultimate form of the international monetary system will be either (1) a single centrally-managed world currency universally used by all mankind or (2) a new federation of national systems not unlike the present arrangements but managed by a new world bank or what we may call a supracentral bank that would control the supply of recognized international reserves and be to national central banks as national central banks are to their domestic commercial banks; or the second solution may be seen as a halfway-house to the first. The original I.M.F. Agreement did not attempt to control the world supply of reserves directly, but instead purported to regulate them by a formal though rather ambiguous linkage of all currencies to gold without any real commitment to gold-convertibility; in practice it was based on the dollar-exchange standard. More recently the Special Drawing Right (SDR) was introduced, and promoted rather half-heartedly as the eventual replacement for gold as the foundation for a new international system. It may well be that the SDR, or something like it, will some day assume this role, but for the present it and other Fund entitlements constitute a relatively small part of the world's total supply of international liquidity or of officially-recognized external reserves; holdings of several partly-cooperating-and-partly-competing key currencies constitute by far the largest and most-rapidly-growing portion.

The creation of external reserves through the operation of the Fund as an international financial intermediary is treated in section 2 of Chapter 9 below. However, since in practice key-currency reserves are more important, the application of the theory of financial intermediation to their generation and use must also get careful consideration. This subject is introduced in section 3.3 of this chapter as part of what we hope is a useful summary of and contribution to the theory of international reserves as currently understood, and two major aspects are treated in sections 1 and 3 of Chapter 9. The first of these aspects relates to the creation of the key-currency reserves through direct credits from one central bank to another; it is introduced before the treatment of credit-expansion through the Fund partly because it may occur independently of recourse to the Fund's resources—it may be either a substitute for or a supplement to Fund drawings —and partly because it helps to explain reserve-creation through the Fund: for the Fund acts as an intermediary partly by providing its members with access to the currencies of other nations, as well as by providing a new international money of its own. (Reserve positions in the Fund are part of its members' *external reserves* but in their present form are not international *money*. The same was originally true of SDR's, though there is now full freedom to transfer them from one participant to another and hence they are both an international reserve and an international money.) The second aspect deals with a form of financial intermediation in which international reserves may be created by market forces through intermediaries over which no national or international authority presently exercises effective control, in contrast to reserves created by a responsible central bank or an international organization, either of which may be expected to consider the global implications of the actions being taken.

Parenthetically, it may be noted that the discussion in this and the two following chapters differs from that in previous chapters in that explicit attention must be paid to a major policy problem that has plagued the international community as a whole and virtually every country individually in recent years, namely the difficulties encountered in attaining all their major economic objectives simultaneously. Three of the most important of those objectives are a high level of employment, stable prices, and a viable balance-of-payments position. As explained in Chapters 8 and 9 below, mutually-acceptable adjustments in their balance-of-payments positions would be relatively easy to achieve if all or most countries could attain the two domestic objectives, so the problem is primarily a domestic one for each country individually; it is only an international problem in the sense that most nations share it. The essence of it is a true dilemma: presently-known techniques for expanding output and employment also add to inflationary pressures, and presently-known techniques for reducing inflation also (and more effectively) reduce output and employment. We may call the phenomenon The Fearsome Dilemma, because it is so widespread and appears to be so intractable.[1]

The workings of domestic financial intermediaries and systems can be analyzed without specific reference to The Fearsome Dilemma, even though it is primarily a domestic problem, because it will be the same team of national officials who must make the decisions on how much credit-expansion to allow, what policies to follow in other areas, and what compromises must be made when all domestic objectives are not fully realizable in a given timeframe. Decisions about international monetary relationships, in contrast, must be arrived at by consensus among disparate national teams whose problems and priorities may be or may be perceived to be quite different. There may indeed be strong differences of opinion within national decisionmaking teams—those between central-bank officials and treasury officials are notorious occupational hazards of economic policymaking, and other public and private interests may also have divergent views—but the essence of government in a sovereign state is the ability to resolve such conflicts in some way and come to a definitive policy conclusion. There is no similar sanction that can be relied on to bring agreement among sovereign powers on policy issues that materially affect their domestic economies, and it is therefore impossible to ignore The Fearsome Dilemma when discussing international monetary issues.

Before proceeding further, however, we will consider offshore banking. In itself offshore banking may be seen as merely a geographical displacement of domestic financial intermediation, and this would be quite adequate in a sanely-operating world in which all or most countries were reasonably successful in pursuing their major policy objectives, for offshore banking in any given currency is normally linked to domestic banking and central-banking in essentially the same way as the operations of domestic non-bank financial intermediaries. However, the common use of key currencies as

[1] See A.N McLeod, "The Fearsome Dilemma: Simultaneous Inflation and Unemployment", *Banca Nazionale del Lavoro Quarterly Review*, no. 131, December 1979.

external reserves, plus the fact that key-currency countries can and do fall into balance-of-payment difficulties, make a combination that partly insulates offshore banking from domestic banking controls and permits an expansion of world reserves with little or no effective restraint.

2. Offshore Banking[2]

2.1. Introduction

In all previous discussion of the principles of financial intermediation we have tacitly assumed that transactions are carried out exclusively in the currency of the country in which the institutions are domiciled. In practice this need not be the case. Banking and other forms of financial intermediation can be, and often are, carried out in one national jurisdiction but denominated in the currency of another or others. We may call this "offshore banking". An offshore bank is carrying on an operation that is in all respects parallel to that of any bank domiciled in the country of the currency so used (the home country), except that its activities happen to be physically located abroad (in the host country).

Offshore banking must be carefully distinguished from the common practice of internationally-operating banks carrying on domestic banking business in a number of countries in the domestic currencies of the host countries. For analytical purposes each of these branches and affiliates must be considered to be a domestic bank operating in the country where it is domiciled.[3]

The simplest case of true offshore banking arises where the currency of one country is used as the legal tender or the customary tender in another. Several currencies, including the U.S. dollar, the Australian dollar, and the South African rand, are so used in countries that are politically independent of the currency-issuing country. In this case bank deposits denominated in the foreign currency can be "created" and used domestically just as if they were denominated in a separate local currency.

However, the typical case of offshore banking relates to what are commonly called Euro-currencies—particularly Euro-dollars, though

---

[2] In this section the term "bank" is used in the ordinary sense of a commercial bank as defined on page 6 above. However, the discussion applies *mutatis mutandis* to the operations of other financial intermediaries, the issuance of bonds or other securities denominated in currencies other than that of the host country, and similar offshore financial activities.

[3] Like any other domestic bank in a particular location, however, branches and affiliates of internationally-operating banks may carry on offshore banking in one or more currencies as well as domestic banking in the currency of the host country.

Euro-sterling and other Euro-monies are also recognized. The name comes from the fact that much of the business occurs in London and continental-European financial centres, but it is inaccurate. A good deal of the banking in U.S. dollars outside U.S. jurisdiction takes place in Canadian financial centres through Canadian banks, and essentially the same phenomenon occurs in smaller financial centres throughout the world. Offshore sterling balances have been a feature of international banking for generations, dating from the time when sterling was the world's major key currency, and offshore banking in a great variety of other currencies is quite widespread on at least a local or regional basis in many parts of the world. In some middle-eastern countries, for example, banks may carry on a banking business in a score of currencies besides their local currency—not just dollars and sterling [4] and major currencies such as the deutschemark and the Swiss or French francs but also Indian and Pakistan rupees, Egyptian pounds, and a number of others. At one time British gold sovereigns circulated actively in some of these countries, and bank deposits might be denominated in sovereigns, sometimes distinguishing between "queenheads" (Victoria) and "kingheads" (Edward VII and George V), or "Edwards" and "Georges" separately.[5] Sometimes foreign-exchange-control prohibitions of the importation of a given country's own currency notes (to make evasion of control more difficult) led to separate offshore deposit accounts payable in the notes of these currencies and deposit accounts payable in cheques or drafts; because of the more limited usability of notes, they would sell at a considerable discount compared to cheques.

2.2. The Location of Banking Operations

There is nothing in the fractional-reserve principle to link the location of a given financial intermediary with the country that issues the currency in which it operates or with the location of the customers it will serve. The main requirements are (1) the ability to attract and hold balances denominated in a particular currency, (2) the ability to employ the funds profitably, and (3) the ability to repay the depositer according to the contract. It is not even necessary that any material portion of the intermediary's assets—neither its loans nor its investments nor its reserves—be in same currency as its liabilities, provided that in practice it can demonstrate its ability to repay on demand or when the liability matures. However, it is clear that all these considerations, and many others besides, do

---

[4] When sterling foreign-exchange-control regulations were highly complex, as in the early 1950's, they offered deposit balances in several types of sterling.
[5] The rationale was that the older coins would be somewhat lighter because of wear and therefore less valuable.

affect the competitive ability of an intermediary in a particular location to attract and serve customers.

The demand for banking services denominated in a given currency and domiciled in any particular locality, whether domestic or offshore, is largely a function of convenience factors and price factors. Some of the offshore demand comes, of course, from natural or juridical persons seeking tax-havens for some or all of their operations, and some from more questionable sources seeking a refuge for undeclared income or ill-gotten gains where they will be free from the prying eyes of the law-enforcement officers of their home countries. But the great bulk of the demand comes from normal considerations of administrative convenience, yield differentials, and the like.

Offshore chequeing deposits in specific locations may be useful for certain purposes, largely but not exclusively for offshore transactions, and in this case convenience is likely to be the main determinant of location. However, term and notice deposits constitute the bulk of offshore-bank obligations, and they tend to come in "wholesale" quantities—either relatively large individual deposits or the relending by one bank of funds it has acquired at the retail level. These balances are likely to go where they earn the most—other things beings equal, of course, such as the strength, soundness, and reputation of the bank concerned. Typically, offshore banks deal in large deposits, are not subject to minimum reserve requirements or maximum interests rates on either deposits or loans, and are not directly involved in the expense of operating the home country's payments mechanism, so they can trade profitably at narrower interest differentials between deposits and loans than domestic banks. Also, offshore deposits are not subject to the exchange controls and other interventions the home country may impose on its domestic banks. The Russian authorities are generally considered to have made a major contribution to the development of the offshore-dollar market after World War II because they wanted U.S.-dollar balances for trading and other purposes but did not want them at the mercy of the U.S. government, which had impounded their funds under the Alien Property Custodian during the war.

On the other hand banks domiciled abroad are at a disadvantage in other respects in attracting deposits: they are at the mercy of foreign-exchange controls imposed by their hosts, banking practices and standards of supervision may be less satisfactory (or simply less well-known), applicable legal considerations are different, and so on. An important consideration may be the fact that there is no recognized lender of last resort for offshore banks. In general it may be argued that the major international banks would support one another and could count on help from their respective central banks in an emergency, because default on any part of any major bank's obligations (whether in domestic currency or a foreign currency and whether at home or abroad) would threaten that nation's entire financial structure. The fact is, however, that effective lender-of-last-resort support must be available virtually without notice if it is ever needed at all, and offshore banks have never yet been put to a major test.

2.3. The Mechanics of Expansion

The mechanics of credit expansion through offshore banks are exactly the same as those of credit expansion through domestic financial intermediaries.[6] For concreteness we will discuss the process in terms of the U.S. dollar, which currently dominates offshore financial markets in most parts of the world for a variety of reasons, including its role as the dominant key-currency, external-reserve medium, and intervention currency since World War II, and the quantity of dollars flowing into the hands of residents of other countries as a result of persistent deficits in the U.S. balance of international payments.

Deposits with U.S. banks serve the same function in offshore-dollar banking that gold coin or other standard money serves in the domestic credit-expansion sequences presented in previous chapters. In strict parallel with Table 1.1 on page 15 above, you may think of deposits in and loans by offshore banks being made in drafts on U.S. banks. The amount of credit expansion produced will be determined in exactly the same way, i.e. by the coefficients of substitution between offshore-domiciled deposits and domestically-domiciled deposits, the effective reserve ratios offshore banks find it necessary to hold,[7] and the leakages out of the system (which in this case we may ignore because we have in effect postulated a closed system). Thus, if the coefficient of substitution was 10 per cent and reserves of 5 per cent were kept entirely with U.S.-domiciled banks, an increase of $1,000 in domestically-domiciled deposits would generate $110.49 in offshore-domiciled deposits; $5.53 of the original domestically-domiciled deposits would be diverted into additional reserves for offshore banks, so total dollar balances in the hands of the general public would rise by $1,104.97.

The next step is to note that transfers into, out of, and among offshore-domiciled dollar accounts need not be effected in drafts on U.S. banks,

---

[6] For an excellent account of these mechanics, and a refutation of some common misunderstandings of offshore banking, see Milton Friedman, "The Euro-Dollar Market: Some First Principles", *The Morgan Guaranty Survey*, October 1969.

[7] Reserves directly attributable to their offshore-dollar liabilities may be small or negligible since the dollar balances they would hold with their banking correspondents in any case, for general international settlement purposes, would probably suffice without supplementation.

but may be effected by other means as well—cheques written on offshore-dollar accounts by the depositors, drafts drawn by offshore banks on themselves or on offshore banking correspondents, or any other instruments by which transfers of any form of bank money can be made. A payee's account with an offshore bank is credited upon the presentation of any valid payment-instrument denominated in U.S. dollars, whether drawn on a U.S.-domiciled bank or branch or on an offshore bank; the instrument is cleared to the payor's bank for debit to his account; and the second bank must give equivalent value to the first in some mutually-agreeable way. Similarly, a cheque or other instrument drawn on an offshore bank will be cleared to the payor's bank for settlement in essentially the same way whether it is deposited with a domestically-domiciled bank or branch or with an offshore bank. If the volume of transactions among a group of offshore banks (or a combination of offshore and domestic banks) justifies a mutual clearing arrangement then only the net balances will need to be settled; if not, each item will be settled individually. In either case the settlement may be made in the form of a transfer on the books of a U.S. bank (perhaps in Federal Reserve funds, perhaps in commercial-bank funds), and this will probably be the case if one of the parties is a U.S.-domiciled bank or branch, but other modes of settlement are also possible. One offshore bank may be willing to accept settlement in the form of a credit to its correspondent account in U.S. dollars with the other, or in the form of a draft on a third offshore bank. Another possibility is that settlement will be effected by the transfer of balances in another currency at an agreed exchange rate on the U.S. dollar. Even if the settlement is effected in U.S. funds, they may be obtained in the foreign-exchange market by the tender of either the offshore bank's domestic currency or a third currency instead of by drawing down a deposit with a banking correspondent.

Dollars on deposit with offshore banks are thus fully convertible into and interchangeable with dollars on deposit with any U.S. bank, just as a deposit with a New York bank is convertible into and interchangeable with a deposit in a Los Angeles bank. The recipient of a cheque or other instrument is primarily concerned that he can get cash for it promptly or that in due course the indicated amount will be credited to his own deposit account and will become available for such uses as he wishes; as long as he is reasonably sure that the cheque will be honoured on presentation, and has means of recourse if it is not, he does not care about the location or other characteristics of the bank on which the cheque is drawn.

The substance of it is that there is a continuing flow of receipts into and payments out of offshore-domiciled bank deposits which is exactly similar to and in part overlaps the flow of receipts and payments into and out of domestically-domiciled bank deposits. It is closely parallel to, but perhaps more independent than, the similar flow into and out of domestically-domiciled near-bank deposit accounts. Offshore-domiciled bank deposits and domestically-domiciled near-bank deposits can grow or decline for exactly the same reasons even if domestic commercial-bank deposits are held constant. And of course the new lending thus made possible will generate exactly the same expansion of income as that described in Chapters 4, 5, and 6 above.

3. External Reserves

3.1. The Monetary Economics of External Reserves

A general consensus on the theory of external monetary reserves can not yet be claimed, but one may be in the making, which parallels the theory of domestic money in a number of important respects. One version of it may be summarized in the six following points:

1. External reserves consist of whatever media are conventionally accepted for that purpose by the international community. At present this includes gold, certain national currencies (mainly the U.S. dollar), reserve positions in the International Monetary Fund, and Special Drawing Rights in the Fund.[8] The national currencies included (key currencies) are commonly used as international monies.

2. The essential characteristic of external reserves is their convertibility into goods and services at competitive prices, not convertibility into gold or some other reserve asset. A national currency (whether an international money or not) may be so converted either directly through purchases or payments in its domestic market or indirectly by being exchanged for another national currency with which purchases or payments may be made, and other external reserves may be converted similarly.

3. The demand for external reserves in general (meaning reserves-to-hold) is a function of the income and the wealth of the holders, of the interest rates and other returns available on them, and of other factors as well. The demand for a particular reserve medium is a function of the same factors plus its availability and any special advantages or

---

[8] If there are two or more acceptable reserve media, a version of Gresham's Law will apply when anything happens that disturbs the coefficients of substitution among them: the demand for a preferred medium (e.g. gold) will rise, while that for an inferior medium (e.g. a soft currency) will fall, especially if its purchasing power and therefore its ability to protect the holder against future contingencies is seen to be declining because of inflationary price rises.

disadvantages compared to other media. Actual holdings of reserves in general or of a particular reserve medium in excess of demand at any given moment (undigested reserves) are reserves-to-spend, except to the extent that they are more-or-less-willingly held to accommodate the issuer or to stabilize the market or for any reason other than the reserve needs of the holder, in which case they ought to be classed as loans to the issuer; but this distinction is not generally recognized, and all balances denominated in a conventionally-acceptable reserve currency are formally counted as available international reserves.

4. The supply of monetary gold is relatively inelastic. The supply and useability of Fund reserve positions and SDR's is controlled by the Fund, which has the potential of becoming or being converted into a supracentral bank, but does not presently play that role and could not do so unless alternative sources of recognized reserves (especially key-currency balances) were brought under control. The supply of key-currency balances to the authorities of other countries is very elastic, not only in the sense that they are credit-based and therefore their total supply is elastic but also in the sense that their availability to other monetary authorities out of a given total supply is elastic: demand for reserve purposes is small relative to the total supply of the currency, and creditworthy monetary authorites can add to their holdings at will and at moderate cost [9] by bidding for them on the capital markets of the issuing country.

5. The existing supply of conventionally-accepted reserves at any given moment is virtually indestructible, except by either (a) the repayment of borrowed reserves or (b) the tendering of key-currency balances for purchases or payments in the issuing country, since their use normally entails merely a change of ownership.

6. There is no longer any firm link between a country's actual holdings of external reserves and its domestic money supply (i.e. it is permissible to let reserves fall to or below zero for good cause), so a loss of reserves need not impose any domestic financial restraint.

3.2. The Indestructibility Principle

As just noted, The Indestructibility Principle discussed on pages 141ff

---

[9] Since running down reserves is a feasible alternative (within limits) to external borrowing, the net cost of holding reserves may be identified with the difference between the interest payable on a marginal increase in long-term debt and the interest earnings on reserves, i.e. the difference between long-term and short-term interest rates in reserve-currency markets.

above applies to external-reserve media in much the same way as to domestic money. If a surplus of actual over desired reserves arises, regardless of the form reserves take or why the surplus occurs, the effects on the international community are closely parallel to the effects of a surplus of domestic money on the national economy: it will generate rising money-income, rising nominal wealth, and, beyond some point, inflationary price increases.[10]

A modest and unrepeated surplus of external reserves in the world at large may be absorbed fairly quickly and with little adverse effect under favourable circumstances. If the recipients of surplus reserves follow monetary policies based on automatic links between external reserves and the domestic money supply, their resultant domestic credit expansions will of course generate new import demand and thereby pass a large part of their new surpluses on to others; there will be modest expansionary effects on the world economy, which may be deemed desirable or undesirable according to whether the current situation would otherwise be or not be deflationary. If the recipients follow demand-management policies and are successfully maintaining full employment and stable prices, however, there should be no difficulty in absorbing the increase in external reserves and neutralizing its effects. In either case the adjustment will be greatly assisted if real incomes are rising in the world as a whole, for that will help to raise the demand for reserves and thus absorb the surplus without any materially-adverse effect on price levels.

A large surplus of external reserves is another matter, and a persistently-recurring surplus is far worse. National authorities that are on the horns of The Fearsome Dilemma will almost certainly feel free to follow more expansionary policies than they otherwise would, for the acquisition of surplus reserves will relieve or reduce any balance-of-payments constraints and tip the balance of priorities in favour of their full-employment objectives; the surplus will be passed on, not neutralized. Stocks of undigested reserves will build up in all countries, just as stocks of undigested domestic money may build up in the hands of local residents in the sequences described in previous chapters, with similar results. In the domestic-money case there will be an expansion of money-income that will not end until the undigested balances either leak away to pay for exports or are added to someone's balances of money-to-hold. In the external-reserve case, closed-economy conditions will obtain for the world as a whole. The only equilibrating force will be the expansion of money-income in all or

---

[10] If the surplus of reserves arises because some country finds it necessary to borrow to cover a balance-of-payments deficit, and that country later succeeds in restoring its desired reserve position and repaying its borrowings, the effects of the initial increase in reserves will of course be reversed.

most countries, which should eventually lead to an increase in demand for reserves; but this might operate very slowly, because inflation will be steadily reducing the purchasing power of key-currency reserves and encouraging national authorities to minimize their holdings.

The Indestructibility Principle may be modified in important and beneficial ways, however, when world reserves contain a significant credit element. A reformed system in which the supply of international reserves was managed by a supracentral bank, for example, would presumably be able to avoid any serious surplus, or to eliminate it promptly if one did occur. A system that includes credit-based key-currencies as part of the world supply of reserves also permits the relatively painless absorption of surplus reserves; indeed, subject to an important proviso, prompt absorption is virtually assured by the automatic mechanism described in the immediately-following section. If this mechanism fails, however, then The Indestructibility Principle operates as ineluctably with key-currency reserves as with any other form.

3.3. Key-Currency Systems

The extensive use of key currencies as international monies and international reserves is an important feature of today's international monetary system. The practice had its origins in the operational decisions of practical men, not in either formal international agreements or academic theorizing, and can be traced a long way back in history. In the 19th century sterling evolved into the dominant key currency, but its status was weakened by World War I and has largely evaporated since World War II. Contrary to common belief, the so-called Bretton Woods Agreement in 1944 did not assign the stellar role to the dollar; the participants merely recognized that the practical realities of world finance had already thrust that role upon it. Both sterling and the dollar started their key-currency roles as gold-exchange-standard currencies, but subsequently lapsed into inconvertible-key-currency standards.

Experience shows that stable and efficient international monetary arrangements can indeed be built on such a foundation, provided the key-currency country's exports remain fully competitive on world markets. Such a system has the enormous advantage of providing a supply of reserves for the rest of the world that is elastic both upwards and downwards.[11] Other countries, singly or in total, can vary their reserves to meet

---

[11] Technically, the key-currency country need hold no reserves itself, since by hypothesis its residents can obtain foreign goods and services by tendering their own currency for them; as a practical matter, however, it may be expedient for it to hold "owned" reserves of its own, especially if other key currencies compete for recognition as reserve media in the eyes of third countries. Historically, such reserves were typically held in specie or bullion, but

their needs instead of fitting their money-income to the Procrustean Bed of an inelastic reserve medium. On the one hand, as noted in item 4 on page 162 above, any creditworthy country should be able to add to its key-currency reserves-to-hold at modest cost. On the other hand, there is an automatic mechanism by which surplus balances of the key currency (and therefore a surplus of reserves in general, if alternative reserve media are available as well) can be eliminated: their ready convertibility into unre-quited key-currency exports, i.e. exports of goods and services paid for by tendering its own IOU's (claims on its banking system) rather than in kind. Any country finding itself with more total reserves than it considers neces-sary may use the excess to make purchases on world markets, or may permit economic expansion at home until rising imports dissipate the excess. All or part of the purchases may be made in third countries, thus passing the surplus on to them, but in due course the international spending stream will return it to the key-currency country in return for exports of those goods and services for which it has a comparative advantage. The only exception is that, because of rising incomes or other factors, some countries may decide to absorb part of the surplus by adding it to their external reserves, or private interests may choose to add to their willingly-held balances of the key currency.

Under these conditions, therefore, a surplus of reserves can exist only temporarily, no matter how it arises or who holds it or how it is held. The surplus funds may arise from increased key-currency-country imports, from key-currency investments abroad, from other countries borrowing the key currency in its domestic or offshore financial markets for public or private investment or consumption, or in some other way for some other purpose; they may be held by official bodies, by business enterprises, or by private citizens; they may be in the form of the obligations of banks, other financial intermediaries, public or private bodies, or other residents of the key-currency country, or in corresponding offshore obligations, or as physical holdings of accepted alternative media such as gold or SDR's, or otherwise. In any case, if the holders view them as money-to-spend rather than money-to-hold, then in due course they will either use them them-selves for purchases in or payments to the key-currency country, or sell them to others who wish to do so, or pay them over to third parties who will face similar choices.

However, such a system is vulnerable to economic misadventures or mismanagement in the key-currency economy. Uncompetitive export

---

holdings of other currencies (even just counter-claims on some of the countries that hold their reserves in the key currency) will do, for they will provide access to foreign goods and services when needed.

industries and consequent balance-of-payments deficits in other countries show themselves as a loss of reserves, but in key-currency countries they show themselves as a build-up of surplus balances of the key currency in the hands of non-residents. Residents can continue to buy imports by tendering their own national currency in payment, but the self-cancelling mechanism by which these balances should be surrendered in exchange for unrequited exports breaks down. Non-resident holders of these balances may still use them for purchases in third countries, but this merely passes the surplus on to others. In effect the key-currency country finances its balance-of-payments deficit by the issue of irredeemable international money and thereby spreads inflationary pressures throughout the world, just as an irresponsible national government can generate domestic inflation by financing its fiscal deficit through the issue of domestic fiat money or by borrowing from its central bank.[12]

The expansion of external reserves as a result of a key-currency balance-of-payments deficit is not limited to the amount of the deficit, however. The net tender of their national currency by residents of the key-currency country in payment for imports constitutes only the primary expansion of this form of external reserves for other countries, just as the overissue of a domestic reserve-money constitutes only the primary expansion of domestic credit; in both cases there is a secondary expansion, which may be much greater than the primary, as some portion of the primary increase gravitates to banks and other financial intermediaries in the form of expanded cash reserves in the domestic case, and to offshore intermediaries in the international case. This aspect will be considered in greater detail in section 3 of Chapter 9.

Nevertheless, unwanted accumulations of key-currency reserves do not make universal price inflation inevitable. A strong economy finding itself with surplus reserves which it can not "get rid of" though "the purchase of some product or other" except by permitting more domestic expansion than is compatible with its price-stability goals may choose to hold excess reserves indefinitely, in which case the excess holdings cease to be true reserves and become an involuntary loan to the issuer of the key currency that is in surplus supply. Self-denying actions of this kind on the part of one or more countries may materially lessen the impact of excess international reserves, and a concerted effort by most major countries might effectively neutralize them indefinitely, but any equilibrium so obtained would be unstable; a stable solution would require either effective control over, or the demonetization of, the offending reserve medium.

[12] An excess supply of any overvalued currency may arise in similar fashion, for example if exchange controls or other obstacles impede its conversion into unrequited exports of the issuing country, but this will not contribute materially to world inflation if the currency is not a recognized international money.

CHAPTER 8

THE EXTERNAL REPERCUSSIONS
OF DOMESTIC POLICIES[1]

1. Introduction

At a number of points in previous chapters we have introduced open-economy models, but we have generally had to limit them to constrained-equilibrium conditions in which we ignored the external repercussions. A relatively minor exception is to be found in section 1.2.2 of Chapter 6 above, where we did look briefly at the asset-structure of a final-equilibrium position in a two-country model. It is now time to attack the problem of general equilibrium as it applies to international economic relationships. It must be stated at once, however, that it will only be possible to treat it in quite broad macroeconomic terms, because a fuller exposition would be beyond the scope of this book.

The term "external repercussions" is generally interpreted to mean the entire chain of economic events set in motion by a given event or policy-action in an open economy—the immediate effects on the exports or imports of other countries, the secondary effects on their incomes through the foreign-trade multiplier, the tertiary effects on their imports and therefore on the exports and the income of the first country, and the infinite but presumably-converging series of endogenously-generated responses thus initiated. It is closely related to, and perhaps merely a more elaborate version of, the mechanism of adjustment of the balance of international payments. In *The General Theory* Keynes referred to the possibility that "our own country may recover a portion of [the import] leakage through favourable repercussions due to the action of the multiplier in the foreign country in increasing its economic activity."[2] Subsequently the concept was further elaborated by Machlup[3] and others.

---

[1] Virtually all the material presented in this chapter, except the algebraic presentations in sections 2.3 and 3.3, was published in the June 1975 issue of the *Banca Nazionale del Lavoro Quarterly Review* (no. 113, pp. 172–186) under the title "The Essential Conditions for International Economic Stability"; the editor's permission to use it here is gratefully acknowledged.

[2] J.M. Keynes, *The General Theory of Employment Interest and Money*, London, Macmillan and Co. Ltd., 1936, p. 120.

[3] F. Machlup, *International Trade and the National Income Multiplier*, Philadelphia, Blakiston, 1943.

Table 8.1. An Illustration of Income Repercussions

Phase or Period	A's Economy					B's Economy				
	Exports (1)	Income (2)	Imports (3)	Savings (4)	Reserves (5)	Exports (6)	Income (7)	Imports (8)	Savings (9)	Reserves (10)
I (1)		(1,000)								
I (2)		3,333	667	333	− 667	667	1,667	500	167	+ 667
II (1)	500	1,667	333	167	+ 500	333	833	250	83	− 500
II (2)	250	833	167	83	− 333					+ 333
II (3)					+ 250					− 250
.										
(4) = Σ∞₁	1,000	3,333	667	333	+ 333	667	1,667	500	167	− 333
III = I+II	1,000	6,667	1,333	667	− 333	1,333	3,333	1,000	333	+ 333
IV (1)	250	833	167	83	+ 250	167	833	250	83	− 250
IV (2)	188	625			− 167		625	188	63	+ 167
IV (3)					+ 188					− 188
.										
(4) = Σ∞₁	1,000	3,333	667	333	+ 333	667	3,333	1,000	333	− 333
V = III+IV	2,000	10,000	2,000	1,000	0	2,000	6,667	2,000	667	0
VI	3,000	15,000	3,000	1,500	0	3,000	10,000	3,000	1,000	0
VII = V+VI	5,000	25,000	5,000	2,500	0	5,000	16,667	5,000	1,667	0

Notes. It is assumed that A's marginal propensity to import is 0.2, B's is 0.3, and A's and B's marginal propensities to save are both 0.1. In Phase I the expansion is generated by the domestic income-multiplier operating on exogenous domestic spending of $1,000 in A. In Phase II the expansion at each step is generated by the export multiplier operating on the net expansion of A's and B's exports in the preceding step or phase. In Phase IV B's expansion at each step is generated by the domestic income-multiplier operating on credit-financed spending equal to B's net retained reserves at the end of the previous step ($333 at IV(1), $250 at IV(3), etc.), and A's expansion is generated by the export multiplier operating on A's net gain of exports in the preceding step. Phase VI repeats Phase V for an exogenous domestic expenditure of $1,000 in B.

2. The External Repercussions of Domestic Spending

2.1. A Numerical Example

Let us postulate a trading world composed of two countries, A and B, each of which earns its income from a combination of domestic production and export sales, and spends its income on a (presumably somewhat different) combination of domestic production and imports. The discussion will be in terms of the spending multiplier, without specifying whether a given increase in the spending stream is due to new capital formation or something else. The exports of each country are identical with the imports of the other, and their respective holdings of foreign-exchange reserves are a component part of their accumulated financial savings out of past income; but a change in reserves may include borrowing by one from the other as well as changes in owned reserves in the form of either gold or claims on the other country. We will identify "equilibrium" as meaning equilibrium in the current account of the balance of payments (exports of goods and services equal imports of goods and services), as if there were no capital movements except changes in official reserves; if you wish, however, you may reinterpret it as incorporating a net flow of private capital in either direction, with the flow of financial capital being kept in step with the flow of real capital by appropriate interest-rate differentials and other parameters.[4]

Now suppose that, starting from an underemployment partial-equilibrium position, A undertakes income-supporting expenditures of $1,000 at Phase I (1) of Table 8.1, using the dollar as a *numeraire* in which to express magnitudes denominated in the local currencies of both countries. If A's marginal propensity to import is 0.2 and its marginal propensity to save is 0.1 then its income-multiplier will generate income of $3,333 and imports of $667 at Phase I(2), which means that B's export earnings will increase by $667.[5] This is identical to the constrained-equilibrium position of earlier chapters, except that we now explicitly identify the new export earnings of B, which will start a multiple income-expansion there.

---

[4] Using the common notation of Y for income, C for consumption, X for exports, I for investment (capital formation), M for imports, and S for savings, so defined that $Y =$ (is earned from) $C + X + I =$ (is spent on) $C + M + S$, the equilibrating condition is that $I + X = S + M$, subject to the constraint that there is no unwanted change in external reserves (which in this formulation are included in the capital account of the balance of payments). This may be rewritten as $M = X + (I-S)$ if domestic capital-formation exceeds domestic saving and therefore a net capital inflow is required, or as $X = M + (S-I)$ if domestic saving exceeds domestic capital-formation and therefore some domestic saving must find an outlet abroad.

[5] Compressing the expansionary sequence into a virtually-instantaneous multiplier may be justified in the same way as in sections 4 of Chapter 1 and 2.2.1 of Chapter 5 above—i.e. by postulating an initial overexpansion that is partly reversed later.

The external repercussions begin in earnest in Phase II. If B's marginal propensity to import is 0.3 and its marginal propensity to save is 0.1 then its export multiplier will generate income of $1,667 in Phase II(1), and new imports of $500, which means an equivalent increase in export income for A. At Phase II(2) this leads to new income of $1,667 and new imports of $333 for A; and so on. By the end of Phase II a further $3,333 has been added to A's income, and a like amount of new income has been generated in B.[6]

Combining Phases I and II as Phase III, we find that A has added $6,667 to its income and $1,333 to its imports, B has added $3,333 to its income and $1,000 to its imports, and A has lost reserves of $333 to B—all as a result of the initial injection of $1,000 in new spending in A. A new equilibrium of sorts has been attained, in that the marginal increments of mutually-induced expenditures have approached zero in both countries, and under some circumstances both countries may be willing to tolerate the exchange flows. For example, A may be willing to borrow from B to support incomes in a temporarily-depressed sector which is expected to recover in due course.

However, perhaps B is encouraged to permit credit expansion as a result of the unexpected addition to its reserves; and let us suppose that the monetary authorities permit the expansion to continue until all the newly-acquired reserves are exhausted. In terms of the usual credit-expansion sequence-analysis we may suppose that at Phase IV(1) B's financial system initially lends the net free reserves it has accumulated in Phases I and II, i.e. $333, and that this is spent domestically and generates income of $833. This will add $250 to B's imports, i.e. to A's exports, which in turn will generate income of $833 and imports of $167 for A at IV(2). The result is that B still has excess reserves of $250 (i.e. $333 - $250 + $167), which the financial system now lends out to be spent as before, and which generates additional income for B of $625 at IV(3); and so on. In the end we find an additional $3,333 of income is generated for A and a like sum for B in this phase. Thus at Phase V we find that A's income has increased by exactly the amount one would expect if it were a closed economy instead of an open economy, and in addition B's income has risen by two-thirds as much.[7]

---

[6] This is a coincidence; as derived in section 2.3 below, in Phase II A's income is to B's as B's marginal propensity to import is to the sum of A's marginal leakages—i.e $Y_a : Y_b = m_b : (m_a + s_a)$.

[7] Note that these are not standard income-multipliers but compound total-income-multipliers like those discussed in section 2.2 of Chapter 4 above.

Parenthetically, we may note that the course of events in Phase IV will be materially modified if B retains a foreign-exchange reserve of some given percentage of the increase in its financial assets that is generated by the expansionary sequence.[8] If the reserve ratio is 100 per cent then there will be no credit-induced expansion at all, and the level of all variables in the table at Phase V will be identical with their levels at Phase III. If the reserve ratio is zero then the expansion will be as shown in Table 8.1. If the ratio is less than 100 per cent but greater than zero the expansion will be at some intermediate level.

Even the situation at Phase V is not the end of the story. Suppose that B is now encouraged to emulate A and undertakes to stimulate new domestic spending by another $1,000. Phases VI and VII of Table 8.1 show the eventual results, assuming that A now permits credit expansion in the same way B did in Phase IV. Total exogenous spending of $2,000 by A and B combined will bring an increase of $41,667 in world income, which implies a compound multiplier of somewhat more than 20.

2.2. Policy Implications

The policy implications of this model are as diverse as the circumstances in which A and B may find themselves at the start of the first sequence, as the changes that may occur in these circumstances in the course of the subsequent events, and as A's and B's possible reactions. However, the various phases into which the sequences have been broken in our model permit us to examine a number of major possibilities.

In a world in which inflation is not a problem and both A and B are in an underemployment position at the start, both should welcome A's initiative. Up to Phase III A tends to gain rather more than B, unless B's marginal propensity to import is considerably smaller (its income-multiplier is considerably greater) than A's, so B will have an incentive to emulate A and initiate some domestic income-supporting measures of its own. Also, unless either A or B achieves full employment earlier, both will benefit from the domestic credit expansion occurring in Phases IV and VI.

In combination, therefore, these different initiatives offer a flexible way in which a general equilibrium acceptable to both A and B could be reached. By a judicious blend of variations in the amount of income-supporting expenditures initiated in A and B, and variations in the amount of additional credit-induced expansion permitted in each country

---

[8] The foreign-exchange-reserve ratio here relevant is the ratio of a change in foreign-exchange reserves to a change in the total of all financial claims generated in the expansion, not just the ratio to the change in the central bank's monetary obligations nor to the change in the "money supply" however defined.

separately, it should be possible to achieve approximately full employment in both economies. If this position involves a permanent and unwanted drain of reserves from one to the other then it should be relatively easy for them to agree on measures to restore balance. The essential point will be to shift some resources from production for export to production for domestic consumption in the surplus country, and the other way around in the deficit country, without causing more than a temporary departure from full employment in either country. Technically it would be possible to use tariffs, exchange controls, import quotas, or perhaps still other techniques to effect the balance-of-payments adjustment and assist in the transfer of resources, but an agreed exchange-rate change would seem to be the least painful procedure and the one most compatible with the money-and-market mechanism.[9]

If B is experiencing inflationary pressures, however, it will not welcome the spill-over of demand from A at Phase I. As long as full employment is not threatened thereby, B will almost certainly suppress Phase IV and may endeavour to offset Phase II by restrictive domestic policies. Conceivably B may be able in this way to maintain domestic price stability without a material increase in unemployment.

In a world of unacceptably-high inflation and unacceptably-high unemployment, which is unfortunately the position of most countries today, the problem becomes more difficult. Both A and B may be supporting their domestic spending streams in an effort to achieve a tolerable position between the two horns of The Fearsome Dilemma. Each may feel that its own domestic expansion is fully justified in order to maintain domestic incomes at the level it considers appropriate under the circumstances, and may welcome the expansion in Phase II even if it suppresses Phase IV, but the combined effects will be far more stimulating than either may realize. Each will presumably be thinking in terms of its open-economy income-multiplier (assuming that reasonably accurate estimates of their respective marginal propensities to import and to save are available), i.e. 3.3. in A's case and 2.5 in B's, but in fact A's spending will generate a much higher multiplier even if Phase IV is suppressed (double the expected value, in our numerical example) and will also generate new income for B of some additional amount, as at Phase III. Similarly, B's spending will generate a much higher multiplier than expected (in our example it too will be double the expected value), and will also generate new income for A by some additional amount, as can be demonstrated through a process exactly parallel to Phases I and II of Table 8.1 with B instead of A taking the initiative.

[9] If the rate of price increase in one country were persistently greater than in the other then of course some form of continuous or periodic adjustment of exchange rates would be necessary.

Each country will be able to demonstrate that a substantial portion of its inflationary pressures is imported. Neither will be satisfied with the level of its employment or the rate of its inflation, hence there is little hope that they can agree on measures to end whatever exchange drain may be occurring; what would suit the surplus country will appear to the deficit country to be an invitation to permit even more unemployment, and what would suit the deficit country will appear to the surplus country to be an invitation to permit still more inflation. Failing a breakthrough that will permit more effective differential control over the price and the quantity components of the spending stream, it is difficult to visualize any solution that will be even close to a stable equilibrium for either country.

2.3. Algebraic Formulation

As in footnote 4 on page 169 above, we will use the conventional notation of Y for income, C for consumption, M for imports, X for exports, S for savings, m for the marginal propensity to import, and s for the marginal propensity to save, with the addition of R for external reserves and r for the ratio of the increase in required reserves to the increase in domestic financial assets (i.e. $r = R / S$). Subscripts a and b will indicate whether a symbol refers to Country A or Country B, and further numerical subscripts will indicate the successive time-periods where relevant. Each upper-case symbol will be interpreted as representing discrete increments in a specific time-period or sequence of time-periods (including infinite sequences), but can be reinterpreted as a rate of flow.

New spending of one unit in A at Phase I(1) generates $Y_{ai2} = 1 / (m_a + s_a)$ and $M_{ai2} = m_a / (m_a + s_a)$ at I(2), which is turn reduces R_a and adds to X_{bi2} and to R_{bi2} (i.e. $X_{bi2} = R_{bi2} = -R_{ai2} = m_a / (m_a + s_a)$). B's export multiplier now generates $Y_{bii1} = m_a / (m_a + s_a) \cdot 1 / (m_b + s_b)$ and $M_{bii1} = m_a / (m_a + s_a) \cdot m_b / (m_b + s_b)$, and produces $X_{aii1} = R_{aii1} = M_{bii1}$ at II(1). A's export multiplier in turn generates $Y_{aii2} = m_a / (m_a + s_a) \cdot m_b / (m_b + s_b) \cdot 1 / (m_a + s_a)$ at II(2), and so on.

This give a common ratio of $m_a / (m_a + s_a) \cdot m_b / (m_b + s_b)$ for the various converging series thus initiated; using the standard algebraic formula for summing such series to infinity, we derive a multiplier of $(m_a + s_a)(m_b + s_b)/(m_a \cdot s_b + s_a \cdot m_b + s_a \cdot s_b)$ to be applied to the first term in each sequence for A and B to get the values at II(4)—except that R_{aii4} and R_{bii4} are derived from M_{aii4} and M_{bii4}. Hence, setting $m_a \cdot s_b + s_a \cdot m_b + s_a \cdot s_b = K$, we derive $Y_{aii4} = m_a \cdot m_b / K(m_a + s_a)$ and $Y_{bii4} = m_a / K$.

173

Since Phase III = I+II, we also derive $X_{a_{iii}}(=M_{b_{iii}}) = m_a \cdot m_b/K$, $Y_{a_{iii}} = (m_b + s_b)/K$, $M_{a_{iii}} = m_a(m_b + s_b)/K$, $S_{a_{iii}} = s_a(m_b + s_b)/K$, $R_{a_{iii}}$ $(= -R_{b_{iii}}) = X_{a_{iii}} - M_{a_{iii}} = -m_a \cdot s_b/K$, $Y_{b_{iii}} = m_a/K$, and $S_{b_{iii}} = m_a \cdot s_b$ $/K$. Alternatively, we can derive these Phase III values (except $R_{a_{iii}}$ and $R_{b_{iii}}$) from the common ratio and the first terms of Phase I (2) or II (1) as the case may be.

If in Phase IV B permits credit expansion and credit-financed spending sufficient to leave reserves of r. S_{b_v} at Phase V, the results can be derived in the same step-by-step sequence as at Phase II, starting with the lending and spending of the initial free reserves of $(1-r)R_{b_{iii}}$. Alternatively, the equilibrium position (Phase V) can be calculated from the postulate that if $R_{b_v} = r.S_{b_v}$ then $X_{b_v}(=M_{a_v}) - M_{b_v} = r \cdot S_{b_v}$. But $M_{a_v} = M_{a_{iii}} + M_{a_{iv}}$, $M_{b_v} = M_{b_{iii}} + M_{b_{iv}}$, and $M_{a_{iii}} - M_{b_{iii}} = R_{b_{iii}} = m_a \cdot s_b/K$. Hence $M_{a_v} - M_{b_v} = M_{a_{iii}} + M_{a_{iv}} - M_{b_{iii}} - M_{b_{iv}} = M_{a_{iv}} - M_{b_{iv}} + m_a \cdot s_b/K$. Therefore $M_{a_{iv}} - M_{b_{iv}} = r.S_{b_v} - m_a \cdot s_b/K$. But $S_{b_v} = S_{b_{iii}} + S_{b_{iv}} = m_a \cdot s_b/K + s_b \cdot Y_{b_{iv}}$, $M_{a_{iv}} = m_a \cdot Y_{a_{iv}}$, $Y_{a_{iv}} = m_b/(m_a + s_a) \cdot Y_{b_{iv}}$, and $M_{b_{iv}} = m_b \cdot Y_{b_{iv}}$. Hence $m_a \cdot m_b/(m_a + s_a) \cdot Y_{b_{iv}} - m_b \cdot Y_{b_{iv}} = r.m_a \cdot s_b/K + r.s_b \cdot Y_{b_{iv}} - m_a \cdot s_b / K$. Solving for $Y_{b_{iv}}$, we get $m_a \cdot s_b(m_a+s_a)(1-r) / K$ $(r.m_a.s_b+s_a \cdot m_b+r..s_b)$; and from this, using the ratio of Y_a to Y_b in Phase II, we derive $Y_{a_{iv}} = m_a \cdot s_b(1-r)/K(r. m_a \cdot s_b + s_a \cdot m_b + s_a.m_b + r \cdot s_a \cdot s_b)$. If $r = 0$ these reduce to $Y_{a_{iv}} = m_a.s_b / s_a.K$ and $Y_{b_{iv}} = m_a.s_b(m_a+s_a) / s_a \cdot m_b.K$.

Since Phase V is the sum of Phases III and IV, the corresponding values can be found by addition. If $r = 0$ then Y_{a_v} reduces to $1/s_a$, Y_{b_v} reduces to $1/s_a \cdot m_a/m_b$, and their sum (the world total) reduces to $(m_a+m_b)/s_a \cdot m_b$.

Thus, if we assume that in both countries the long-run-equilibrium external-reserve ratio applicable to a marginal increase in domestic liquid assets (or savings) is zero, then in Phase V A's total-income-multiplier becomes the reciprocal of its marginal propensity to save, the same as if A were a closed economy. The initial injection of income in A will also produce a total-income-multiplier for B equal to the product of A's and the ratio of their respective marginal propensities to import. The world's total-income-multiplier will be the sum of A's and B's, which reduces to the sum of the two marginal propensities to import divided by the product of A's marginal propensity to save and B's marginal propensity to import; if the two import propensities are approximately equal this will be approxi-

174

mately double A's total-income-multiplier. Note that A's total-income-multiplier is invariant with respect to its own marginal propensity to import and with respect to both of B's marginal leakages, that B's is invariant with respect with its own marginal propensity to save but not with respect to either one of A's marginal leakages, and that their sum (the world total) is invariant to B's marginal propensity to save.

The values for Phase VI can be found in the same way as those for Phase V by interchanging the roles of A and B. Phase VII is then found by adding Phases V and VI. If we retain the assumption of zero marginal external-reserve ratios and postulate that B also initiates income-supporting expenditures equal to A's, as in Phase VI of Table 8.1, then in the final position (Phase VII) the world total-income-multiplier becomes the arithmetic mean of its Phase V and Phase VI values. More generally, if A's and B's initiatives are quantitatively different, the combined Phase VII world total-income-multiplier will be the weighted arithmetic mean of the Phase V and the Phase VI values.

3. The External Repercussions of a Balance-of-Payments Initiative

3.1. A Numerical Example

Instead of undertaking a domestic income-supporting expansionary programme, suppose A takes action to effect an "improvement" of $1,000 in its balance of payments, either by expanding its exports or by diverting domestic spending from imports to domestic goods. Presumably the purpose will be either to stimulate the domestic economy or to end an exchange drain that threatens the viability of an existing support programme. We need not postulate what technique A uses—import tariffs or quotas, export subsidies, exchange-rate depreciation or devaluation, or what—but we may specify that the monetary values in the table are in terms of a common *numeraire* after allowing for any change in exchange rates that may have been involved. Essentially the same principles apply as in the income-supporting sequence, but the results are complicated by the negative impact on B's income.

Table 8.2 illustrates what will happen. In Phase I A achieves a net gain of income amounting to $3,333 and a net gain of reserves amounting to $333, which means that B suffers a net loss of $333 in both export earnings and exchange reserves. If B initially reacts passively then at Phase II(1) its export multiplier produces a loss of income of $833, and consequently a reduction of $250 in imports. This sets off a contractionary sequence which ends with a loss of income of $1,667 for each of A and B at Phase II(5). Combining Phases I and II as before, we find that at Phase III A has lost half its initial gain of income and reserves and B has lost as much

175

Table 8.2. An Illustration of Balance-of-Payments Repercussions

Phase or Period	A's Economy				B's Economy			
	Exports (1)	Income (2)	Imports (3)	Reserves (4)	Exports (5)	Income (6)	Imports (7)	Reserves (8)
I	1,000	3,333	667	+333	−333			−333
II(1)	−250	−833	−167	−250	−167	−833	−250	+250
II(2)	−125	−417	−83	+167	+83	−417	−125	−167
II(3)				−125				+125
II(4)				+83				−83
⋮								
II(5) = $\sum_1^\infty$	−500	−1,667	−333	−167	−333	−1,667	−500	+167
III = I+II	500	1,667	333	+167	−667	−1,667	−500	−167
IV	−500	−1,667	−333	−167	−333	−1,667	−500	+167
V = III+IV	0	0	0	0	−1,000	−3,333	−1,000	0
VI	−1,000	−5,000	−1,000	0	0	0	0	0
VII = V+VI	−1,000	−5,000	−1,000	0	−1,000	−3,333	−1,000	0

Notes. Marginal propensities are as in Table 8.1. In Phase I A's expansion is generated by the diversion of $1,000 in spending from B (an increase in A's exports or a decrease in imports). In Phase II the contraction at each step is generated by the export multiplier operating on the net loss of exports in the preceding step. In Phase IV a step-by-step contraction is generated as the reverse of the expansion illustrated in the same phase of Table 8.1. Phase VI repeats Phase V for a retaliatory trade diversion of $1,000 by B.

income and as much reserves as A has gained.[10]

Now (Phase IV) suppose B is constrained to deflate its economy in order to end the drain on its foreign-exchange reserves. By a process that is just exactly the reverse of that set out in the corresponding phase of Table 8.1, B must deflate its income by $1,667, i.e. until its imports are reduced relative to its exports by an amount equal to its reserve drain in Phase III. This will reduce its imports (and hence A's exports) by $500, which will cause a deflation of $1,667 in A's income and a reduction of $333 in A's imports. On balance, therefore, B loses exports of only $333 but loses imports of $500 in this phase, for a net gain of reserves of $167.

The overall result of Phase V, therefore, is that the initial "improvement" in A's balance of payments is reduced to zero, and the net effect of its action is to reduce B's exports (and imports) by the amount of the initial "improvement" A achieved in Phase I(1). This of course entails a loss of $3,333 of income to B, which is the product of A's initial trade diversion and the reciprocal of B's marginal propensity to import.

As in the income-expansion case, the outcome in Phase IV will be materially modified if B alters its foreign-exchange reserves in a fixed ratio to increases and decreases in its accumulated financial assets. Just as in Table 8.1 an increase in the reserve ratio brought a reduction in Phase IV of the expansion, so in this case it brings a reduction in the contraction: some of the foreign exchange that must be given up is released from previously-required reserves as B's stock of financial assets is reduced. If the reserve ratio is zero the results are as in Phase V of the table; if 100 per cent, they are unchanged from Phase III; if between zero and 100 per cent, there will be an intermediate additional contraction.

Now suppose that, instead of passively accepting the adverse effects of A's attempt to "improve" its balance-of-payments position, B decides to retaliate in kind. On the same assumptions as before, including the assumption that A is impelled to deflate in the same way as B did in Phase IV, in the end B will achieve neither an increase in income nor an improvement in its balance of payments but A will lose exports of $1,000 and its income will thereby be deflated by $5,000. At the end of this compound sequence of events (Phase VII) neither country achieves an "improvement" in its balance-of-payments position but each suffers a loss of income amounting to the product of the other's diversion of trade and the reciprocal of its own marginal propensity to import.

---

[10] It is a matter of hypothesis that B's loss of reserves is equal to A's gain, but it is merely a coincidence that B's loss of income in Phase II is the same as A's and half A's gain in Phase I; with different values for the various marginal propensities these proportions might be greater or less.

3.2. Policy Considerations

Trade-diversion tactics have long been known as beggar-my-neighbour[11] policies, whose principal intent is to export unemployment. They invite retaliation, benefit no one, and harm everyone.

In a deflationary context A does gain somewhat in Phase III, and B will be well advised not to permit a credit deflation (as in Phase IV) if it can possibly sustain the persistent exchange loss that A's action has saddled it with: the result will be only to reduce its own domestic income still further, for which the elimination of A's ill-gotten gains will be poor compensation. Indeed B might be very well follow the enlightened policy of expanding its domestic spending stream, as we supposed A did in Phase I of Table 8.1. That will aid A also, thus returning good for evil, but B's reward is a further drain on its foreign-exchange reserves. At best, if A responds as we supposed B did in Phase IV of Table 8.1, this new drain on B's reserves will disappear; but B will still be left with the original drain inflicted by A, and under the circumstances A seems unlikely to agree to any rational way of ending it. Sooner or later, therefore, B is likely to decide to emulate A and endeavour to export some of its unemployment.

However, a combination of expansion at home with trade-diversion against B might be a rational policy for A under certain conditions (or a corresponding combination for B). Suppose both A and B are experiencing underemployment conditions, but B refuses to participate in a joint programme of expansion and does not permit any credit expansion at Phase IV. A would then find itself with a persistent exchange drain at the rate of $333 per period, which it might not be able to sustain indefinitely, and would be adding to B's income at the rate of $3,333 per period (Phase III of Table 8.1). Now let A undertake a trade diversion, as in Table 8.2, sufficient to end its exchange drain. In terms of our numerical example it would require a diversion of $2,000 to improve A's position by $333, assuming that B did not impose a credit deflation on itself (which seems a reasonable assumption, since B has failed to permit a credit expansion on the basis of its original gain in reserves). This would give A a net income of $10,000, yet leave B no worse off then before—B would get new exports of $2,000 from A's increased income and imports, just replacing the exports lost through A's trade-diversion initiative.

If B is experiencing inflationary pressures at home it may welcome A's initiative, as long as it brings no material increase in its own unemployment level. However, it is quite probable that the effect will be felt more as a reduction of output and employment than as an easing of price pressures,

---

[11] Presumably reflecting today's greater permissiveness towards words that used not to be seen in print, someone has rechristened this phenomenon the "bugger-my-neighbour" policy.

and B can not permit this to go very far—presumably it already has as much unemployment as it can tolerate under the circumstances. It would therefore appear that B will be quite as ready to retaliate against A's efforts to divert trade in an inflationary context as in a deflationary context.

3.3. Algebraic Formulation

Diversion of one unit of imports to domestic production, which may be treated as an exogenous increase of exports for A and a like loss of exports for B at Phase I, generates $Y_{a_i}=1/(m_a+s_a)$ and $M_{a_i}=m_a/(m_a+s_a)$; this produces $R_{a_i}=1-m_a/(m_a+s_a)=s_a/(m_a+s_a)$, and $R_{b_i}=-R_{a_i}$; it also means a like net loss of income for B. B's export multiplier then generates $Y_{b_{ii1}}=-s_a/(m_a+s_a).1/(m_b+s_b)$ and $M_{b_{ii1}}=-s_a/(m_a+s_a).m_b/(m_b+s_b)$ at II(1), thus producing $X_{a_{ii1}}=M_{b_{ii1}}$. Hence $Y_{a_{ii2}}=-s_a/(m_a+s_a).m_b/(m_b+s_b).1/(m_a+s_a)$, $M_{a_{ii2}}=-s_a/(m_a+s_a).m_b/(m_b+s_b).m_a/(m_a+s_a)$, and $Y_{b_{ii3}}=-s_a/(m_a+s_a).m_b/(m_b+s_b).m_a/(m_a+s_a).1/(m_b+s_b)$. Thus in Phase II of Table 8.2 the common ratio is the same as in Table 8.1, i.e. $m_a/(m_a+s_a).m_b/(m_b+s_b)$, and each series in this phase can be summed by multiplying the initial term by $(m_a+s_a)(m_b+s_b)/K$, where $K=m_a.s_b+s_a.m_b+s_a.s_b$ (as in section 2.3 above); $Y_{a_{ii5}}=-s_a.m_b/(m_a+s_a)K$, $Y_{b_{ii5}}=-s_a/K$, etc., and $R_{a_{ii5}}=X_{a_{ii5}}-M_{a_{ii5}}=-s^2{}_a.m_b/(m_a+s_a)K$. At Phase III, i.e. I + II(5), $Y_{a_{iii}}=s_b/K$, $Y_{b_{iii}}=-s_a/K$, and $R_{a_{iii}}=s_a.s_b/K$.

If B deflates because of its exchange loss and A accepts the consequent erosion of the "improvement" in its balance-of-payments position achieved in Phase III then in Phase IV B must "improve" its balance-of-payments position by the amount of reserves lost in Phase III *less* the reserves that will be released from the deflation of its previously-accumulated savings. This can be derived by the same step-by-step sequence as in Phase II, starting with a deflation that attempts to reduce imports by the amount of the reserve deficiency at Phase III. Alternatively, the equilibrium position (Phase V) can be calculated from the postulate that if $R_{b_v}=r$. S_{b_v} then $X_{b_v}-M_{b_v}=r$. S_{b_v}. From this, paralleling the procedure in the income-supporting case, we can derive $Y_{b_{iv}}=-s_a$. $s_b(m_a+s_a)(1-r)/K(r.m_a.s_b+s_a.m_b+r.s_a.s_b)$ and $Y_{a_{iv}}=-s_a.m_b.s_b(1-r)/K(r.m_a.s_b+s_a.m_b+r.s_a.s_b)$. If $r=0$ these reduce to $Y_{a_{iv}}=-s_b/K$ and

179

$Y_{b_{iv}} = -s_b(m_a+s_a)/m_b.K$, and by addition of Phases III and IV we get $Y_{a_v}=(s_b-s_b)/K=0$ and $Y_{b_v}=-s_a/K-s_b(m_a+s_a)/m_b.K=-1/m_b$ for Phase V. Phase VI is derived in the same way as Phase V, with B instead of A initiating a trade diversion; and Phase VII is the sum of Phases V and VI.

CHAPTER 9

THE CREATION OF EXTERNAL RESERVES

1. Loans between Central Banks

1.1. A Numerical Example

The world's supply of international monies and close substitutes therefore is expanded when one central bank borrows from another. In principle the increase is temporary, of course, and will be reversed when the loan is repaid, but in the meantime it may have important effects on the world's reserves and on the generation of money-income. Furthermore these economic effects are essentially the same whether it is generally-accepted international money that is created (i.e. if the lending central bank is a key-currency issuer) or whether the newly-created claims take some other form, since the borrowing central bank gets access to international reserves in one way or another whereas even if the lending central bank directly or indirectly lends some of its own reserves it will not feel constrained to take the restrictive domestic actions it might if its reserves were depleted by an equivalent drain through the foreign-exchange market.

Several techniques are available by which one central bank may extend credit to another. The lending bank may rediscount commercial or other bills for the borrowing bank, buy securities or other assets from its portfolio or buy up the borrower's currency in the foreign-exchange market (presumably under the terms of a repurchase agreement); or it may simply make a deposit in its own currency with the borrowing bank. These various techniques involve somewhat different accounting entries on the books of the banks in question, but the net effect on the lending bank is either to increase its monetary liabilities and its assets by the same amount or to reduce one asset (e.g. gold bullion, or claims on a third central bank) and to increase another (e.g. claims against the borrowing bank, or assets acquired from it); and the net effect on the borrowing bank is to increase its holdings of either the lender's currency or a third currency, and simultaneously to reduce some other asset or incur some new liability. For simplicity, however, let us suppose that each bank records the transaction as equivalent additions to its assets and its liabilities, even though when the loan is denominated in a third country's currency the lending bank must be prepared to see its own reserves promptly depleted by virtually the full amount of its loan, just as if it were a domestic commercial bank lending to a commercial customer.

Table 9.1 uses a set of T-square accounts to illustrate lending by both key-currency and non-key-currency central banks, and to compare the

Table 9.1. Loans Between Central Banks: A Schematic Illustration[1]

		(1)	(2)	(3)	(4)	(5)	(6)	(7)
COUNTRY A—Borrower								
Central Bank of A								
A Gold	1			−100				−100
Due from: Central Bank of B	2	+£ 50	+100		−100			—
Central Bank of C	3	+£ 50	+100			−100		—
Domestic assets	4						+300*	+300
L Due to: Central Bank of B	5	+£ 50	+100					+100
Central Bank of C	6	+£ 50	+100					+100
Domestic banks	7			−100	−100	−100	+300	—
Commercial Banks in A								
A Primary reserves	8			−100	−100	−100	+300	—
L Deposits	9			−100*	−100*	−100*	+300	—
COUNTRY B—Lender[2]								
Central Bank of B								
A Gold	10			+ 40				+ 40
Due from: Central Bank of A	11	+$100	+100					+100
Domestic assets	12						−120?*	−120?
L Due to: Central Bank of A	13	+$100	+100		−100	{ −100		—
Central Bank of C	14				+ 60	+ 60 }		+ 20
Domestic banks	15			+ 40	+ 40	+ 40	−120?	—?
Commercial Banks in B								
A Primary reserves	16			+ 40	+ 40	+ 40	−120?	—?
L Deposits	17			+ 40	+ 40	+ 40	−120?	—?
COUNTRY C—Lender								
Central Bank of C								
A Gold	18			+ 60				+ 60
Due from: Central Bank of A	19	+DM200	+100					+100
Central Bank of B	20				+ 60	{ −100		+ 20
Domestic assets	21					+ 60 }	−180?*	−180?
L Due to: Central Bank of A	22	+DM200	+100		−100			—
Domestic banks	23			+ 60	+ 60	+ 60	−180?	—?
Commercial Banks in C								
A Primary reserves	24			+ 60	+ 60	+ 60	−180?	—?
L Deposits	25			+ 60	+ 60	+ 60	−180?	—?
MEMORANDA:								
International monies[3]	26		+200	—	− 40	−140	—	+ 20
International liquid assets[4]	27		+400	—	− 40	−140	—	+220

[1] The Central Bank of A borrows $100 from the Central Bank of B and $100 from the Central Bank of C in columns 1 (where they are recorded in local currency) and 2 (converted into dollars as a *numeraire*), then draws down and spends pre-existing gold reserves in column 3, B's loan in column 4, and C's loan in column 5. In column 6 all three central banks undertake offsetting open-market operations. Column 7 records the cumulative results. The initiator of a sequence is indicated by *.

[2] A key-currency country. [3] Gold plus key-currency holdings of non-residents of B; lines 1+2−3+10 +18+20. [4] International monies plus official claims repayable in key currencies; lines 26+11+19.

results with what would happen if the borrowing central bank simply ran down its pre-existing reserves; the currency of the borrowing country (A) is designated as the pound (£), that of the key-currency country (B) as the dollar ($), and that of the second lender (C) as the deutschemark (DM), on the arbitrary assumption that £1 = $2 = DM4 on the exchange market. In column 1 the Central Bank of A borrows $100 from the Central Bank of B and a further $100 from the Central Bank of C, though the Central Bank of C's entries would be essentially the same if the second loan were denominated in deutschemarks. Each lender simply writes up a liability item "due to" and an asset item "due from" the Central Bank of A, while the Central Bank of A makes corresponding entries "due from" and "due to" its creditors. By hypothesis each loan is denominated in dollars,[1] but naturally each bank keeps its accounts in its own currency. For clarity, however, all these amounts are converted into dollars as a common *numeraire* in column 2, and this practice is followed in the subsequent columns.

Columns 1 and 2 bring out an important aspect of interbank borrowing: you can't tell from their balance sheets alone which bank is lending to which, nor what currency the loan is denominated in. All banks solicit correspondent and other balances "due to" other banks, and in turn hold correspondent and other balances "due from" other banks, and all bank deposits are basically debtor-creditor relationships even though they are not normally looked on by either party as loans; when one bank does lend to another, therefore, it is likely to appear on both balance sheets as simply an exchange of deposits. In fact real-life balance sheets may be much less revealing than our schematic ones; no distinction may be made between balances due from banks abroad and banks at home, and balances due to other banks at home and abroad may not be distinguished from other deposits. However, the banks themselves will know all right. The lending

---

[1] Presumably this will suit the Central Bank of B best for its loan, and the borrower will have little choice but to agree. The Central Bank of C might have preferred to denominate its loan in deutschemarks as a protection against a possible depreciation of the dollar, to which the borrower could hardly object as long as deutschemarks were either freely convertible into dollars or readily acceptable for international settlements. Another possibility is that the Central Bank of C may denominate its loan in dollars, as here assumed, but transfer them immediately to the Central Bank of A on the books of the Central Bank of B. A third possibility is that C's currency may be accepted by A and used to pay for imports from C; the net effect, however, is simply to displace key-currency earnings C would otherwise have made, so there will be no difference in substance. A fourth possibility is that C's currency may be used for purchases in D, E, ... if the payees in those countries so agree. To the extent this occurs C's currency becomes an international money; but it may be so accepted primarily because it can be promptly used by the recipients to make payments in C, so its international-money status may be limited in both amount and duration. More complex arrangements may also be negotiated to meet particular needs, e.g. simultaneous spot and forward transactions in one or more currencies.

and the borrowing bank will each know that the latter is likely to draw down its balance due from the former promptly, otherwise it would not have had to borrow, and each will know that the former is unlikely to draw down its balance due from the latter before its scheduled maturity unless there is an unexpected change in their relative positions.[2] In our example the Central Bank of A needs dollars and deutschemarks to enable its commercial banks and their customers to make payments in B and C, but residents of B and C can get all of A's currency they want in the market.

It may be noted that alternative lending techniques that provide the Central Bank of A with the same volume of usable external reserves may result in the creation of a significantly-different volume of international monies and other forms of international liquid assets. The technique illustrated in Table 9.1 results in the creation of $200 of international money and $200 of other liquid assets, as shown in the memorandum accounts (lines 26 and 27) at the foot of column 2. Had the Central Bank of C's loan been denominated in deutschemarks instead of dollars the volume of liquid assets created would still have been $400, but the volume of international monies would have been only $100 since by hypothesis the deutschemark is not an international money; and had the Central Bank of C directly transferred dollars to the Central Bank of A the figures would have been $300 and $100 respectively. However, these differences are purely a reflection of accounting conventions and the necessarily-arbitrary definition of what is and what is not an international money; it is unlikely that they would make any significant difference in the actions of any of the participants.

1.2. Phase I Repercussions

We may interpret columns 1 and 2 of Table 9.1 as representing merely precautionary borrowing to end or forestall a speculative run on A's currency even though its balance of payments is essentially in equilibrium, in which case we may disregard the remaining columns as irrelevant. It is more instructive, however, to suppose that the borrowed reserves are intended to permit the continuance of domestic policies in support of full employment or other domestic economic goals by meeting the resultant external drain over some given period of time. It is only as reserves are actually drawn down and spent that there will be any identifiable effect on incomes and income-related variables at home and abroad.

Columns 3, 4, and 5 represent the start of the series of external reper-

---

[2] All of this applies to commercial banks as well as central banks, and most of the techniques of interbank borrowing discussed above also apply.

cussions thus set in motion, and are analogous to the sequence depicted in Phase I of Table 8.1 above. As a result of A's domestic-income-supporting measures its residents pay £150 ($300) more for imports and net capital transfers than they receive in exports over some finite period; they draw down their balances at their commercial banks (line 9) to buy the foreign exchange, and their banks draw down their reserve balances at the Central Bank of A (lines 7 and 8) to obtain the exchange for their customers. In its turn the Central Bank of A draws down its pre-existing gold holdings and its two external loans (lines 1, 2, and 3) to meet these drawings. If we interpret our model as a three-country world we may then postulate that A's external payments are made to B and C in the ratio of, say, 2:3. Residents of B will want to be paid in dollars and residents of C in deutschemarks, but by hypothesis the Central Bank of A can obtain either currency in exchange for gold, or can pay out dollars directly from and buy deutschemarks out of its balance due from the Central Banks of B and C, thereby providing its commercial banks and their customers with the appropriate currencies.

Payments made to exporters in B and C will be deposited with their commercial bankers (lines 17 and 25), thus adding to the latters' primary reserves (lines 15 and 16 in B, 23 and 24 in C). Regardless of how it is financed, every £50 of A's deficit will add $40 to the bank deposits of residents of B (line 17), $60 to the external reserves of the Central Bank of C (lines 14 and 20), and DM120 to the bank deposits of residents of C (line 25); but the method of financing the deficit does affect the world supply of international money and international liquidity. If reserves are held and payments made in gold or some other commodity-money or in some claim whose total is independently determined, as in line 1, 10, and 18 of column 3, there can be no change in the world supply of international money or liquidity attributable to that payment (lines 26 and 27). (Had the Central Bank of A borrowed gold instead of dollars in column 1 then of course there would have been an increase in the world supply of international liquidity, even though there would have been no increase in international money, but there would be no change attributable to payments made with the gold.) If settlement is made in a credit-based international money, however, there may well be changes in both totals, The Indestructibility Principle notwithstanding; and the ultimate results will be identical regardless of how the credit-based money is obtained.

Any net payment by residents of A to residents of B that is effected in B's currency (line 17) brings a transfer of the Central Bank of B's monetary obligations from nonresidents to the domestic cash reserves of B's commercial banks, as the Central Bank of A either draws directly on its own reserves (line 13 of column 4) or draws down its loan from the Central Bank of C (first entry in line 14 of column 5), thereby converting international monetary balances into domestic monetary balances. (In column 5 there is a further reduction of $100 in international money and international liquidity, but this is merely a reversal of the temporary creation of offshore-dollar balances on the books of the Central Bank of C; it would not have occurred if the loan had been denominated in deutschemarks and only converted into dollars as the Central Bank of A drew it down to meet its external drain, or if the dollar balances at the Central Bank of B had been transferred immediately to the credit of the Central Bank of A.)

Note that the entries in column 4 will be exactly the same if the Central Bank of A is drawing down previously-existing balances of its own instead of newly-borrowed funds, or if it is spending dollars obtained by the sale of gold. The shrinkage of international monies and liquidity in this fashion is a thoroughly healthy phenomenon: it is a concrete illustration of the self-cancelling mechanism that converts excess holdings of a key currency (or any other currency) into goods and services in a smoothly-functioning world, as discussed in section 3.3 of Chapter 7 above. The bad news comes only when we turn to a world in which The Fearsome Dilemma rears its ugly head, as in section 1.4 below.

1.3. Phases II and IV with Optimistic Assumptions

Presumably A can not allow the deficit in its commercial-banks' primary reserves (lines 7 and 8 of columns 3, 4, and 5) to precipitate a credit contraction, otherwise it would not be constrained to pursue the domestic-income-supporting measures that led to the external drain, so in column 6 of Table 9.1 its central bank must undertake offsetting open-market operations (lines 4 and 7). What happens thereafter depends mainly on conditions in B and C. As a first (optimistic) hypothesis let us suppose that both B and C are successfully maintaining full employment and stable prices; accordingly their central banks also undertake offsetting open-market operations (lines 12 and 21) to forestall any expansion in Phases II and IV, which would presumably have inflationary domestic effects.

Column 7 summarizes the cumulative results. In effect the Central Bank of A has converted $300 of external assets into domestic assets; the Central Bank of C has converted domestic assets into external assets to the amount of 60 per cent of A's deficit; and the Central Bank of B has not only converted domestic into external assets equivalent to 40 per cent of A's deficit but also added a further $20 to its external assets and a like sum to its external liabilities. The world supply of international money is $20 greater than it was when the Central Bank of A began to borrow, and international assets have grown by an additional $200 (i.e. by the claims the Central Banks of B and C now have against the Central Bank of A).

More generally, the world supply of international *money* will be increased by C's portion of A's deficit that is paid for in a credit-based currency obtained by borrowing (or by running down previously-held balances), and will be decreased by the spending of any key-currency loan from the Central Bank of C to the Central Bank of A. Alternatively, and equivalently, it will be increased by the Central Bank of B's loan to the Central Bank of A, but decreased by the portion of A's deficit that becomes unrequited exports for B. This may work out to a net reduction if C's share of world trade is relatively small (B's unrequited exports are relatively large), C's loan relatively large, or B's loan relatively small. The world supply of international *liquidity* will be increased by the sum of all loans from the Central Banks of B and C to the Central Bank of A, plus the increase (or minus the decrease) in the supply of international money.

In addition, of course, B and C will gain international reserves to the amount of any portion of its deficit that A pays for in gold or similar assets. If either B or C or both purchase gold from A, the immediate effect for all three will be merely an exchange of one foreign asset for another. As A spends the proceeds, however, they will in part be extinguished for B's unrequited exports and will in part accrue to the Central Bank of C, where they may be seen to be available for further loans to A.

The situation represented in column 7 of Table 9.1 is analogous to that at the end of Phase I in Table 8.1 above, since the repercussions in Phases II and IV have been suppressed. Both B and C can sustain their positions indefinitely, but A must effect some structural readjustment in its economy if it is to achieve full equilibrium (unless it has suffered a merely-temporary setback). However, since by hypothesis B and C are able to maintain both full employment and stable prices, the presumption is that A should sooner or later be able to end its external deficit without prejudicing its domestic objectives; presumably it is using the time it is buying through foreign borrowing to make whatever re-allocation of resources is necessary. Under the postulated conditions we may also suppose that any consequential adjustments in the trade and resource-allocation patterns of B and C can be accommodated without too much difficulty, so we have the optimistic scenario described on pages 171f above, and a viable equilibrium is possible for the trading world as a whole.

1.4. Phases II and IV with Pessimistic Assumptions

As a second and more pessimistic hypothesis let us suppose that B or C, or both, are having difficulty achieving their employment and price-stability objectives simultaneously. This makes the situation more fluid, and no pat solution can be offered; that is the reason for the questionmarks after certain entries in columns 6 and 7 of Table 9.1. We may add a further postulate that conditions are approximately similar in both B and C: each faces The Fearsome Dilemma in about the same severity, and each is getting its usual share of world exports. Each will be reluctant to forgo the expansionary effects normally associated with an export surplus, and will presumably be more willing to risk some increase in price-pressures than if its balance-of-payments position were weaker. This again is analogous to Phases II and IV of Table 8.1, but in this case it is likely that at least some and perhaps a good deal of the credit expansion there illustrated will be permitted to occur.

A third and still more pessimistic hypothesis has conditions materially worse in the key-currency country, B. To take an extreme case, suppose that B's exports have become noncompetitive at the margin on world markets. A's external deficit will be directed to C, and when the Central Bank of A runs down its key-currency balances, as in columns 4 and 5 of Table 9.1, the entire proceeds will accrue to C (and therefore to the Central Bank of C's balance due from the Central Bank of B) and none will accrue to commercial banks in B: lines 26 and 27 of column 7 will read $+100$ and $+300$ respectively. (At this point it is irrelevant how the Central Bank of A gets the key-currency balances it runs down—whether by borrowing, by the sale of assets, or from pre-existing balances of its own.) If C finds its key-currency holdings greater than it needs, the only way it can use them up is by finding some fourth country willing to accept them in payment for exports; but the implication is that other countries will also have more of the key currency than they need. This leads back to the discussion of key-currency-country deficits in sections 3.3 of Chapter 7 above.

1.5. Algebraic Formulation

There is not much purpose in setting up a general algebraic representation of negotiating and recording a loan agreement between two central banks; that has more to do with accounting conventions and banking practices than with economics, and an *ad hoc* algebraic formulation of a particular arrangement can easily be derived if desired. In Table 9.1, for example, the Central Banks of B and C create deposit balances in favour of the Central Bank of A, denominated in the key currency and equal to their respective loans, which may be designated L_1 and L_2 respectively; the world supply of international monies is thereby increased by L_1 and L_2, and international liquid assets by the same sum plus the lending banks' counter-claims on the borrowing bank or a total of $2(L_1+L_2)$. Had the Central Bank of C simply bought up a corresponding amount of A's currency, or immediately transferred to the Central Bank of A a sum equal to L_2 from its claims on the Central Bank of B, the world supply of international monies would have increased by only L_1 and international liquidity by $2L_1+L_2$; the immediate effect is different, but when C's loan is actually drawn down the difference disappears.

The numerical illustration in Table 9.1 may be generalized to include the drawing-down and spending of pre-existing reserves in key currencies as well as gold and borrowed funds. Let G be the Central Bank of A's loss of pre-existing holdings of gold and other fixed-supply international monies, L_0 the loss of pre-existing holdings of the credit-based key currency, L_1 the amount borrowed from the Central Bank of B and spent, and L_2 the amount borrowed from the Central Bank of C and spent; by hypothesis, A's balance-of-payments deficit is $G+L_0+L_1+L_2$. Now let n be the portion of A's deficit spent in B and $(1-n)$ the portion spent in C (or divided among all the remaining members of the trading world, namely C, D, E, . . .), subject to the constraint that $0 \leq n \leq 1$. As the Central Bank of A draws down and spends its loan from the Central Bank of C (column 5 in the table) the latter must draw down a like sum from the Central Bank of B, which immediately reduces the international money supply and international liquidity by the amount of L_2, but this merely reverses the temporary expansion that occurred when the Central Bank of C chose to write up its loan on its own books rather than transfer some of its own key-currency balances to the Central Bank of A immediately.

If the Central Bank of A draws on its gold reserves to meet its deficit then the Central Bank of B will receive nG and the Central Bank of C will receive $(1-n)G$, and each will add the gold it receives to its assets as well as crediting its commercial banks with an equivalent addition to their reserves. If payment is made in B's currency B's commercial banks will receive the same credit to their reserve accounts, but it will take the form of a simple transfer on the books of the Central Bank of B of an equivalent amount previously due to the Central Bank of A, so the sum of $n(L_0+L_1+L_2)$ will be converted from international money to domestic money. At the same time, however, A's key-currency payments to C will remain in the category of international money, in the form of a transfer on the books on the Central Bank of B amounting to $(1-n)(L_0+L_1+L_2)$, and the Central Banks of A and C's pre-existing balances due from the Central Bank of B will be reduced by L_0 and L_2 respectively. The net change in the world's supply of international monies (which will be entirely in credit-based components, and will equal the net change in the Central Bank of B's balance due to the Central Banks of A and C since by hypothesis any induced change in its domestic liabilities is offset by open-market operations) will therefore be $(1-n)(L_0+L_1+L_2)-L_0-L_2$, which reduces to $L_1-n(L_0+L_1+L_2)$ and is positive if $n < L_1 / (L_0+L_1+L_2)$. The net change in international liquidity is the net change in international monies plus the Central Banks of B and C's claims on the Central Bank of A (i.e. L_1+L_2) or $2L_1+L_2-(1-n)(L_0+L_1+L_2)$ and is positive if $n < (2L_1 + L_2) / (L_0+L_1+L_2)$. The net change in the Central Bank of C's key-currency reserves reduces to $L_0+L_1-n(L_0+L_1+L_2)$ and is positive if $n < (L_0+L_1) / (L_0+L_1+L_2)$.

Table 9.2. Drawings on the I.M.F. General-Resources Account: Schematic Illustrations[1]

Central-Bank Accounts	Lending by B				Lending by C			
	Reserve tr.		Credit tr.		Reserve tranche		Credit tranche	
	(1)	(2)	(3)	(4)	(5)	(6)	(7)	(8)

COUNTRY A—Borrower
Central Bank of A

		(1)	(2)	(3)	(4)	(5)	(6)	(7)	(8)
A	Foreign exchange	1 +100	+100	+100	+100	+100	+100	+100	+100
	IMF reserve position	2 −100		−100		−100		−100	
L	Use of IMF credit	3	+100		+100		+100		+100

COUNTRY B—Lender[1]
Central Bank of B

		(1)	(2)	(3)	(4)	(5)	(6)	(7)	(8)
A	IMF reserve position	4 +100	+100						
L	Monetary obligations to:								
	Central Bank of A[3]	5 +100	+100	+100	+100	(−100)	(−100)	(−100)	(−100)
	Central Bank of C[3]	6				(+100)	(+100)	(+100)	(+100)
	Use of IMF credit	7		−100	−100				

COUNTRY C—Lender
Central Bank of C

		(1)	(2)	(3)	(4)	(5)	(6)	(7)	(8)
A	Foreign exchange	8				−100	−100	−100	−100
	IMF reserve position	9				+100	+100		
L	Use of IMF credit	10						+100	+100

Memoranda:

		(1)	(2)	(3)	(4)	(5)	(6)	(7)	(8)
International money[4]		11 +100	+100	+100	+100	—	—	—	—
International reserves[5]		12 +100	+200	—	+100	—	+100	−100	—

[1] Columns 1, 3, 5, and 7 represent borrowings in A's reserve tranche, columns 2, 4, 6, and 8 in its credit tranche.

[2] A key-currency country.

[3] Merely accommodating transfers, honouring instructions from the Central Bank of C, are shown in parenthesis.

[4] Lines 1+8 or 5+6.

[5] Lines 1+2+4+9.

2. Using the Facilities of the I.M.F.

2.1. Drawings on the General Resources Account

Table 9.2 summarizes the various types of transactions that may be effected through what is now known as the General Resources Account of the International Monetary Fund, and the effects on the reserve-positions of members. In this case the various columns represent alternative types of Fund transactions;[3] they do not represent a sequence of events over time, nor show what use the borrowing nation makes of its newly-acquired reserves. Transactions are denominated in whatever you think is the most appropriate *numeraire* for a given period—U.S. dollars, gold, SDR's, or any new *numeraire* that may be devised in due course. In all cases A, a non-key-currency country, is the borrower and acquires foreign exchange from the Fund in exchange for its own relatively-soft currency.

In columns 1 to 4 inclusive the lender is B, a key-currency country, and in all four cases there is a net increase in international money by the amount of B's loan, because the Central Bank of B must expand its monetary obligations in order to redeem some part of its non-interest-bearing demand note payable to the Fund in order to honour its commitment to provide its currency to other members. If both A and B are operating in what are now their reserve tranches but were originally their gold (or super-gold) tranches, or within their reserve positions in the Fund[4] (column 1), or both in their credit tranches (column 4), there is no net change in Fund reserve positions, and therefore the total change in world reserves is equal to that in the supply of international money. However, if B is operating in its reserve tranche and A is operating in its credit tranche (column 2) there is a net increase in Fund reserve positions equal to the loan, and in the opposite case (column 3) there is a net decrease. The consequence is that, while the world supply of international *money* rises by the amount of B's loan in all four cases, total world *reserves* are unchanged in column 3, rise by the amount of the loan in columns 1 and 4, and rise by double the amount of the loan in column 2.

---

[3] Except for "Monetary Obligations to Banks", the balance-sheet items schematically illustrated in the table appear in the country pages of the monthly issues of the Fund's *International Financial Statistics* for each member country. In addition the Fund shows certain memorandum accounts which are not included in the table: the credit tranche position, distinguishing between stand-by credits and other credits; drawings outstanding, distinguishing among compensatory, buffer-stock, and other drawings; and the member's quota in the Fund.

[4] Strictly speaking the two terms were not synonymous: a member's "reserve position in the Fund" comprises its gold and super-gold tranche and its net lending to the Fund outstanding under the General Agreement to Borrow and under certain *ad hoc* arrangements with individual countries.

In columns 5 to 8 inclusive the lender is C, whose currency is relatively hard but not a key currency. There is no increase in the world supply of international money, because C merely transfers some of its existing balances in B's currency to A and receives credit at the Fund in exchange;[5] the entries in the accounts of the Central Bank of B depict merely accommodating transactions in response to the Central Bank of C's instructions, as has been indicated by putting the figures in parenthesis. If both A and C are in their reserve tranches (column 5) or both in their credit tranches (column 8) then there is no net change in Fund reserve positions, and total world reserves as well as the world money supply are unchanged. However, if A is in its credit tranche and C is in its reserve tranche (column 6) there is a net increase in Fund reserve positions (and therefore in world reserves) equal to the loan, whereas in the opposite case (column 7) there is an equal net decrease.

The table does not illustrate a drawing by a key-currency country. If B draws for balance-of-payments reasons, the implication is either that its currency has been displaced by another in the key-currency role or that it is voluntarily limiting the accumulation of its currency in the hands of non-residents; in either case B will replace A in the table and some other country (say, C) will replace B. However, a drawing by a strong key-currency country may be made for the sake of other members: reducing its reserve-tranche position will replenish the Fund's holdings of its currency. In that case B will draw down and hold a selection of other currencies in exchange for a reduction in its Fund reserve position. There will be no increase in the supply of international monies, no net change in B's reserve holdings, and no net increase in world reserves unless the countries whose currencies are drawn are in their reserve tranches, but that will be immaterial— the object of the exercise would be not to provide new world reserves directly but to permit renewed lending by the Fund.

To summarize, there is a net expansion of international monies when the lender is a key-currency country, but not otherwise. There is also an equal increase in Fund reserve positions if the lender but not the borrower is in

<hr>

[5]   Two important intermediate steps are omitted from the table, as they immediately cancel one another out. The first step is that the Central Bank of C must expand its monetary obligations in order to honour the Fund drawing, in exactly the way just described in the case of a direct drawing of B's currency. The second step is that the Central Bank of C immediately exchanges its own national currency for B's currency (i.e. cancels out its own new issue and transfers the equivalent amount of B's currency to A out of its own reserve balances). However, as an alternative the Central Bank of C may simply write up a balance due to the Central Bank of A, as in Table 9.1; in this case there will be a temporary further increase in international money, which will be reserved as the funds are drawn down and spent.

the reserve tranche, an equal decrease if the borrower but not the lender is in the reserve tranche, but no change if both lender and borrower are in the reserve tranche or the credit tranche. The change in world reserves may therefore vary from a decrease equal to the loan to an increase of double the loan.

2.2. Use of SDR's

There is of course a net increase in the external reserves or liquidity of each participating member country, and of the world as a whole, when SDR's are allocated—that is the object of the exercise. However, the direct use of SDR's for payments by one participant to another, as freely permitted under the Second Amendment to the Articles of Agreement (1978), is in all respects similar to a payment by the transfer of gold or any other form of owned reserves: there is no change in total world reserve holdings or liquidity.

Nevertheless the use of SDR's may still entail a net increase in world liquidity under some conditions, and normally did so after they were first introduced. The First Amendment (1969) put severe limitations on direct member-to-member transfers, and obligated the Fund to designate a trans-feree to provide a "currency convertible in fact" (now a "freely usable currency") when so requested by a member wishing to use its holdings of SDR's. That procedure is still an essential part of the system. A currency so obtained may be used either to make settlement directly or to acquire a second currency that can be so used. If the currency first obtained happens to be a recognized international money (B's currency in our example) then of course its use will have the effects illustrated in column 4 of Table 9.1, but if not (if it is C's currency) then it must be exchanged for some international money, as in column 5. This is as if a country wishing to use its reserves of gold (or for that matter silver or wheat or any other commo-dity) first sells them for B's or C's currency; whether additional inter-national reserves are or are not created at that stage depends on whether the commodity in question is recognized as a form of international money, but what happens thereafter will be independent of that rather arbitrary deter-mination.

Furthermore the SDR could become the vehicle for the further expan-sion of international liquidity if certain versions of the so-called " substi-tution account" that have been proposed from time to time are put into effect. One proposal is to allow members to voluntarily deposit officially-held key-currency reserves with the Fund in exchange for a new type of claim denominated in SDR's. This offers two possibilities for a greater-than-expected expansion of international liquidity. First, it might enshrine the continued monetization of key-currency balance-of-payments deficits. To counter that it would be necessary to deny access to the substitution account for any newly-acquired balances of key currencies after some agreed cut-off date. Even then inflation could continue for some time, because the amounts deposited would presumably be still-undigested reserves, unless the use of all or part of the claims in question could be frozen and only liquidated gradually over a suitable period of time. Conceivably this could be done as part of a self-denying international agreement by the major (or perhaps all) countries in the interests of international monetary reform, but not by voluntary participation. Second, if these difficulties were overcome and a primary expansion of the new SDR claims was accomplished, there might be a secondary expansion of the sort that may occur with the obligations of any financial intermediary.

Evidently it is *not* proposed to issue new SDR's in exchange for the key currencies deposited, but simply to provide depositors with claims *denominated* in SDR's. The distinction is largely irrelevant, as the simple model used in Chapter 1 above demonstrates. The critical questions would be (1) who would be entitled to hold these claims, and (2) why would they want to hold them? In the terminology introduced in Part One above, what would be the acceptance ratio of the new claims in terms of "SDR's proper", and what would be the coefficients of substitution between them and other forms of international liquidity? Voluntarily-acquired claims denominated in SDR's must be attractive to the holder and must be honoured according to the contract or they will be useless. Presumably the sole holders initially would be national monetary authorities, though a case can be made for wanting extensive holdings by private interests so the Fund, acting as a supracentral bank, could conduct open-market operations in them. Private holders might see them as attractive investments because they would offer a partial hedge against exchange-rate risks, but only if they paid a competitive interest rate and enjoyed a broad and active market; they might accept redemption in national currencies at current exchange rates, as they do now for existing private claims denominated in SDR's, but effective supracentral bank open-market operations would require that they be redeemable in SDR's or the equivalent. National monetary authorities might accept them as an alternative form of external reserves, competitive with gold, "SDR's proper", key currencies, and other reserve media, in which case much the same exchange-hedging and interest-return considerations would apply as for private holders; in addition, however, they would need to be assured that they could liquidate their claims for "SDR's proper" or some other acceptable reserve medium when needed for balance-of-payments reasons. Thus the new claims must be good substitutes for "SDR's proper", and they must be suitable vehicles for borrowing-and-lending contracts—certainly between entities in the private sector, and presumably between national central banks or other monetary authorities as well. Therefore all the requirements for a credit expansion through these SDR claims will exist, closely paralleling the primitive model of credit expansion presented in section 2.2 of Chapter 1 above: a model in which the financial intermediary's obligations need not be "money".

2.3. Spending the Foreign Exchange Obtained though the I.M.F.

If A spends the foreign exchange it obtains through its access to either the General Resources Account or the SDR-designation procedures of the International Monetary Fund, as distinct from merely holding it for precautionary reasons, the results are identical with those of using any similar form of reserves obtained in any other way. In particular, the world's supplies of both international monies and international reserves will be reduced by the amount paid over to the residents of key-currency countries for unrequited exports, as illustrated in column 4 of Table 9.1.

Under the optimistic assumptions of section 1.3 above, B and C will continue to add to their external reserves as long as A's deficit continues, but this will eventually be ended or even reversed by corrective domestic measures in A, perhaps aided by complementary adjustments in B and C. Under the pessimistic assumptions of section 1.4, however, no mutually-acceptable solutions may be found. In terms of Table 9.1, The Fearsome Dilemma may prevent A from correcting its balance-of-payments position, and may also prevent B and C from fully offsetting the inflationary impact on their economies (column 6). The outlook becomes even more pessimistic if B is experiencing balance-of-payments difficulties as well as A; this will tend to ease A's balance-of-payments problem, but probably at the cost of intensified inflationary pressures, and will mean that C must finance not only all of A's deficit but B's as well.

2.4. Influence on Domestic Policy Decisions

In principle the effects of the expansion of international reserves through the General Resources Account of the Fund are closely parallel to those of the expansion of reserves through swaps and other forms of lending between central banks or through other international credit transactions, but institutionalizing these credit arrangements through the Fund does introduce an important new element. The Fund is an international financial intermediary, and it alters the nature of the obligations of ultimate borrowers to primary lenders at the international level just as a domestic bank or other financial intermediary does at the domestic level. When the Central Bank of B lends directly to the Central Bank of A, as in columns 1 and 2 in Table 9.1, what is receives in exchange is a claim against a particular soft-currency country; it is unlikely to consider such a claim as an addition to its useable reserves, or to be more lenient in its domestic policies because of it. But when the Central Bank of B lends to the Central Bank of A through the intermediacy of the Fund as in column 1 of Table 9.2 the claim it receives is fully recognized by all parties as an eminently respectable reserve asset, and its holding of that asset may very well lead it to a more relaxed stance in its domestic monetary policy.[6]

Nor is that the end of the matter. All member countries may quite properly look to their claims to Fund credit, qualified as they may be by the need to justify drawings in the credit tranches, as being reliably available to meet real balance-of-payments needs; that was the purpose behind providing these facilities in the first place. Thus they will be ready to consider these credits as reasonably good substitutes for owned reserves for precautionary and even for speculative purposes as distinct from transactions purposes. In other words these credit facilities make a member nation content to see its owned reserves decline somewhat below the level it would otherwise wish to maintain.

3. Key-Currency Borrowings

Just as domestic commercial banks can borrow reserves and thereby expand the domestic money supply or avoid contracting it, so the international community can borrow reserves and thereby expand the world supply or prevent a decline. In the domestic case the borrowed reserves are at the discretion of the central bank, which has adequate powers to eliminate or reduce them if that is what current economic policies call for (keeping in mind the difficulties of attaining multiple policy goals simultaneously), but in the international case there is as yet no responsible body with the authority to decide what level of external reserves is appropriate for the world at large or with the power to contain the supply within any limit that might be set or agreed upon. For borrowings between central banks or between a national authority and the I.M.F., explored in sections 1 and 2 of this chapter, there is nevertheless some degree of international control: these borrowings and lendings are in the hands of presumably-responsible officials who ought to be well aware of the economic implications of their actions, and the procedures that govern the transactions are regulated by explicit or implicit international agreements. These procedures are not foolproof, but they do make some attempt at taking account of

---

[6] Drawings are actually taken in national currencies because that is what is currently required for participating in foreign-exchange markets, but they give rise to generalized claims on the Fund; the drawee country gets an improvement in its reserve position in the Fund, and the drawer may repay in any currency acceptable to the Fund, provided the Fund's holdings of it are not thereby raised above its issuer's quota.

the public interest in the world at large.[7]

The possibility of unregulated reserve-expansion through borrowing arises primarily because of the use of the key currencies as international monies, and operates primarily through normal financial markets. Paradoxically, it is the obverse of a major virtue of the key-currency system: the fact that the supply of reserves is elastic. It is not true, though often asserted, that key-currency balance-of-payments deficits are necessary to provide the rest of the world with reserves; even if the key-currency country's balance-of-payments is in surplus, the authorities in other countries can normally add to their reserves at moderate cost through the operation of key-currency financial markets, as noted in item 4 on page 162 above. However, two other factors that are also inherently desirable in their own right contribute to the possibility of unregulated reserve-expansion: the great increase in offshore banking in recent years, and the fact that international borrowing for balance-of-payments reasons has become eminently respectable. Offshore banking adds flexibility to world financial markets, and in principle poses no more threat to domestic money-management in any given country than the competition of domestic non-bank financial intermediaries. Borrowed external reserves, within reasonable limits, provide a highly useful cushioning device while more permanent corrective action is taken to remedy whatever fundamental difficulty has led to a balance-of-payments deficit; the main problem is that the international community has been reluctant to specify and enforce those reasonable limits. What makes it possible for these three essentially-favourable features of modern financial arrangements to coalesce into an engine of world inflation is the fact that a key-currency system is vulnerable to the economic misadventures or mismanagement of that currency, leading to balance-of-payment deficits.

As long as the key-currency country's exports remain sufficiently competitive on world markets, the self-cancelling mechanism described in section 3.3. of Chapter 7 will clear the market of any surplus or undigested

---

[7] The illustrations of inter-central-bank borrowing and Fund borrowing given in sections 1 and 2 above are in terms of key-currency procedures, but would not be materially altered if the use of key currencies as international monies was abandoned. Lending between central banks would proceed as with country C in column 5 of Table 9.1, using any other form of international reserves instead of B's currency. So might borrowing through the Fund's SDR-designating procedures, though a more likely alternative is that this procedure would lapse, especially if the SDR itself were made the main reserve medium. Drawings on and repayments to the General Resources Account could still be made in much the same way as they are now, using SDR's or whatever other reserve medium was internationally agreed upon (which might be simply a formalized claim against the General Resources Account, instead of the rather artificial SDR).

balances of the key currency that may temporarily accumulate in the hands of non-residents, no matter how they arise or who holds them or how they are held. When the self-cancelling mechanism falters, however, the situation alters drastically. Borrowing by residents or non-residents in the financial markets of the key-currency country for use abroad (which will be artificially encouraged if domestic interest rates are kept below comparable rates elsewhere) will add to the undigested key-currency balances circulating abroad or accumulating in the hands of the monetary authorities of other countries as a result of the deficit on current account that insufficiently-competitive exports imply. These surplus balances will gravitate to the offshore banking system, where they will constitute a primary expansion of deposits, add to bank liquidity and reserves, and provoke a secondary expansion of loans and deposits, because this banking system will now be substantially insulated from the monetary policies of the key-currency country's central bank. The supply of this type of external reserves to other countries may thus come to be largely determined by the appetite of the international community for key-currency borrowing—including not only private interests planning investment projects or takeovers or other activities anywhere in the world, but also national authorities seeking to finance their balance-of-payments deficits. That appetite will presumably be stimulated by the inflationary pressures to which the unregulated expansion of international reserves makes a major contribution. Each participant may be acting quite rationally from his own point of view, but the composite effect will be inimical to all.

Part Four

ELABORATIONS AND INFERENCES

CHAPTER 10

SUPPLEMENTARY COMMENTS

1. Credit Expansion

1.1. Deposit Creation

In a credit-money-using society, a bank typically grants loans by simultaneously expanding its assets and its liabilities. It takes a promissory note or the equivalent from the borrower and records that as an asset (a debit to his loan account); if it is a bank of deposit, it gives him in exchange a credit to his deposit account (a liability); if it is a bank of issue, it tenders him its own banknotes (which are simply its IOU's, and must also be recorded as liabilities). Many writers have identified this procedure as the source of "created" credit. However, that is a misinterpretation of the facts. The procedure in question certainly is a particularly useful one for banks, but it is not the source of their ability to expand credit; as the examples in Part One amply demonstrate, credit can be expanded through banks or any other type of intermediary even if the loan is taken in standard money.

A borrower from a bank of deposit will presumably write cheques against his newly-increased bank balance quite soon, which will be promptly deposited to the accounts of his payees at other banks. Those other banks are sure to present the borrower's cheques through the clearinghouse and demand settlement in standard money or the equivalent, so the lending bank will lose reserves almost as soon as if the loan had been taken in standard money. (The same is true of a loan made by one particular branch of a bank in a branch-banking system, though in that case the cash reserves of all branches of the same bank may in effect be pooled and redeposits at other branches will reduce the drain on the bank as a whole.) It will be cold comfort to the individual banker that his free reserves will now be deposited with a competitor, or even to the manager of a branch that part of them will go to other branches of his own bank, for that will add nothing to the resources from which his bank or branch must earn its keep. Nor can the banking system as a whole benefit, unless the total cash reserves available to it have been increased in some way; otherwise any expansion by one bank must be offset by contraction at another or others.

Pretty much the same is true of loans granted by banks of issue, though in this case there is some possibility that the lending bank may be able to expand its circulation at least temporarily.[1] Banknotes will be continually

---

[1] The fabled "wildcat" bankers of nineteenth century U.S.A. exploited the possibilities to the full. They promised to redeem their notes on demand in specie, but maintained their redemption offices in remote and inaccessible places "among the wildcats". Such a banker

being paid into and withdrawn from all banks in the system, and the public will actively or passively express its preferences among the competing note-issues by passing on less-desirable notes in a variation of Gresham's Law. In many such banking systems the individual banks will promptly return their competitors' notes through the clearing system in exchange for standard money, just as they would a cheque on another bank, so the lending bank must have adequate reserves to cover its loans. Even if each bank's notes are acceptable as cash reserves for the others, as in the cross-pyramiding situation illustrated in section 3.3 of Chapter 2 above, the public will be able to enforce its coefficients of substitution not only to limit the total note issue but also to limit the share accruing to each individual bank; a disproportionate expansion of one bank's issues will deplete its cash reserves just as surely as if its competitors returned them directly, though perhaps somewhat more sluggishly.

Furthermore the ability to "create" its own obligations by simultaneously "writing up" loans and liabilities is *not* unique to banks; other intermediaries can do it too, and actually do so to at least some limited extent. When a non-bank lender promises a mortgage loan to a borrower (who wishes, say, to make an offer to buy a property) he is in effect adding to both his assets and his liabilities simultaneously, regardless of whether he opens corresponding ledger accounts at that point or merely writes an office memorandum or only makes a mental note; and like any banker he had better have free cash reserves or ready access thereto in order to meet his commitment when the purchase formalities are completed and the mortgagor wishes to draw down his loan. Like an individual banker, he will face an immediate cash drain of (as far as either can tell) 100 per cent of the loan. Unlike the banker, of course, he can not expect any material part of the loan to be redeposited with his own or any similar intermediary; but, as already noted, the individual banker does not get much direct benefit from these redeposits either.

"Writing up" its own obligations is nevertheless a highly useful lending technique for a bank, and a largely impractical one for a non-bank, because banks (as we have rigourously defined them) are issuers and servicers of an immediately-useable means of payment whereas non-banks are not. Chequeable deposits and banknotes are money-proper, a bank's stock-in-

might travel through a frontier area buying up local produce at good prices but paying in his own notes; by the time his victims found the notes worthless, or only acceptable at a heavy discount, he was out of reach. Competing banknote issues were discounted by the public according to popular perception of their redeemability in standard money—an interesting application of The Revaluation Effect.

trade, and the debits and credits to the borrower's chequeing account with his bank become just a part of the normal flow of payments through the banking system, hence loans in the form of credits to such an account or in the form of the physical transfer of the bank's IOU's are administratively convenient to both the bank and its customer. Loans in the form of the IOU's of (say) an insurance company, or a credit on its books, would not be administratively convenient to either the borrower or the lender, because the former needs money-proper and the latter is not in a position to service that kind of obligation.

1.2. Reversibility

In principle the process of credit expansion is as easy to reverse as to set in motion; any loss of ultimate standard money through an external drain or for any other reason, any shift of the public's coefficients of substitution towards money-proper or standard money or ultimate standard money (such as a rise in liquidity-preference), any adverse change in lenders' evaluations of economic prospects, any decision by the monetary authorities to reduce credit or to curtail its expected rate of expansion, or any other adverse change in conditions can set in motion a multiple contraction of claims on and loans by particular financial intermediaries or by the financial system as a whole. In practice, however, the expansionary and the contractionary sequences are not nearly as symmetrical as they appear. For the most part our models ignore the time element in the equilibrating process; once we introduce a time dimension, we find that contraction may be much more difficult and painful than expansion.

Even the expansionary process normally requires considerable time before it achieves its full effects, starting with the appearance of additional free reserves in the system, but no-one is under financial pressure to act hastily. Lenders may quietly show greater receptivity to new loan requests, and in the meantime may buy securities on the open market in order to keep their funds fully employed, which will tend to reduce interest rates and signal easier credit conditions. Borrowers and potential borrowers must then assess their oppportunities for using additional funds, negotiate loans from lenders, and set new spending plans in motion. It will probably take some additional time before the additional loans are fully drawn down and spent, but in due time a new equilibrium will be reached; credit will have expanded to the full extent permitted by the public's coefficients of substitution and the other controlling parameters, and any temporary investments by financial intermediaries in marketable securities will have been resold to the public.

However, suppose the financial intermediaries find themselves substantially under-reserved and under pressure to regularize their positions quickly.[2] Their first defence of course will be to liquidate some of their secondary reserves and their portfolios of longer-dated securities, but overly-rapid sales will depress prices unduly. New loans and loan renewals may be refused, and unused lines of credit may be cancelled or reduced; but if that is still not sufficient then demand and other terminable loans may have to be called. Especially-good borrowing customers, feeling the credit pinch through reduced cash flows, may nevertheless be allowed to draw down unused lines of credit; the possibility of such emergencies is one of the reasons for wanting a generous line in the first place, but such drawings intensify the pressure on weaker borrowers to repay. Some borrowers may be able to curtail their activities smoothly, or to get temporary loans else-where (at higher rates of interest), or draw on personal resources, but still others may be forced to liquidate their positions prematurely and at serious losses or may be forced into bankruptcy. Lenders may have to accept losses too, due to bankruptcies of their debtors and the forced sales of collateral security on depressed markets. If these losses become wide-spread or if the bankruptcies involve major firms, then the solvency of financial intermediaries (including the banks) may be threatened. Instead of contracting smoothly, the credit structure may become frozen into largely-uncollectible debts. All economic activity will then be seriously hampered until the losses can be digested, some measure of confidence restored, and a start made at repaying those debts that have not been terminated by bankruptcies, foreclosures, or the like.

The problems of credit-contraction are particularly acute in a financial system that is based on more-or-less automatic convertibility into a commodity-money. Unless the intermediaries contract credit promptly and decisively when they find themselves under-reserved, the problem will almost certainly prove self-aggravating: fears that the intermediaries' primary reserves or the nation's external reserves may be exhausted before the situation can be corrected may lead to a rush for the ultimate standard money (an internal gold drain or an external drain or both) and thus intensify the original shortage of reserves.[3] Mere rumours may start the contraction going even though the economy and the financial system are

---

[2] The necessary contraction is progressively greater if the reserve-deficiency occurs at the non-banks, the banks, or the Bank of Issue, because that implies a progressively greater portion of the total credit pyramid must be dismantled.

[3] A particularly spectacular example occured in 1931 when a major customer of the Kredit-Anstalt in Austria got into difficulties and brought the bank down with it. The aftermath drove the Austrian currency off the gold standard, then spread an infectious panic across Europe that did the same for a succession of other currencies, including sterling. That episode, and not the crash of the U.S. stock markets in 1929, is usually counted in Europe as the start of The Great Depression.

both entirely sound. The search for defences against such capricious credit contractions has been a major factor in the evolution of central-banking and money-management techniques in the domestic sphere, and in the persistent but still-faltering attempts to improve the international monetary system.

1.3. Limits to Expansionary Sequences

For the most part our models tacitly assume (a) that domestic credit-and-income expansions end when the intermediaries' reserves of standard money (or ultimate standard money) are reduced to zero, and (b) that in open-economy models the authorities successfully maintain relatively stable exchange rates by supplying some form of ultimate standard money at an approximately-fixed price on demand. Under these assumptions an unlimited inflation can not occur in a closed economy unless both the acceptance ratio approaches unity and the reserve ratio approaches zero, and in an open economy not even then.[4]

In the real world, of course, neither of these assumptions may obtain. The authorities may cease to support the exchange rate or to ensure the convertibility of the standard money into ultimate standard money, and may do so even before their reserves are exhausted; in this case there is no determinate limit to the expansion, except as the authorities may arbitrarily impose one. Alternatively, the authorities may borrow external reserves abroad and allow the credit expansion to continue (or avoid a contraction, if the expansion has already overshot the equilibrium position) and still maintain fixed exchange rates.

2. Money-Proper

2.1. The Definition of Money

There is no single monetary aggregate or other entity that can be uniquely identified as constituting "the" money supply, in the sense that it would be universally accepted as appropriate in all circumstances. No matter where

---

[4]   It is technically possible to derive an unlimited expansion of domestic assets (but not money-incomes) in an open economy under fixed exchange rates by postulating a *reductio ad absurdum* extension of the perfectly valid proposition that some borrowing may be for liquidity reasons instead of to finance immediate spending. Let borrowers retain *all* their borrowings as unused balances; the loans and redeposits will have no effect on incomes, but may inflate both sides of the intermediaries' balance sheets without limit. (In the equations on pp. 125ff above set $a=1$, $d=r=(1-n-z)=0$, and m at any positive figure, then let n approach zero; Y will remain invariant at some positive figure in the income version and at zero in the substitution version, but Ad, K, and L will increase without limit.)

one contemplates setting the boundary between money and near-money, one is bound to find one or more types of financial claim or other object just outside that boundary that are close substitutes for one or more of the sub-categories within the boundary. A non-chequeing savings account at a commercial bank is a good example; it is so readily exchangeable for a credit to a chequeing account at the same bank as to make it virtually indistinguishable for most practical purposes. Another important example was to be found in many countries during World War II and for some years thereafter, when the monetary authorities were committed to supporting the prices of some or all government securities at more-or-less-fixed levels; in effect, such securities in the hands of the public were freely inter-changeable with bank deposits and currency, because the banking system had to monetize them on demand. More generally, many financial claims are readily convertible into money-proper *at a price*, and hence may reasonably be counted as spendable funds for some purposes.

As a practical matter, therefore, it may often be best to take a flexible attitude and consider a series of subtotals from which we may select the one that is most useful for the purpose at hand. There is not much choice but to do some aggregating of financial claims of varying moneyness, just as we often have to aggregate other not-entirely-similar economic entities, because the number of variables we would have to deal with would be intractably large otherwise, but the best aggegration to use for one purpose is not necessarily the best for another. For some analytical purposes we may properly insist on confining our attention to hand-to-hand currency whose genuineness can be determined by objective tests, for other purposes we may include chequeing deposits, for some others term and notice deposits, and so on. In practice we may make a further distinction between chequeable and non-chequeable deposits at institutions officially recognised as "banks" in a particular juris-diction and similar deposits at other institutions, not because there is any real difference in their nature or use but simply because statistical information is available in greater detail and with greater promptness for the officially-recognized institutions.

Notwithstanding these qualifications, however, the fact remains that a significant categorical distinction can be made between those objects and claims that are customarily used to settle transactions in a given economy at a given time, and those that are not. This distinction is the essence of Robert-son's definition of money, quoted on page 5 above. The case for this defi-nition is argued in section 2.3 of Chapter 6 above. Granted that any definition must be arbitrary in some degree, this one seems less arbitrary than any reasonable alternative.

2.2. The Upper Limit to the Money Supply
The stock of any commodity available at any given time is finite, and its

annual increase is limited to its total annual production less current consumption; the upper limit to the supply of a commodity-money such as gold is therefore finite, and usually increases slowly. These are desirable features from the point of view of restraining inflation, but undesirable features if "the needs of trade" grow more rapidly than the stock of the monetary commodity. Given the persistent growth of real income and the shift from subsistence to money-and-market economies during most of recorded history, the needs of trade have certainly grown more rapidly than the supply of traditional commodity-monies not only on average but also in all but a relatively few short periods of inflation; chronic deflation has been avoided by more-or-less-continuous modifications of pure commodity standards or "metallist" monies. These modifications have usually involved credit-based monies of one kind or another, which by now have completely displaced commodity-monies in most jurisdictions.

The supply of a credit-based money is by nature elastic, though it may be constrained by rules or conventions of some kind, such as convertibility into a stipulated commodity-money. In actual historical experience these constraints left the financial system subject to periodic panics and credit-freezes, which typically began when some incident precipitated a "run" to convert credit-based monies into full-bodied coin; central banking and money-management evolved out of the search for remedies for these evils. There is no upper limit to the supply of a managed credit-based money, except as the judgment of money-managers imposes one. In principle this has eliminated the risk of a deflation caused by a shortage of money, but it has also eliminated the (admittedly-imperfect) defence against inflation that metallism and metallist adaptations offered. In practice, unfortunately, it is presently giving us something of both evils simultaneously: the depressed levels of output and employment that used to be associated with severe *de*flation, combined with the distortions generated by persistent *in*flation. This is described as The Fearsome Dilemma on page 155 above. It would appear that solving this policy problem will be one of the major challenges to policy-oriented economists in the foreseeable future.

2.3. The Lower Limit to the Money Supply

It would appear that the lower limit to the supply of money-proper in any money-and-market economy must be well above zero, to cover normal transactions needs. In the days of full-bodied coinages Hume's self-balancing specie-flow mechanism was supposed to ensure that each trading nation's money supply was adequate, but it was based on two assumptions that did not necessarily hold true: that prices would adjust fairly flexibly to the available money supply, and that all transactions were effected in coin of the realm or the equivalent. In the early stages of European colonization of the Western Hemisphere there were persistent complaints of a shortage of coin, and there is circumstantial evidence to support these complaints in the variety of expedients the colonists resorted to—direct barter between agricultural producers, fishermen, etc. and merchants, the monetary use of merchants' tokens and IOU's or of tobacco or beaver pelts or other commodities, etc. More generally, commodity-monies seem to have been invented independently in a number of cultures whenever systematic exchanges of goods grew large enough to justify them, often in the form of some staple commodity such as salt (so used within living memory in parts of Africa), or some object deemed to have intrinsic value in that particular culture. It is not unreasonable to look on the history of money as a continuing series of adaptations to society's persistently-increasing needs for a satisfactory supply of means-of-payment.

This line of thought suggests that a new form of money will be invented if the supply of currently-accepted monies proves inadequate. Thus in unsettled times in Europe after World War II, and in prisoner-of-war camps even earlier,[5] cigarettes had an astonishly-wide vogue as a commodity-money. Somewhat less exotically, Kaldor has described a hypothetical situation in which the authorities try to reduce spending by limiting the note circulation, with the result that major business firms pay their employees in chits (promissory notes) that then circulate as money.[6] Something very like this happened in the U.S.A. during the so-called bank holiday from 7th to 13th March 1933, when all banks in the country were closed. Well-known individuals as well as business firms issued "scrip", vouchers, promises to pay, IOU's, which gained a considerable currency; doubtless the practice would have been rapidly expanded and systematized if the emergency had lasted much longer. However, all these examples have an air of desperation about them, or at best the "make-do" pragmatism of frontier days; they offer little prospect of providing effective instruments of commerce and finance in a sophisticated money-and-market economy, or of offering a serious threat to the central bank's control over the financial system.

A more technical discussion of the lower limit to the money supply, or how a society can economize on money-proper, may be begun in terms of the old-fashioned but still-useful equation of exchange, in either the Fisher version ($MV=PT$) or some variant of the Cambridge version (which can be transliterated as $M=KPT$ without serious distortion). Reducing the quantity of money (M) a country needs to operate at a given level of real income and a stable price-level means either (a) reducing the volume of

[5] R.A. Radford, "Economic Organization of a P.O.W. Camp", *Economica*, Vol. XII, November 1945, pp. 189–201.

[6] N. Kaldor, "The New Monetarism", *Lloyds Bank Review*, July 1970, pp. 6f.

transactions to be effected in cash (T) or (b) increasing the velocity of circulation (V in the Fisher version) or decreasing the public's desired stock of money-to-hold (K in the Cambridge version). The first involves factors that are outside the scope of this book, such as the vertical integration of firms or other structural changes in the production function that would substitute internal bookkeeping entries within a single entity for external payments to third parties. These same factors might simultaneously affect V and its reciprocal, K. More significantly, V and K would also be affected by such things as the average pay-period for wages and salaries, the smooth articulation of receipts and payments, the public's habits in the use of credit to postpone payments, the proximity or dispersion of regional and other markets within the economy, the rapidity of transportation and communications, the sophistication of the financial system, etc., as extensively covered in the monetary theorizing of the first third of the twentieth century.

However, current financial trends raise some doubts about the long-run validity of this conventional wisdom. We have already noted (page 146 above) an example of how the sophistication of the financial system can affect K (and V): some portion of the public's money-to-spend may be temporarily converted into near-money if there are suitable liquid short-term vehicles available. This includes not only business balances accumulated from receipts pending payments for wages and salaries, materials, etc., but also consumer balances not needed till later in the pay-period. A credit-based monetary system makes it possible for an economy's supply of money-proper and its supply of near-money to fluctuate inversely in the short run no matter how their long-run changes may be related, in contrast to the situation with an invariant stock of commodity-money (such as a full-bodied coinage). It may well be that a sufficiently-detailed study of current financial statistics would show that some such inverse movements already occur, but if they do they have not yet proven great enough to attract attention. Nevertheless some changes in payment practices that are already in process, and others envisaged for the future, raise the possibility that the supply of money-proper as we know it today may eventually become much more volatile.

The rapid spread of the use of credit cards by individuals in the third quarter of the 20th century, in both their personal and their business capacities, has already brought many payments that used to be made in hand-to-hand currency into the realm of monthly settlements by cheque, and has consolidated many payments that used to be made by cheque at various times in the pay-period into a single monthly payment. Now suppose that further technical advances akin to the electronic settlement of accounts through point-of-sale computer terminals, even now being tested in practice, eventually make it possible to use credit cards for virtually all purchases—

perhaps even newspapers and bus fares.[7] In this way all private and many business demands for money-proper could be reduced to or towards zero, except for the monthly or other periodic settlement of the accumulated debts.

Business firms have the same incentives to economize on their cash holdings, and they may enjoy some economies of scale and other advantages in money management. Perhaps trade associations and chambers of commerce could eventually bring about the perfect articulation of all inter-firm payments by scheduling them for the same day (or even the same hour) of each week or month or other settlement period. Logically, the settlement of all credit-card and other accounts-due from individuals should be scheduled simultaneously.. This would reduce the need for anyone to hold any money-proper at all to one day (one hour? one minute?) in each payment-period.

Given the ability of a credit-based monetary system to expand and contract the supply of money-proper at will, we have in effect postulated a situation in which there would be no money-proper in existence except for a brief settlement period. In fact the whole process might be reduced to an instantaneous clearing procedure (perhaps through computer records), in which case no money-proper need be created even for an instant. Money-proper as we know it would have been eliminated, and with it "banks" as we have defined them. However, the near-money obligations of commercial banks would remain, and their basic function (intermediation) would not be affected by a mere change in the mechanism for inter-personal and inter-firm settlements, for this would seem to be a natural adaptation of their present role in operating the payments mechanism, including inter-bank clearing houses.

Fantastic? Impossible? Well, a mechanism that could make this possible already exists and is in use, though on a tiny scale compared to what would be required for the entire elimination of money-proper as we now know it. Indeed it could be adapted for use without requiring perfect articulation of the timing of payments, or even any improvement over the present degree of articulation. The mechanism in question is something called "daylight overdrafts" or "overcertification". Typically the borrower is a reputable security dealer who has contracted to buy a certain quantity of securities,

---

[7] Replacing cheques by electronic signals as the means of effecting transfers between one bank account and another is not the point here; its principal effect will be to *speed up* settlements somewhat and eliminate the debit float that now inflates deposit balances in the interval between the deposit of a cheque to the payee's account and its debiting to the payor's account. What we are here postulating is the adaptation of similar techniques to the enlargement of the scope for the use of credit cards to *defer* settlement for a larger portion of the community's total monthly transactions.

probably a new issue being offered on the market for which settlement is to be made on a certain day, which he has already contracted to resell to customers who have subscribed to the issue through him. The amount may be quite substantial relative to his normal needs for working capital, but he will need it for only a matter of hours because his customers are pledged to pay him as soon as he delivers them their securities, and his receipts will exceed his buying costs by the amount of the commissions he will receive on his sales. Furthermore he will have good loan collateral: not only the securities in process of being sold but also considerable capital of his own, a substantial inventory of marketable securities of various kinds, and perhaps direct or indirect access to the central bank in case of need as part of the arrangements under which he is willing to carry an inventory of government securities for resale to the public. The solution is for his banker to certify his cheque for the amount required (in effect, to give him an overdraft), confident that this cheque will be covered before the end of the day by the deposit of the cheques the dealer will receive from his customers when he delivers their securities to them; the banker charges a stipulated fee or commission for this service.

There would seem to be no technical difficulties in adapting over-certification to meeting the need for sharp fluctuations in the volume of money-proper envisaged in reducing the average amount outstanding towards zero. In order to participate in the system individuals and businesses would have to hold at least enough liquid financial assets at the end of the payment-period to settle their debts, just as they now must hold enough money-proper, except to the extent that their credit standing permitted them to postpone settlement by paying an agreed rate of interest on their outstanding balances (as can now be done through lines-of-credit with a banker or a credit-card issuer). The monetary authorities might well feel it necessary to take official cognizance of the practice instead of ignoring it as they pretty well do now, perhaps by insisting that banks maintain minimum cash reserves against the maximum amount of their overdrafts on each and every day, but it is difficult to see why this should be necessary; surely the main requirement would be to ensure that any debtor had to make good promptly by liquidating suitable financial claims.

So money-proper as we have known it could conceivably disappear without disturbing the spending stream. But would that really mean that society was able to get along without "money proper" in any sense, or merely that we would have to redefine money-proper? Credit expansion could still go on through whatever financial intermediaries remained, and would need to be controlled just as now. Far from being curtailed, the role of some at least of these intermediaries might be greatly expanded; the acceptance ratio of some type or types (collectively) of claims on them must approach or reach unity. The authorities might subject at least the

211

more important of these claims—those liquid enough to be used in settling net debtor positions, or otherwise acceptable as collateral for daylight overdrafts—to the same sort of constraints that now apply to the obligations of the institutions that are officially recognized as "banks" in a given jurisdiction.

In such a system could we logically object to extending the term money-proper to any claim that could serve as the basis for a daylight overdraft? At one time many economists denied that chequeable deposits were money, and in the course of sorting that out there was some confusion between whether the argument was over the cheque as such or over the chequeable deposit. It is now generally accepted that it is the deposit, not the cheque by which it is transferred to another holder, that is money-proper. In the hypothetical situation we have now envisaged the daylight overdrafts or the inter-personal and inter-firm clearings or whatever other settlement techniques might be used would be simply the instrument by which transfers would be effected, and in this sense would be on all fours with cheques as we now know them; what would be transferred would be net debits[8] or credits to individuals' or firms' accounts with various financial intermediaries, and therefore such credits on their books would have the same right to be classed as money-proper as chequeable deposits do now.

---

[8] Net debit as well as net credit positions might be involved between any of these financial intermediaries and their customers because there would be nothing to prevent them granting loans (including ordinary overdraft loans, not to be confused with the new daylight overdrafts involved in the new payments process) to their customers in return for a suitable interest charge in just the same way banks do at present. Even now some cheques are cleared to the overdraft accounts of bank customers (loan or debit balances on the books of the bank) instead of to deposit accounts (credit balances on the books of the bank).

CHAPTER 11

SELECTED POLICY INFERENCES

1. Domestic Credit Expansion

1.1. Portfolio Adjustments

Some inferences from our models have been incorporated in the text of Chapters 1 to 9 inclusive, mostly relating to analytical rather than policy matters. However, a number of additional inferences merit mention, especially some relating more directly to questions of policy.

In most of the illustrative examples used in this book the initial disturbance that sets the expansionary process in motion is the appearance of a given quantity of new or newly-released standard money in the economy—either directly in the hands of the general public or soon put there by loans. The operative force is the public's attempts to restore its desired mix of financial assets, which fuels an expansion that must continue until a new equilibrium is achieved and the new or newly-released standard money is just absorbed by the currency drain, the external drain, and the reserves of financial intermediaries. However, we may draw a second inference as well: *anything* that causes the public's actual holdings of *any* asset to be above (or below) its desired holdings will constitute a "disturbance" and will set a corrective sequence in motion.

Columns 2, 3, and 4 of Table 3.2 above, and the discussion thereof on the following pages, illustrate a disturbance in the form of an introduction of additional marketable securities; the new issues are accepted voluntarily by the public, but that requires some readjustments in its holdings of other financial assets, and interest rates and other parameters are also affected as part of the adjustment process. A more dramatic example would be a decision by a government to pay its employees or its suppliers by tendering government bonds instead of cash, as impecunious governments have sometimes done in the real world; the recipients would be forced to sell some or all of their bonds for whatever they would bring, in order to cover their living or business expenses, thus producing a sharp negative revaluation effect on them (and probably on other domestic financial claims as well, because of competitive pressures). Or, suppose the government deposited its bonds with an "open-end" near-bank and induced it to credit the accounts of the employees and suppliers at face value with their proportionate shares of the resultant claims against it. If these claims were payable on demand, the claimants would presumably withdraw all or most of their entitlements at once; the depository would have to sell the bonds or others assets to meet the drain on its resources, and would suffer the negative revaluation effects instead of the government's creditors. If the claims were payable after the lapse of some time, the creditors would first have to sell or borrow against their claims on the best terms they could; then at maturity the depository would have to meet the drain as before. In this case the capital losses would be shared in some way between the government's creditors and the depository. In all three cases third parties might make capital gains or suffer capital losses on any claims they bought from the original creditors.

Thus we may derive a third inference: even in this static-equilibrium application of the model, claims that are generally acceptable as money-proper have a special status—and so therefore do their issuers, the banks. *Ceteris paribus*, any disturbance that takes the form of or induces an arbitrary increase in bank credit will involve a parallel expansion of other forms of credit; but, *ceteris paribus*, any disturbance that takes the form of an arbitrary increase in non-bank credit will probably have adverse side-effects on other forms of non-bank credit, or on the interest rates and other parameters that influence the public's coefficients of substitution, or both.

1.2. Pyramiding and Central-Bank Control

Simple pyramiding is of course the foundation of central banking. Examples of cross pyramiding are still to be found, as when a bank is permitted to count balances with its correspondents as part of its required reserves (or counts them as part of its customary reserves), but the practice does not appear to pose serious problems in a system managed by an efficient central bank. Interest now centres on compound pyramiding, which is widespread, and on the possibility that it may be further extended. The mechanics of the matter were presented in section 4 of Chapter 2 above; the main question remaining is whether the central bank can control the total credit expansion in the domestic financial system despite the activities of near-banks and other financial intermediaries over which it does not have any direct influence.

Within the context of overall economic policy, the central bank has unequivocal control over its own total liabilities through its rediscounting and open-market policies; these liabilities comprise (a) notes in circulation with the general public and (b) the primary reserves of the banks; provided the public continues to hold an appreciable and relatively-stable portion of its financial assets in the form of banknotes or other claims on the central bank, therefore, the bank can control the volume of credit in the system no matter how the public chooses to hold the remainder of its financial assets. In effect the central bank limits the expansion of bank credit to accommodate those needs that are not met by non-bank credit, though that is not how it will appear to the various participants. In the first instance the central bank will limit the growth of the primary reserves of the banks according to its perception of general credit conditions, or its target growth rate for a particular monetary aggregate or a selection of aggregates, or whatever other policy guide it deems appropriate. However, its ultimate aim will be to promote that level of money-income which will accord with the best compromise official policymakers can achieve between their full-employment and their price-stability goals. Normally the permitted increase in bank credit will dominate the growth of money-income in the short run, as argued in section 2.2 of Chapter 6 above, and the public's allocation of its current savings will determine the parallel growth of non-bank credit and its feed-back effects on money-income. If there is a substantial unexpected increase (or decrease) in the public's allocations of current savings to the non-banks there will be a corresponding change in their loans and therefore in money-income, and the central bank will have to revise its guidelines accordingly. If the public is not merely allocating more of its current savings to the non-banks but also attempting to shift previously-acquired bank balances as well, then at first The Indestructibility Principle will tend to maintain the existing level of bank credit while permitting a surge of non-bank credit; that will have inflationary effects on money-income, and the central bank will have to reduce the assets and liabilities of the banks by contracting its own liabilities and thereby reducing the primary reserves available to them.

The effects on the balance sheets of the various financial intermediaries may be illustrated by reference to Table 2.5 on page 59 above, reinterpreting the savings and loan associations as a composite of all non-bank sources of credit. Suppose the appropriate increase of credit in a given period would be about 15,000 francs, but innovations of some kind sharply reduce the role of chequeable deposits and shift the public's marginal coefficients of substitution from $0.08 : 0.72 : 0.20$ (as in column 3) to $0.10 : 0.00 : 0.90$ (as in column 6), so credit threatens to rise by about 23,000 francs: by limiting the expansion of its own loan portfolio to 745 francs and its note-issue to 1,745 francs the Bank-of-Issue-turned-central-bank can limit the expansion of bank deposits to 1,441 francs (all of which will be required by the non-banks as their primary reserves), non-bank obligations to 14,408 francs, and total loans to 15,009. This will work even if the non-banks can get by with no marginal increase in their reserves, in which case their obligations would rise by 25,000 francs if the central bank did not intervene; by limiting its loans to 600 francs and its note-issue to 1,600 francs it will reduce the credit expansion to 15,000 francs—600 at the central bank, 14,400 at the non-banks, none at the banks. The worst possible case would be one in which the public was induced to transfer a substantial portion of its pre-existing claims on the banking system to the non-banks, which may be illustrated by letting the coefficient a become negative and increasing *b* correspondingly in column 6. If the central bank took no action then the banks would continually reexpand their assets and liabilities while non-bank credit grew continuously, but an appropriate limitation on the note-issue would bring whatever contraction in bank obligations was necessary to offset the growth of non-bank obligations.

Furthermore, the direct influence of central-bank policies really applies not to "banks" as strictly defined on page 6 above but to "commercial banks". No doubt this is due to pragmatism, empiricism, and historical accident rather than to theoretical insight, but it makes monetary policy more immediately effective. The near-money obligations of commercial banks may be as large as or larger than their money-proper obligations, and are more-or-less comparable in nature to those of their nearest competitors; they should therefore be able to retain a substantial share of the public's total financial assets even if the role of chequeable deposits is sharply curtailed. If their competition for funds is handicapped by laws or regulations that penalize them unfairly, then the laws or regulations should be changed. If on the other hand their competitors have a legitimate advantage in offering services or types of obligations that are not deemed appropriate for commercial banks, then the limitations on commercial-bank activities are surely justified.

A potentially-more-serious problem relates to financial intermediaries that offer chequeable deposits or the equivalent but are not formally classed as "banks" for official purposes, and are not required to keep primary reserves in the form of claims on the central bank. We may identify the officially-recognized banks as "regulated" commercial banks and the others as "unregulated" (or less-stringently-regulated) banks. In most countries the latters' share of the public's chequeable deposits is relatively small and seems likely to remain so, because their regulated competitors are larger and more prestigious and are better able to serve the needs of large firms and wealthy individuals. As a matter of principle, however, we can not rule out the possibility that they might gain sufficiently in stature to pose a real threat not only to the regulated banks but also to the central bank's effective control over the financial system. Their transferable and non-transferable obligations are equivalent to the chequeable and non-chequeable obligations of the regulated banks, so the "worst case" hypothesis noted above becomes at once more plausible and more serious: they could conceivably displace the regulated banks entirely as custodians of the public's financial assets and reduce the latters' role to that of custodian of their primary reserves. If their obligations were able to substantially displace not only the regulated banks' chequeable deposits but also the central bank's notes, as suggested on page 62 above, effective central-bank control of the financial system would really be threatened; a point would come sooner or later at which regulatory or legislative changes would be necessary.

The unregulated banks do have certain competitive advantages of their own, though at first glance they may seem relatively insignificant. It is sometimes argued that they have a cost advantage in that they may be able to get by on a smaller primary reserve ratio, i.e. with a smaller portion of non-earning assets, but this is not necessarily the case; the reserves they require for a given type of obligation may approximate those of the regulated banks. Their main advantage is not in the *amount* of their reserves but in the *nature* of them: they may be mainly in the form of deposits with the regulated banks. In normal times this advantage is unimportant, because they must pay competitive rates for their funds and can not charge materially more for their loans than other lenders. In a period of severe credit restraint, however, the difference could become very important. The central bank can squeeze the primary reserves of the regulated banks as tightly as it wants, even though that may cause very high interest rates, because it can make the supply completely inelastic at any level it chooses; the regulated banks may have to call loans and reduce the lines of credit they have granted their borrowing customers. But the supply of reserves to the unregulated banks will remain elastic: as long as they are prepared to pay market rates of interest (high though they may be), they can readily add to their reserves by bidding deposits at the regulated banks away from the general public.[1]

If they are prepared to bid aggressively for funds in a credit squeeze, therefore, the unregulated banks can meet all the credit needs of their borrowing customers—even take on new customers—and exact high enough returns on their loans to give them their customary spread above the cost of the funds, because in such circumstances the availability of credit may be far more important to borrowers than its cost. Indeed, it may be very good strategy for them to do so, for it may enable them to expand their share of the market permanently; business borrowers will highly appreciate their ability to honour or even expand their lines of credit while the regulated banks are having to contract theirs. The immediate effect will be that the central bank will have to put still greater pressure on the regulated banks, thus further enhancing the advantages of their unregulated competitors.

---

[1] The unregulated banks will of course need some banknotes as till-money, so some part of their reserves will consist of claims against the central bank, but if necessary they can draw down their balances with the regulated banks to get more, for the latter must maintain the ready convertibility of their obligations into standard money. In practice, however, it is unlikely that this would happen; the high interest rates this scenario implies would presumably induce the public to reduce its holdings of standard money to a minimum in exchange for earning assets, so both regulated and unregulated banks should have a net inflow of notes.

Of course, the regulated banks could prevent the encroachment of their unregulated competitors by agreeing among themselves not to serve them. However, this might contravene anti-trust or restriction-of-trade legislation. Also, other financial intermediaries are good customers of banks even though they compete for some types of business, since they have good cash flow, substantial deposit balances, and ample liquid collateral to support lines of credit; any given bank will therefore find it profitable to accept their accounts in normal times, and will then find it difficult to terminate the relationship in difficult times (which are likely to be relatively brief). As for the authorities, they may be expected to intervene with legislative or regulatory changes if the expansion of credit by the unregulated banks appears to be undermining effective credit management; the obvious answer is to make each type of public claim on all intermediaries subject to the same reserve requirements and other constraints. Specifically, all chequeable or transferable claims should be subject to an identical reserve ratio in central-bank funds, and the reserve requirements for other claims should be equivalent in nature and amount regardless of the intermediary with which they are held.[2] But, why wait for a crisis before making this logical change? There is no reason for permitting different intermediaries to operate similar facilities under disparate rules.

Offshore financial assets denominated in a particular currency are in principle under the same indirect control of the central bank as claims on unregulated domestic banks and non-bank financial intermediaries, for similar reasons. The appetite of both residents and non-residents for offshore financial assets so denominated is regulated by coefficients that are simply a subset of those that regulate their appetite for all financial claims in that currency. The position of offshore banks is similar to that of unregulated domestic banks, but their geographic location makes their services less competitive with regulated domestic banks for effecting domestic payments, so they are a less-serious threat to the central bank's control.[3] However, offshore financial claims denominated in a key currency acquire a substantial measure of independence if the issuing country's exports lose competitiveness in world markets, for the reasons and with the

---

[2] There would be administrative difficulties for the central bank if it were required to operate reserve accounts for many small intermediaries, perhaps of purely-regional significance, but several alternatives could be devised. One possibility would be that small intermediaries be required to join an association of some kind and hold their reserves with that association, which in turn would hold reserves with the central bank equal to 100 per cent of its members' deposits. Another possibility would be to allow small intermediaries to hold their reserves with the regulated banks, and to require the latter to maintain 100 per cent reserves against them with the central bank.

[3] This might conceivably change, of course, if electronic transfers of funds became economical not only locally but also over long distances.

consequences noted in section 3.3 of Chapter 7 and section 3 of Chapter 9 above.

1.3. Intermediaries in Small Open Economies

In the open-economy models we have previously used in the context of constrained-equilibrium applications we have noted a consistent relationship between the external drain and the secondary expansion of domestic financial assets. In conformity with The Leakage Principles, if imports and savings are the only leakages from an expansionary sequence then the external drain and the secondary increase in domestic financial assets will be in the ratio of the marginal propensities to import and to save (i.e. $m{:}s$), and the sum of the two drains will be equal to the initial "disturbing" injection of funds. Applying these relationships to a situation in which the initiating factor is the granting of a loan (L) equal to the free reserves of the financial system as a whole, we conclude that the loan will result in an external drain (loss of reserves) amounting to $mL / (m+s)$ and the addition of $sL / (m+s)$ to domestic financial assets.

Now note that the marginal propensity to spend is usually quite large relative to the marginal propensity to save. Second, for our purposes we are subsuming saving in the form of the direct acquisition of capital goods in the propensity to spend and are concerned only with the propensity to save in financial forms, which is presumably smaller than the total propensity to save. Third, the more open an economy is the larger the ratio of spending on imports to total spending is likely to be; indeed this is a useful index of the openness of an economy. In combination these three points make a persuasive case for believing that the external drain will increasingly dominate the secondary expansion of domestic financial assets as we make our model more and more open.

Whatever may be the propensity to allocate savings to the acquisition of foreign claims, it will reinforce the likelihood that the external drain will dominate the increase in domestic financial assets. Furthermore the probability is that the propensity to acquire foreign claims will tend to increase as the size of our model economy decreases,[4] because it becomes less and less likely that the economy can support a suitable variety of financial intermediaries and therefore the public is likely to invest a larger portion of its savings abroad.[5]

---

[4] The smallness and the openness of the economy are likely to be positively correlated in practice, but they are distinct in principle. For example, a relatively large economy might have highly concentrated comparative advantages in certain industries, and its heavy specialization in those industries would make it correspondingly dependent on imports for much of its needs.

[5] Cf. A.N. McLeod, "The Role of Financial Institutions in Developing Countries: A New Perspective", *The Canadian Banker*, Vol. 77, no. 5, September/October 1970, pp. 8-10.

We may draw some rough conclusions about the relative magnitudes of these two leakages in the real world from material available in the International Monetary Fund's *International Financial Statistics*. The ratio of imports to gross national product seems a reasonable proxy for the average propensity to import, and the ratio of the annual increase in the money supply plus what the Fund calls quasi-money to the increase in gross national product seems a reasonable proxy for the average propensity to add to financial savings; and, as an assumption of ignorance, we may suppose that the marginal propensities are not far from the average propensities for most countries. The first ratio ranges from about 5 per cent for a relatively closed economy like the U.S.A. to about 40 per cent for Canada and some of the smaller industrial nations of Europe and still higher figures for some small open economies.[6] The second ratio ranges around 4 to 6 per cent for many industrial countries, and from about the same level down to about 2 per cent for less-developed countries. On this admittedly-tenuous basis we may tentatively conclude that the ratio of the marginal propensities to import and to save (i.e. d in the notation we used in Part One above) is of the order of unity for a relatively closed economy like the U.S.A., 5 to 10 for medium-sized industrial countries, and considerably higher for more open economies.

An important practical inference from all this is that in a small open economy virtually the entire amount of any net new loan by any resident of the economy—a bank, any other financial intermediary, a business firm, an individual—will leak away fairly promptly as an external drain. In effect, loans in such economies must be deemed to be made in foreign exchange.

2. The Macroeconomics of Credit Expansion

2.1. Managed Disequilibrium

As noted in section 1.1 of this chapter, anything that causes the public's asset-holdings to differ from its desired pattern will induce attempts to eliminate the difference. If it is holdings of physical assets that are involved, the supply of which can normally be changed only slowly, most of the adjustment (initially at least) must take the form of a revaluation of one or more of the assets together with consequential changes in their coefficients of substitution. In the case of financial assets, however, most of the adjustment may

---

[6] Some developing countries, large and small, have quite low ratios of imports to gross national product. Presumably this reflects relatively low standards of living and similar factors, perhaps including a substantial sector of subsistence agriculture. In such cases one may suppose that the marginal propensity to import is considerably higher than the average propensity, especially for income reaching the well-to-do.

take place through changes in their supply, in the credit structure of the economy, in the spending stream, and in the flow of money-income. Changes in the supply or the availability of money-proper are particularly effective in stimulating reasonably-predictable changes in the public's spending and asset-holding patterns; this is what gives monetary policy its power to influence money-income quite directly, and thereby to influence employment, output, and other real variables as well, though less directly and less certainly.

All of which can be summed up in a single inference: monetary policy operates by deliberately creating an imbalance between the public's actual holdings of money and close substitutes for money, on the one hand, and the portfolio of money, other financial assets, and physical assets it would prefer to hold at its current level of money-income, on the other hand, thereby inducing actions that may change the levels of most of these variables and the parameters that link them.

2.2. Created Credit and Forced Saving

Vining's combined credit-and-income-expansion sequence helps to clear up the old misunderstandings that contrasted the supposedly-unique ability of banks to "create" credit (and money) with the limitation of other intermediaries to relending funds saved out of income and deposited with them. The substance of Part One of this book is that credit creation (or expansion, as we prefer to phrase it) can occur in exactly the same way through a wide variety of intermediaries, or even through private lending and borrowing between principals. Vining's analysis offers a further clarification: even when the credit expansion outstrips the income expansion in the short run, as it may do on a considerable scale in the case of bank credit, it must ultimately be saved out of income.

It is also worth noting that Vining's procedure and the elaborations that can be built on it rehabilitate the concept of forced saving. This idea (though not necessarily under that name) was an important aspect of economic analysis from at least the time of Bentham until recently, but it raised some puzzling questions. Money was long seen as merely a veil behind which the real economic forces operated, or at best a facilitator of those basic forces; how was it, then, that money created out of thin air could have important effects on real economic variables? The evolution of monetary theory in the 20th century has progressively enlarged our understanding of the role of money as a major economic variable in its own right, and Vining's analysis completes the demystification: credit-expansion is directly linked to income-expansion in monetary terms, and hence, *ceteris paribus*, in real terms as well. Credit-expansion through banks can indeed be a short-run substitute for saving as a means of financing new spending, and a much more potent and munipulatable source than credit expansion through other intermediaries. Futhermore we can now see not only that the credit so provided must ultimately be saved out of income, but also that it must be saved in the specific form of willingly-held balances of money-proper; additional savings in other forms are virtually certain to be generated in the process. In view of today's preoccupation with instant foods, instant this, and instant that, perhaps we should call the phenomenon "instant pre-saving" instead of forced saving.

2.3. Alternative Guides to Monetary Policy

From the analysis of Parts One and Two above we may draw some inferences for the long-standing debate over whether general credit conditions or some specific monetary aggregate is a better guide for monetary policy, and if the latter then what specific aggregate should be chosen.

We may begin with three points made in section 2.2 of Chapter 3 above. First, changes in a country's stock of real and financial assets, valued at historical cost, and changes in the stock of each particular asset, are functionally related to the flow of money-income.[7] Second, the various alternative vehicles for the employment of savings, including money-proper, are in competition with one another for a share of the savings being generated. Third, interest rates and other rates of return on particular assets are major parameters influencing the public's allocation of its savings among these competing vehicles. There is therefore a strong presumption that the end result will be pretty much the same regardless of whether monetary policy is directed initially to general credit conditions (commonly gauged by the behaviour of interest rates and related parameters) or to some particular monetary aggegate; any difference will presumably be attributable either to leads and lags in certain responses or to extraneous factors that have a special influence on the particular parameter(s) or aggregate(s) chosen as policy guides.

For those who favour monetary aggregates as the proper guide to monetary policy, it is common to base the choice of a particular aggregate partly or wholly on how well fluctuations in it over some selected historical period have correlated with gross national product. This is surely a poor basis. It has long been recognized that a great many economic series correlate very well with gross national product.[8] This must be particularly true of changes in

---

[7] The chain of causation may run in either direction, or in both simultaneously. Thus an exogenous change in income will produce changes in the stock of assets and in the stock of particular assets; but exogenous changes in the composition (or the desired composition) of the stock of assets may provoke changes in the flow of income, with feedback effects on the stock of assets.

[8] Cf. R. Stone, "On the Interdependence of Blocks of Transactions", *Journal of the Royal Statistical Society, Supplement*, Vol. IX, no.1, 1947, pp. 1-32.

the stock of any saving vehicle, including all monetary aggregates, since they are largely functions of national income; relying on such correlations comes close to circular reasoning. Even if we disregard this criticism, however, a strong correlation between a given monetary aggregate and gross national product in the past is not a reliable guide to the future. No monetary aggregate is *solely* a function of income; in part at least it is also a function of interest rates, other rates of return on various real and financial assets, the availability of reliable short-dated and flexible-dated investment vehicles, and other variables, any or all of which may change significantly over time. Money-income, the spending stream, the full array of financial claims, and all the parameters that link them act and react on one another in true general-equilibrium fashion. Better correlation for one monetary aggregate than another with gross national product or net national income in any given timeframe may reflect nothing more than fortuitous changes in some parameter or other, or stronger feedback effects, rather than a positive causal relationship.

The analysis of Part Two above suggests that the volume of loans being granted and spent in the economy as a whole would be a more promising guide to monetary policy than either general credit conditions or any particular monetary aggregate. The ready acceptance of money-proper makes it a preferred instrument of monetary policy, but that does not justify focusing attention solely on the banking system and disregarding other sources of credit. For example, instances have been known in which a sudden loss of confidence in acceptance houses or some other type of financial intermediary has triggered a sudden reduction in their scale of operations and threatened a material reduction in the total credit outstanding in the community, which had to be met by an expansion of bank credit and a partial monetization of pre-existing debts. Had the authorities been monitoring monetary aggregates exclusively, a quite unnecessary credit squeeze would have occurred. In the event they usually did the right thing, due either to monitoring general credit conditions or to recognizing that special circumstances warranted a departure from their normal guidelines; had they been monitoring the total credit outstanding, however, the right action would have been obvious at once.

2.4. Financial Statistics

If the monetary authorities are to monitor a wider range of financial intermediaries than they do now, much more complete and timely financial statistics will have to be compiled. Ideally, all loans granted and spent in the community should be reported week by week, with little delay. Achieving anything like this ideal may of course take a long time, or may prove either too costly or physically impossible, but a beginning should be made. In most jurisdictions the recognized commercial banks are required to report with reasonable frequency and promptness, and similar requirements could gradually be extended to other intermediaries; even delayed or less-frequent reporting of non-bank credit would be helpful, if the data were reasonably complete.

The expanded financial statistics should be compiled on a consolidated basis, in order to avoid double counting. It is standard practice in most jurisdictions to eliminate inter-bank balances and transactions for those banks that are officially recognized and subject to the control of the monetary authorities; the next step would be a similar consolidation of the accounts of all reporting intermediaries. On the liability side, the compilation should include a suitable classification of their obligations, including as a separate category the funds of the shareholders of the reporting institutions. As argued on page 75 above, shareholders' equity should be seen as simply a different category of claim on the intermediary, differing from its debts only in the terms on which the claimants share in the gross earnings and on which they can hope to recover their investment. Debt and equity are distinct entities at law, but meaningful economic distinctions are difficult to make, since they are merely different forms of invested capital.

In principle the same procedure should be extended to non-financial corporations and other juridical entities, in order to sift out the inter-corporate lendings and borrowings and leave only those of the natural persons who are the true principals. However, the consolidation should not be carried to the extent of showing only the net creditor or debtor position of each individual; your net position is the same whether you have $100 in your pocket and debts of $100, or hold nothing and owe nothing, but your room to manoeuvre in the economic sphere is very different.

3. International Intermediation

3.1. The Underestimation of Inflationary Implications
The inflationary implications (for both the domestic economy and the world at large) of policy decisions in individual countries are chronically underestimated, because conventionally-calculated domestic money-income multipliers are systematically understated. The understatement occurs for two reasons:

(1) When the domestic financial system is more-or-less-effectively insulated from the full effects of the external drain, as tends to be the case nowadays, the expansionary sequence closely approximates closed-economy proportions in the short run.

(2) Even if this short-run phenomenon is avoided, the external reper-

cussions of domestic economic policies tend to raise the multiplier sooner or later to something approximating or exceeding its closed-economy value.

3.2. The Essential Conditions for International Equilibrium

There can be no equilibrium in international economic arrangements unless each major nation and the world as a whole is reasonably well satisfied with its lot. That includes such things as the levels and the rates of change of real and money incomes, prices, employment and output, the terms of trade, and the progress being made (particularly in the developing countries) in raising living standards. Any nation, large or small, that is not fairly well satisfied with its position on any of these counts, or with the rate at which conditions are improving, will surely take such action as it can to better its situation. However, any action one nation takes is likely to have direct and indirect effects on others, for good or for ill.

In the early years after World War II it seemed that all or most nations would be able to maintain full employment at stable prices in their own economies, once the distortions inherited from the war and The Great Depression had been overcome. The Fearsome Dilemma was only a small cloud on the horizon; few economists were worried about the moderate upcreep of prices that was clearly discernible even in the U.S.A. and West Germany, which were leading the world in an unparalleled era of prosperity and growth. The optimistic assumptions considered in Chapters 8 and 9 above seemed to apply.

Instead, the performance of virtually all countries deteriorated in the 1960's, and after 1971 the deterioration got progressively worse. Pessimistic assumptions now seem to apply. No mutually-acceptable solution seems possible until The Fearsome Dilemma is solved in the domestic economies of major nations, or until the international community devises generally-acceptable rules for living with it and sharing the economic and social burdens it entails. It may be safely predicted that the search for a solution will prove as pressing a challenge for a new generation of economists as the search for a solution to The Great Depression of the 1930's was for an earlier generation, though any substantial contribution to that search is outside the scope of this book.[9] It is conceivable that a solution will first be found in one or more relatively small economies, but until it is effectively applied in the major trading nations the situation will remain inherently unstable. They must bear the principal responsibility for finding and applying a solution, because of their superior resources and influence.

[9] For some suggestions see A.N. McLeod, "Wanted: A Better Anti-Inflation Strategy", *Queen's Quarterly* [Kingston, Canada], Vol. 90, no. 1, Spring 1983, pp.1–15.

3.3. Reform of the International Monetary System[10]

It is a corollary of the previous section that an effective reform of the international monetary system will not be possible until the essential conditions for international equilibrium are met. However, some modifications of present practices could greatly assist in the process.

Measures to demonetize key currencies in the international sphere and replace them by some reserve medium under effective international control would certainly be desirable. Such a reserve medium would provide a rational instrument for the management of international liquidity by a supracentral bank in much the same way that national central banks now manage the domestic money supply. Some observers have advocated making SDR's the new reserve medium, and converting the I.M.F. into a supracentral bank, but the attempts so far made to move in this direction have not been very promising; the issues of SDR's have been in arbitrary amounts on arbitrarily-chosen dates without regard to the persistent expansion of other forms of international liquidity.

If the I.M.F. or some other international intermediary is to function as a supracentral bank, effectively managing the world supply of SDR's or some alternative reserve medium, two main conditions will have to be met: (1) all other reserve media will have to be demonetized, or at the very least new increments thereof will have to be strictly controlled; and (2) there will have to be some reliable way of *decreasing* the supracentral bank's asset holdings on occasion, as well as increasing them, in order to adjust the supply of reserves to changing world conditions. Moreover, changes in its assets will have to be capable of being made on a relatively delicate scale, and preferably in a way that will be neutral with respect to the reserve positions of particular countries. If the model of domestic central banking is followed, which usually relies on open-market operations and similar techniques, there will have to be broad and active markets in securities denominated in the reserve unit; and the general public will have to participate in those markets on a substantial scale, or the operations of the supracentral bank will overwhelm them.

Other solutions are of course possible. A new international monetary system might be built around a stable key currency—the proposed European Currency Unit (ECU), the deutschemark, a rehabilitated dollar, a revitalized pound, or something else. The main qualifications for the central currency would be three: a broad and efficient domestic financial system, substantial domestic output of a wide range of products (to provide dependable convertibility of the currency into goods and services), and

---

[10] Cf. A.N. McLeod, "Reforming the International Monetary System", *International Journal of Social Economics*, Vol. 10, no. 2, 1983.

extensive interests in world trade (to ensure that the country's policies would not be unduly parochial). There could be worse solutions.

Whatever solution is ultimately found, it will surely be a long time before the details can be worked out and made effective. If the remedy does include a reasonable degree of price stability in the domestic affairs of all or most nations, then exchange rates should tend to stabilize automatically (or it should be relatively easy to stabilize them); even so, it might be a long time before there would be any attempt to reestablish a fixed-rate system. Meanwhile we need international agreement on satisfactory standards for judging exchange-rate levels, satisfactory standards for judging the appropriateness of domestic policies and their impact on exchange rates, and satisfactory means of enforcing compliance with those standards. Surely we can agree, at the very least, that exchange rates must be flexible enough to accommodate differing price trends in the various national economies, but not so flexible as to encourage destabilizing feedback effects on national price levels.

Some authors have suggested an international agreement that interventions in exchange markets by national authorities would be limited to moves designed to shift the market value of the currency towards some agreed reference rate or estimated equilibrium rate.[11] An agreement of this kind would require no major institutional changes, and no major retreat by any nation from its presently-established policies. Since 1971 there have been many instances of substantial and precipitate changes in the relative values of major currencies, sometimes dramatically reversed within a few months; that sort of thing can hardly be considered an example of the functional operation of the market system, so agreement to avoid or limit it should not be too hard to achieve. It is to be hoped, however, that the evolution of standards and practices of this kind would lead to a more substantial consensus in due course.

[11] See for example W. Ethier and A.I. Bloomfield, *Managing the Managed Float*; Princeton, Princeton University, 1975; Department of Economics, International Finance Section, Essays in International Finance No. 128.

ABOUT THE AUTHOR

ALEXANDER NORMAN McLEOD, B.A., M.P.A., Ph.D., is a monetary economist who is experienced in practical applications as well as in theoretical developments. He had a distinguished academic career, being medalist at Queen's University, Littauer Fellow at Harvard, and later a professor at Atkinson College of York University in Toronto, from which he retired in 1977 as Professor Emeritus.

Between these academic periods A.N.M. pursued the practical application of theory. He was an early staff member of the International Monetary Fund, which sent him to several Central American countries on financial missions and seconded him as a monetary adviser to the United Nations Commissioner in Libya in preparation for independence. On leave from the Fund, he was Director of Research for the Saudi Arabian Monetary Agency for two years. Later (1966–69) the Fund's Central Banking Service provided him to Trinidad and Tobago as Governor of that country's central bank. In the meantime he was Chief Economist of The Toronto-Dominion Bank for ten years, and established its Research Department. During that period he was chairman of the Economists' Committee of the Canadian Bankers' Association, which drafted the Association's influential presentation to the Royal Commission on Banking and Finance (the Porter Commission). York University gave him leave of absence to advise the Government of Botswana on monetary matters, which led to the establishment of their new currency and their central bank.

Married, with four sons and a growing assortment of grandchildren, Professor McLeod now writes and works in support of national and international policies that are both socially responsible and economically sound.

Bagehot, W. *Lombard Street: A Description of the Money Market.* London; Henry S. King, 1873.

Beise, S.C. "Are Our Monetary Controls Outmoded?", an address before The Economic Club of New York, 19th November 1956.

Birnbaum, E.A. "The Growth of Financial Intermediaries as a Factor in the Effectiveness of Monetary Policy", *I.M.F. Staff Papers,* Vol. VI, no. 3, November 1958, pp. 384-426.

Bloomfield, A.I. *Monetary Policy under the International Gold Standard: 1880-1914.* New York; Federal Reserve Bank of New York, 1959.

Crick, W.F. "The Genesis of Bank Deposits", *Economica,* no. 20, June 1927, pp. 191-202.

Ethier, W., and Bloomfield, A.I. *Managing the Managed Float.* Princeton; Princeton University, 1975. Department of Economics, International Finance Section, Essays in International Finance No. 128.

Friedman, M. "The Euro-Dollar Market: Some First Principles", *The Morgan Guaranty Survey,* October 1969.

Gurley, J.G., and Shaw, E.S. "Financial Aspects of Economic Development", *American Economic Review,* Vol. XLV, no. 4, September 1955, pp. 515-538.

————— . "Financial Intermediaries and the Savings-Investment Process", *The Journal of Finance,* Vol. XI, no. 2, May 1956, pp. 257-276.

————— . "The Growth of Debt and Money in the United States, 1800-1950", *The Review of Economics and Statistics,* Vol. 39, no. 3, August 1957, pp. 250-262.

————— . *Money in a Theory of Finance.* Washington; Brookings Institution, 1960.

Hawtrey, R.G. *Good and Bad Trade.* London; Constable & Co. Ltd., 1913.

————— . *Currency and Credit.* London and New York; Longmans Green, 1919.

————— . *Capital and Employment.* London and New York; Longmans Green and Co., 1937.

International Monetary Fund. *International Financial Statistics.* Washington; International Monetary Fund, serial.

Kaldor, N. "The New Monetarism", *Lloyds Bank Review,* July 1970, pp. 1-17.

Keynes, J.M. *The General Theory of Employment Interest and Money.* London, Macmillan and Co. Ltd., 1936.

Lamflussy, A. "Radcliffe under Scrutiny: Money Substitutes and Monetary Policy", *The Banker* [London], Vol. CXI, January 1961, pp. 44-50.

Machlup, F. *International Trade and the National Income Multiplier.* Philadelphia; Blakiston, 1943.

McLeod, A.N. "The Mysteries of Credit Creation", *The Canadian Banker,* Vol.66, no.3, Winter 1959, pp. 20–28.

_____ . "Credit Creation in an Open Economy", *The Economic Journal,* Vol. LXXII, September 1962, pp. 611–640.

_____ . "The Role of Financial Institutions in Developing Countries: A New Perspective", *The Canadian Banker,* Vol. 77, no. 5, September/October 1970, pp. 8–10.

_____ . "The Essential Conditions for International Economic Stability", *Banca Nazionale del Lavoro Quarterly Review,* no. 113, June 1975, pp. 172-186.

_____ . "The Fearsome Dilemma: Simultaneous Inflation and Unemployment", *ibid.,* no. 131, December 1979, pp. 377-389.

_____ . "Wanted: A Better Anti-Inflation Strategy", *Queen's Quarterly* [Kingston, Canada], Vol. 90, no. 1, Spring 1983, pp. 1-15.

_____ . "Reforming the International Monetary System", *International Journal of Social Economics,* Vol. 10, no. 2, 1983, pp. 44-61.

Phillips, C.A. *Bank Credit.* New York; The Macmillan Company, 1920.

Plumptre, A.F.W. *Central Banking in the British Dominions.* Toronto; The University of Toronto Press, 1940.

Radford, R.A. "Economic Organization of a P.O.W. Camp", *Economica,* Vol. XII, November 1945, pp 189-201.

Robertson, D.H. *Money.* Cambridge Economic Handbooks II. Fourth ed. London; Nisbet, 1948.

Say, J.B. *A Treatise on Political Economy.* Translated from the 4th ed. of the French by C.R. Prinsep. New American Edition. Philadelphia; Claxton Remsen and Halleffinger, 1880.

Schumpeter, J.A. *History of Economic Analysis.* New York; Oxford University Press, 1954.

Stone, R. "On the Interdependence of Blocks of Transactions", *Journal of the Royal Statistical Society, Supplement*. Vol. IX, no. 1, 1947, pp. 1-32.

Thorn, R.S. "Nonbank Financial Intermediaries, Credit Expansion, and Monetary Policy", *I.M.F. Staff Papers*, Vol. VI, no. 3, November 1958, pp. 369-383.

Viner, J. *Studies in the Theory of International Trade.* New York and London; Harper & Bros., 1937.

Vining, R. "A Process Analysis of Bank Credit Expansion", *The Quarterly Journal of Economics,* Vol. LIV, no. 4, August 1940, pp. 599-623.

Wood, E. *English Theories of Central Banking Control 1819-1858.* Cambridge Mass.; Harvard University Press, 1939.

INDEX